# GEOMETRY OF MARKETS

## Bryce T. Gilmore

*25th Anniversary*
*1975-2000*

**TRADERS PRESS, INC.®**
**PO BOX 6206**
**Greenville, SC 29606**

*Books and Gifts*
*for Investors and Traders*

Copyright© 1989 by **Bryce T. Gilmore**. All rights reserved.

4th Edition - January 2000

1st Limited Edition of 125 copies - January 1989

ISBN 09-34380-55-4

Published by **Traders Press Inc.**®
Cover Design by
**Teresa Darty Alligood**
**Editor & Graphic Designer**

No part of this publication may be reproduced, stored in a retrieval system, or transmitted, in any form or by any means—electronic, mechanical, photocopying, recording, or otherwise—without the prior written permission of the publisher.

All illustrations used in this work have been prepared using the computer software package WAVE TRADER™. Certain routines displayed are proprietary, they are the author's own design. They are also protected by copyright and cannot be legally copied or emulated by other software merchants without prior consent.

WAVE TRADER is available as a commercial package. It is supported to run IBM compatible hardware only.

For information on our books, software and seminars, our contact address and emails are:

Bryce Gilmore
**Bryce Gilmore & Associates Pty Ltd**
6 Heywood Place
Helensvale, QLD
AUSTRALIA 4212
email: bryceg@qldnet.com.au

**AGENTS**
Adest - Sydney, Australia     CycleTrader - Melbourne, Australia
Website - WaveTrader.com     Website - CycleTrader.com.au

*25th Anniversary*
*1975-2000*
**TRADERS PRESS, INC.**®
**PO BOX 6206**
**Greenville, SC 29606**

# Biographical Sketch of Bryce T. Gilmore

Bryce Gilmore first became familiar with trading following a diverse and interesting background in various aspects of business. His career began in Sydney with an accounting firm while he attended university and night school part time. Accounting held no special interest for him and he left that field to find another job that suited his talents and his interests more closely. He eventually became the office manager for a multinational car manufacturer and developed a deep interest in cars, buying and selling used cars as a sideline occupation. This showed his natural interest in and proclivity for trading.

By 1969 he had become the head buyer for a firm in Melbourne, buying up to 50 cars a week. After several successful wholesaling jobs in the car business he went out on his own in 1972. For the next ten years, Bryce operated his own highly successful retail and wholesale car business, specializing in sports cars and prestige vehicles. During this period of "car trading," he bought and sold in excess of 2,500 cars, making profits on over 95% of his "trades." As he gained more experience, his knowledge of how to buy and sell more efficiently grew. He made a number of trips abroad to the USA and UK for the purpose of importing cars. On his last trip, he had become so astute in his ability to "buy low and sell high" that he made profits ranging between $10,000 and $25,000 on each car purchased.

Thus, when Bryce was first introduced to futures trading in 1981, he had already become accustomed to making money trading, and the process of buying and selling for a profit. He quickly "got hooked" on futures trading. His first 6 months of trading were spent "learning the ropes." During this period, he broke even, but gained valuable experience in this fascinating endeavor. Highlights were a $4,500 profit in silver (over a 30 minute period), and a disheartening loss of $15,000 when caught in a "limit down" situation for 3 days.

After this initial period, he began to study system approaches and trend indicators in earnest. His natural propensity for dealing with numbers and probabilities was evidenced by his success in the Australian backgammon championship and his earlier study of all types of casino gambling games. After an exhaustive period of testing, he began system trading in mid-1982 with a friend and over a 7 month period achieved profits of $150,000 on a $200,000 account (50% of which was always held in reserve). His broker was so impressed with their system that he promoted it to his clients. Over the next 3 years Bryce and his friend continued to trade for their own account and for managed client accounts. Results were mixed depending on when one began trading but were profitable overall.

By mid-1985, Bryce began designing WaveTrader software and by early 1986 was regularly picking tops and bottoms using time, price, and trend analysis. From 1986 on he developed a following of other traders interested in his work. By 1987 he began speaking to technical analysis groups about his methods and conducting teaching seminars for his increasing body of WaveTrader users. In an 8 week trading contest he achieved a return of 42% (250%+ annualized) with all trades made on the basis of time and price analysis.

His most famous "market call" was made in 1987 (November 11th) when he called, to the day, the low of the "Ordinaries Index" (a local share market), saying "If the market goes lower than today I will throw all my work out into the street and change my occupation." Today, nearly 13 years later, that index has never been below its November 1987 low. A 1988 article in Stocks and Commodities Magazine explaining and demonstrating his methods led to an increasing worldwide interest in his WaveTrader software, and to his writing this book, "Geometry of Markets," which explains the concepts of price and time analysis. Bryce feels strongly, like Gann before him, that time is the most important market factor, and that his work is the most accurate form of analysis available. His contributions to technical analysis methods have been lauded by such prominent analysts as Larry Pesavento, Phyllis Kahn, and Larry Jacobs.

Today Gilmore continues to share his extensive knowledge of technical analysis and trading with others by conducting seminars, upgrading his work, and putting out current revisions to his original "Geometry of Markets" material. As a point of interest, this book was awarded the coveted title of " Book of the Year" in 1991 by Frank Taucher, publisher of SuperTraders Almanac. Readers who avail themselves of the knowledge it imparts of time, price, and pattern analysis equip themselves with a dynamic tool second to none in the analysis of markets.

**TRADERS PRESS, INC.®**
PO BOX 6206
Greenville, SC 29606

**Publishers of:**

*A Complete Guide to Trading Profits* (Paris)
*A Professional Look at S&P Day Trading* (Trivette)
*Ask Mr. EasyLanguage* (Tennis)
*Beginner's Guide to Computer Assisted Trading* (Alexander)
*Channels and Cycles: A Tribute to J.M. Hurst* (Millard)
*Chart Reading for Professional Traders* (Jenkins)
*Commodity Spreads: Analysis, Selection and Trading Techniques* (Smith)
*Comparison of Twelve Technical Trading Systems* (Lukac, Brorsen, & Irwin)
*Cyclic Analysis* (J.M. Hurst)
*Day Trading with Short Term Price Patterns* (Crabel)
*Exceptional Trading: The Mind Game* (Roosevelt)
*Fibonacci Ratios with Pattern Recognition* (Pesavento)
*Geometry of Stock Market Profits* (Jenkins)
*Harmonic Vibrations* (Pesavento)
*How to Trade in Stocks* (Livermore)
*Hurst Cycles Course* (J.M. Hurst)
*Jesse Livermore: Speculator King* (Sarnoff)
*Magic of Moving Averages* (Lowry)
*Pit Trading: Do You Have the Right Stuff?* (Hoffman & Baccetti)
*Planetary Harmonics of Speculative Markets* (Pesavento)
*Point & Figure Charting* (Aby)
*Point & Figure Charting: Commodity and Stock Trading Techniques* (Zieg)
*Profitable Grain Trading* (Ainsworth)
*Profitable Pattern for Stock Trading* (Pesavento)
*Stock Market Trading Systems* (Appel & Hitschler)
*Stock Patterns for Day Trading* (Rudd)
*Stock Patterns for Day Trading 2* (Rudd)
*Study Helps in Point & Figure Techniques* (Wheelan)
*Technically Speaking* (Wilkinson)
*Technical Trading Systems for Commodities and Stocks* (Patel)
*The Amazing Life of Jesse Livermore: World's Greatest Stock Trader* (Smitten)
*The Professional Commodity Trader* (Kroll)
*The Taylor Trading Technique* (Taylor)
*The Traders* (Kleinfeld)
*The Trading Rule That Can Make You Rich\** (Dobson)
*Traders Guide to Technical Analysis* (Hardy)
*Trading Secrets of the Inner Circle* (Goodwin)
*Trading S&P Futures and Options* (Lloyd)
*Understanding Bollinger Bands* (Dobson)
*Understanding Fibonacci Numbers* (Dobson)
*Viewpoints of a Commodity Trader* (Longstreet)
*Wall Street Ventures & Adventures Through Forty Years* (Wyckoff)
*Winning Market Systems* (Appel)

PLEASE CONTACT TRADERS PRESS TO RECEIVE OUR CURRENT 100 PAGE CATALOG DESCRIBING
THESE AND MANY OTHER BOOKS AND GIFTS OF INTEREST TO INVESTORS AND TRADERS.
*800-927-8222 ~ Fax 864-298-0221 ~ 864-298-0222 ~ tradersprs@aol.com*

## A message from Bryce Gilmore, 21st March 1999

The underlying geometric figure is the one true secret of the universe, it helps explain the binding natural relationships we find within human affairs and the market behavior.

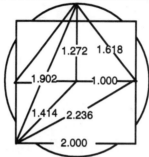

*Geometry of Markets*, was first published in 1989. It contained information about Market Time and Price Geometry never seen in print before the first edition. The original edition was awarded "Trader's Book of the Year Award" by SuperTraders Almanac, one of the most prestigious critics of trading methods and technical systems in the USA. Several thousand copies were sold to traders and technical analysis students worldwide (at prices ranging from US$89 - A$295) while the first and second editions were in print. I have since authored two other books on the same subject, *Geometry of Markets II*, (c) 1993 and my most recent *Dynamic Time and Price Analysis of Market Trends*, (c) 1998 (A$295). It is my wish that this original book, *GOM*, remains in print, as it explains my concepts of time and price analysis before I really felt I had become a specialist at this form of analysis.

I would like to make it known to purchasers of this book that my company has available, for traders who desire a fast and efficient means of conducting computer generated analysis using the principles outlined in this book, a program called WaveTrader/CycleTrader software.

The WaveTrader/CycleTrader software now has 10 years of extra development from the time of this book's initial printing and is Y2K compliant. It runs using the CSIM data format, but is only available from my company and a couple of dedicated agents.

For information on our books, software and seminars, our contact address and emails are:

Bryce Gilmore
**Bryce Gilmore & Associates Pty Ltd**
6 Heywood Place
Helensvale, QLD
AUSTRALIA 4212
email: bryceg@qldnet.com.au

**AGENTS**

| | |
|---|---|
| Adest - Sydney, Australia | CycleTrader - Melbourne, Australia |
| Website - WaveTrader.com | Website - CycleTrader.com.au |

# DEDICATIONS

*To the great analysts past and present.*

*WITHOUT YOUR INPUT THIS WORK WOULD NEVER HAVE BEEN POSSIBLE.*

*To the wave trader users who have supported my work, this is your reward.*

*Use this knowledge wisely.*

## DISCLAIMER

Every attempt has been made to verify the accuracy of the figures and statements contained within this text.

This text is a guide. It is written to show the amateur analyst how to apply the geometric principles of time and price analysis to identify relationships that unfold in markets. Any statements directly connected with investing money, future forecasts, important rules to follow etc., are the opinion of the author.

Throughout this text I make the statement - Technical analysis is a science, trading is an art. This statement again is the author's opinion.

The opinions of the author have been uncannily accurate in the past. This does not mean that they will be accurate in the future. The law requires me to mention this fact. Bryce T. Gilmore the author, or his legal assigns in no event will be liable for direct, indirect, incidental, or consequential damages that should occur through the use of any **methodology, strategy or opinion** outlined in the following text.

GEOMETRY OF MARKETS

Bryce T. Gilmore

Melbourne, Australia.

January 1989

# Table of Contents

1. **THE THEORY BEHIND TIME RELATIONSHIPS IN MARKETS** .................... 1
   - INTRODUCTION .................................................. 1
   - PLANETARY CYCLES ............................................. 2
   - SEASONAL CYCLES OF AN EARTH YEAR (4 SEASONS) ................. 3
   - SEASONAL BEGINNINGS .......................................... 4
   - PLANETARY MOVEMENT ........................................... 5
   - SUMMARY ON IMPORTANT TIMES THAT COULD SIGNAL A CHANGE ....... 6
2. **ANCIENT GEOMETRY & NUMEROLOGY** ................................... 9
   - ANCIENT GEOMETRY ............................................. 9
   - A SQUARE ..................................................... 10
   - A CIRCLE ..................................................... 11
   - A TRIANGLE ................................................... 12
   - A GOLDEN RECTANGLE ........................................... 13
   - A GOLDEN TRIANGLE ............................................ 14
   - THE GREAT PYRAMID OF GIZA .................................... 15
   - PYTHAGORAS & PLATO ........................................... 16
   - ANCIENT NUMEROLOGY ........................................... 17
   - FIBONACCI NUMBER SERIES ...................................... 18
   - LUCAS NUMBER SERIES .......................................... 20
   - POWERS OF NUMBERS ............................................ 21
3. **IMPORTANT STATIC TIME ELEMENTS CAN SIGNAL A CHANGE IN TREND** ......... 23
   - USING MATHEMATICAL TIME ELEMENTS ............................. 23
   - SEASONAL CARDINAL POINTS ..................................... 24
   - CLUSTERS OF TIME ............................................. 24
   - DIVISIONS OF A YEAR .......................................... 25
   - SUMMARY ...................................................... 30
4. **STATIC PRICE INCREMENTS AND LEVELS FOR SUPPORT & RESISTANCE AREAS** .. 31
   - PRICE ELEMENTS ............................................... 31
   - FIBONACCI DEGREE PRICE RISES AND DECLINES .................... 31
   - PRICE LEVELS OF FIBONACCI DEGREE ............................. 32
   - LUCAS DEGREE PRICE RANGES & LEVELS ........................... 33
   - SQUARE OF 144 ................................................ 34
   - SIMPLE SQUARINGS OF TIME AND PRICE ........................... 35
   - COMPLEX SQUARINGS OF TIME AND PRICE .......................... 35
   - USING STATIC PRICE ELEMENTS .................................. 37

## 5. DYNAMIC PRICE LEVELS FOR MARKET SUPPORT AND RESISTANCE ............39

DOUBLE TOPS AND BOTTOMS ........................................39
100% MULTIPLE RISE IN VALUE FROM A LOW PRICE ................42
50% DECLINE IN VALUE FROM A HIGH PRICE .......................43
61.8% to 66.6% DECLINE IN VALUE FROM A HIGH PRICE ............44
SUMMARY OF DYNAMIC PRICE LEVELS ..............................48

## 6. SQUARING PRICE FOR LOCATION OF FUTURE SUPPORT AND RESISTANCE ZONES 49

SQUARING PRICE ................................................49
SQUARING A PRICE RANGE ........................................51
EXAMPLE OF RANGE SQUARING USING SOYBEANS .....................52
SOYBEAN RANGE LEVELS OF EXTREME IMPORTANCE ..................53
MARKET CORRECTIONS ............................................54
SQUARING A LOW PRICE ..........................................55
SQUARING A HIGH PRICE .........................................57
ANY MAJOR TURNING POINT .......................................58
MAJOR PRICE SUPPORT AND RESISTANCE ZONES .....................58

## 7. DYNAMIC TIME SUPPORTS AND RESISTANCES .............................59

PREVIOUS MAJOR RANGE TIMES ....................................59
COMPLETED BULL AND BEAR CYCLES ................................62
BULL MARKET CYCLE .............................................63
BEAR MARKET CYCLE .............................................64
USING RANGE VIBRATION TIMES FOR TRADING SIGNALS ..............65
RANGE VIBRATIONS IN INTERMEDIATE WAVES .......................66
DAILY CHART FOR ACCURACY OF TIME MEASUREMENT .................67
CONFIRMING ORIGINAL FINDINGS ..................................68
ALTERNATIVE CONFIRMATIONS OF TIME SQUARINGS ..................69
THE BOTTOM LINE ON RANGE VIBRATION ............................70

## 8. CHART SCALING OF TIME AND PRICE ...................................71

1 UNIT OF PRICE EQUALS 1 UNIT OF TIME SCALE ..................71
ALTERNATIVE PRICE TO TIME SCALES ..............................72
STOCKS AND SHARES SCALING .....................................74
BEST ADVICE ON SCALING ........................................75
DAILY, WEEKLY AND MONTHLY CHARTS ..............................75
GEOMETRIC ANGLES OF SUPPORT AND RESISTANCE ...................76
ANGLE INTERSECTIONS AND TIME SQUARING ........................77
MY BEST GUIDE TO THE USE OF GEOMETRIC ANGLES .................78
ALTERNATIVE ANGLES USED BY TECHNICIANS .......................79
1.618 AND 0.618 ANGLES OF PRICE TO TIME ......................80
PERCENTAGE OF A PRICE SQUARING TO TIME .......................81

# GEOMETRY OF MARKETS

**9. FUTURE TIME SQUARINGS OF PRICE** .................................................... 83

    SQUARING A LOW PRICE IN TIME ................................................ 83
    SQUARE OF THE 1982 LOW IN THE STANDARD & POORS 500 ......... 85
    SQUARING A HIGH PRICE IN TIME ............................................... 86
    SQUARING A PRICE RANGE IN TIME ............................................ 87
    SQUARING A RANGE TIME TO A FUTURE PRICE ........................... 89
    USE OF THESE METHODS ......................................................... 90

**10. RATIO ANALYSIS OF PRICE RETRACEMENTS AND PRICE PROJECTIONS** ........ 91

    PRICE PROJECTION EXAMPLES IN BULL MARKETS .................... 92
    COMPLEX RETRACEMENTS AND PROJECTIONS IN MINOR WAVES ..... 96
    61.8% EXAMPLE RETRACEMENT IN BEAR MARKETS .................. 102
    The most important future range levels to consistently monitor are :- ...... 104
    Following range retracement and projection levels ..................... 104

**11. GEOMETRIC VIBRATION ANGLES** ............................................................ 105

    VIBRATION ............................................................................ 105
    DISCOVERING MARKET VIBRATION ............................................ 105
    COMMODITY VIBRATION .......................................................... 106
    CALCULATING A VIBRATION RATE ............................................. 107
    DISPLAYING A COMMODITY VIBRATION GEOMETRICALLY ............ 108
    VIBRATIONS IN TRENDS .......................................................... 111
    MARKET SYMMETRY ............................................................... 113
    Summary of important vibration ratios to monitor. ....................... 124

**12. ELLIOTT WAVE ANALYSIS** ...................................................................... 125

    ELLIOTT WAVE STRUCTURES ................................................... 125
    WAVE LABELING .................................................................... 126
    WAVE PATTERNS FORMED ON A BAR CHART ............................. 127
    ELLIOTT WAVE STRICT RULES ................................................. 128
    MAJOR POINTS TO REMEMBER ................................................ 129
    WAVE ANALYSIS .................................................................... 129
    ELLIOTT WAVE CHARACTERISTICS ........................................... 130
    BEAR MARKETS .................................................................... 136
    WAVE ANALYSIS PROCEDURES ................................................ 139
    ELLIOTT WAVE IN PRACTICE ................................................... 140
    ELLIOTT SPEAKS ON GOLD as interpreted by Bryce Gilmore ........... 141
    DJIA Wave count probability ..................................................... 143

## 13. TIME PRICE & SPACE .................................................. 145

    CORRECTLY RECORDING STOCK OR COMMODITY PRICE HISTORY ...145
    COMMODITY PRICE HISTORIES ........................................145
    STOCK PRICE HISTORIES ............................................147
    CALCULATING A RIGHTS ISSUE ADJUSTMENT ............................148
    PRICE IN TIME FROM PAST SHARE PRICE ..............................148
    CORRECT DATA MEANS ACCURATE ANALYSIS .............................148
    TIME PRICE & SPACE ...............................................149
    TIME PRICE & SPACE RELATIONSHIPS TO LOOK FOR .....................162

## 14. STEPS REQUIRED FOR COMPREHENSIVE TIME & PRICE ANALYSIS ............ 163

    STEP 1. RECORD ALL IMPORTANT HIGHS AND LOWS .....................163
    BHP LTD - RECENT HISTORY FACT FILE ..............................164
    CALCULATE TIME VIBRATIONS BETWEEN FACT FILE DATES ...............165
    STEP 2. ELLIOTT WAVE COUNT ......................................167
    WAVE STRUCTURE POST 1987 HIGH $11.10 ............................172
    STEP 3. RECORDING SQUARES OF PRICE SUPPORT AND RESISTANCE 177
    STEP 4. RECORDING MAJOR TIME VIBRATIONS FOR THE FUTURE .....181
    MONITORING STATIC TIME AND VIBRATIONS ON A DAY TO DAY BASIS .187
    FUNDAMENTAL OUTLOOK FOR THIS STOCK ..............................192
    GEOMETRY OF MARKETS - BHP 2nd Edition update JUNE 1989 ........194

## 15. TRADING WITH TIME AND PRICE ANALYSIS .............................. 197

    BULLISH CONSENSUS ...............................................198
    RELATIVE STRENGTH INDICES .......................................199
    FILTER DAILY NEWS ...............................................199
    TIME PRICE & PATTERN ............................................200
    MONITOR UNFOLDING RATIOS OF WAVES WITHIN CYCLES .........205
    SIMPLE PRICE RELATIONSHIPS THAT SIGNAL THE END OF A MOVE ....206

## 16. HELIOCENTRIC PLANETARY CYCLES ..................................... 213

    ELECTRO MAGNETIC FORCES .........................................214
    HELIOCENTRIC ASTRONOMY .........................................214
    TIME IN DAYS FOR EACH STAR SIGN TRANSIT ........................216
    HELIOCENTRIC OVERLAY FOR 14TH DECEMBER 1987 ...................222
    HELIOCENTRIC OVERLAY FOR 26TH SEPTEMBER 1988 ..................223
    HELIOCENTRIC OVERLAY FOR 13TH JANUARY 1989 ....................224
    PLANETARY CYCLES and CONVENTIONAL TIMING ANALYSIS .........226
    STUDY THE PLANETARY CYCLES AS A SCIENCE ........................226
    GEOMETRY OF MARKETS - EPILOGUE .................................227

# GEOMETRY OF MARKETS

## A guide to advanced technical analysis of stocks and commodities.

Geometry is the basis for explaining all things in life's path. Geometry is a science that has been used throughout the ages by great philosophers and scientists, to illustrate the binding mathematical relationships in nature, the cosmos and the human evolution.

Market swing highs and lows are points in time and price, where the PSYCHOLOGICAL imbalance of supply and demand, dictated by traders, reaches its zenith. Market vibration points have a sound natural mathematical basis. By careful study and research it is possible to predetermine these levels. It could be said, that waves of price movement in markets are motivated by fundamental input. However, the unfolding patterns are often predictable and non-random. Time and price ratio analysis of markets is the most reliable approach that I know of, where you can identify and trade changes in market trend on the day they occur. These techniques work on trends of either minor, intermediate or primary degree.

Techniques for analysing price movements in stocks and commodities revealed in this text, use the same geometric measurements and patterns that apply to all other scientific work.

*GEOMETRY OF MARKETS* will give you an insight into the natural order at work in all free trading markets. This information would normally be unavailable for such a reasonable price. Market analysis is reduced to a science by applying graphic representation of the geometry relating price movement in time.

**Bryce. T. Gilmore.**

Melbourne, Australia.

January 1989, revised April 1991.

# THE THEORY BEHIND TIME RELATIONSHIPS IN MARKETS

## INTRODUCTION

Since the early days of man, scholars, philosophers, mathematicians and scientists have endeavored to prove that nature and the universe grow in harmony to some natural law of vibration. Sufficient proof exists that all forms of life and matter vibrate to some natural law of harmonics. In modern times such inventions as the telephone, radio and television rely on the vibration of invisible frequencies transmitted though another medium. These vibrations cannot be seen, heard or felt by us, yet they are part of our daily lives and we now take them for granted. Modern science indicates that all matter emits vibrations. Vibrations start from the Sun which is believed to control the solar system and effect all things. Plants grow in harmony with cycles of the year. Crops planted at specific times of the year grow more favorably than those out of harmony with their most favorably cycle. Life itself, evolves around cycles of the solar system and the planetary aspects. The Moon creates a pattern of rising tides and feeding habits for marine life. Night becomes day and day becomes night, the oceans rise and fall, economic conditions expand and contract, the path of life continues to unfold in some strict relationship with the past.

Since every natural occurrence in nature revolves and evolves around cycles and vibrations, they can be accurately measured. The principles that apply in all forms of nature also apply to the markets, these things are merely a reflection of human nature and the ingenuity of man himself.

NATURAL TIME CYCLES

## PLANETARY CYCLES

The center of our solar system is the sun. The planets of our solar system revolve around the sun in set cycle periods. These cycle periods are known as a PLANETARY YEAR.

|  |  |
|---|---|
| Earth | 365 Days 7 Hours or 1 Year |
| Mercury | 87.9 Days or 0.24085 Year |
| Venus | 224.7 Days or .61521 Year |
| Mars | 687 Days or 1.88089 Years |
| Jupiter | 4332.7 Days or 11.862 Years. |
| Saturn | 29.45772 Years. |
| Uranus | 84.01529 Years. |
| Neptune | 164.7883 Years. |

Each orbit around the sun completes a cycle. Individual planets travel around the sun at a different speeds, each cycle is similar to a wheel within wheels, especially when one views the proceedings from the the sun; the center of our solar system. At times the planets pass through aspects, ie., they could be opposite in line with the sun, or other planets, or even in line and each on the same side of the sun. These various aspects have a significance in our work as they are cyclic. They are explained at length in the latter stages of this work. For the moment it is only necessary for you to be aware that these cycles exist.

## LUNAR PHASES

The moon orbits around the earth every 29.53 days and passes though two major phases; new moon and full moon.

A new moon occurs when the moon is in complete darkness (this is when the moon travels between the earth and the sun. A solar eclipse occurs when the new moon coincides with a lunar node [crossing of the ecliptic path of the earth's orbit around the sun]). The full moon occurs when the moon is at its brightest. This is around the time of its cycle when it's opposite the sun.

NATURAL TIME CYCLES

# SEASONAL CYCLES OF AN EARTH YEAR (4 SEASONS)

The orbital cycle of the earth dictates seasonal changes. These changes often effect the patterns of human nature as the climate moves from warm to cold. Producers can only grow some agricultural crops at certain times of the year. Due to weather inconsistency some years are years of abundance and others are years of shortage. Depending on the stocks being stored as carry over, prices will rise and fall and form a cyclic pattern. Natural resources are also affected by seasonal demand. Production will be more prolific at certain times of the year due to climate, economic conditions and demand by industry.

A good example of seasonality is the way the cost of Oil rises during a particularly cold winter. Seasonal tendencies help to form cyclic patterns in most markets.

The 90 degree annual astrological dates are strong times for change. Their significance is greatly enhanced when other planetary cycles such as full or new moons, planetary conjunctions or oppositions coincide with their anniversaries.

### FIG 1.1    ILLUSTRATES NATURAL SEASONAL TIMES FOR CHANGE.

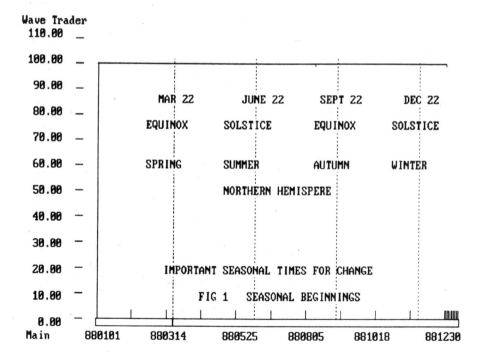

NATURAL TIME CYCLES

## SEASONAL BEGINNINGS

**21/22nd March EQUINOX** when the sun crosses the equator into the northern hemisphere, day and night have an equal length. This the 0 degrees CARDINAL point of the year.

**21/22nd September EQUINOX** when the sun crosses the equator into the southern hemisphere, day and night have an equal length. This is the 180 degree CARDINAL point in a year.

**21/22nd June SOLSTICE** when the sun reaches its highest position in the sky over the northern hemisphere. This is the longest day and also the 90 degree CARDINAL point in the year.

**21/22nd December SOLSTICE** when the sun reaches its lowest position in the sky over the northern hemisphere. This is the shortest day and also the 270 degree CARDINAL point in the year.

These dates are important to watch as they often signal a cyclic change in the markets. Past research shows they are very reliable. Also two other times of the year that Gann warned were important to watch for a change in trend are the perigee and the apogee, ie., around January 4th and July 5th each year. The perigee and apogee are explained in a later chapter dealing with the planets.

The astrological year begins at the MARCH 22nd EQUINOX. This is when the sun crosses the EQUATOR into the northern hemisphere. This time is known as 0 degrees when dividing the year into a 360 degree circle. This is the time of the sun entering the house of ARIES.

There are 12 signs of the zodiac and each 30 degree progression through the circle of one year takes us into another star sign of the zodiac.

| SIGNS OF THE ZODIAC | POSITION IN DEGREES |
|---|---|
| **ARIES** | **21st MARCH 0-360 degrees CARDINAL sign of FIRE** |
| TAURUS | 21st APRIL 30 degrees FIXED sign of EARTH |
| GEMINI | 21st MAY 60 degrees COMMON sign of AIR |
| **CANCER** | **21st JUNE 90 degrees CARDINAL sign of WATER** |
| LEO | 21st JULY 120 degrees FIXED sign of FIRE |
| VIRGO | 21st AUGUST 150 degrees COMMON sign of EARTH |

## NATURAL TIME CYCLES

**LIBRA**            **21st SEPTEMBER** 180 degrees **CARDINAL sign of AIR**

SCORPIO          21st OCTOBER 210 degrees FIXED sign of WATER

SAGITTARIUS     21st NOVEMBER 240 degrees COMMON sign of FIRE

**CAPRICORN**     **21st DECEMBER** 270 degrees **CARDINAL sign of EARTH**

AQUARIUS        21st JANUARY 300 degrees FIXED sign of AIR

PISCES            21st FEBRUARY 330 degrees COMMON sign of WATER

From a cyclic viewpoint we should remember these dates as they can often have a profound effect on human behavior for reasons beyond our comprehension.

**FIG 1.2 ILLUSTRATES THE ORBITAL PATHS OF VENUS, EARTH, MARS, JUPITER AND SATURN AS THEY PROGRESS THROUGH THEIR PLANETARY YEARS.**

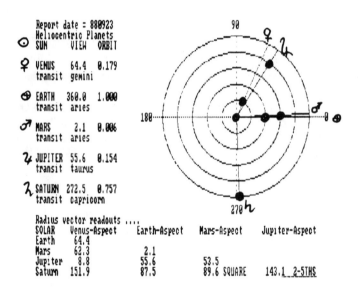

Each planet moves faster or slower in relationship to its wheel, regular cycles of relationships in position to each other often develop for a time. These cycles have been used by man to predict future changes in years past, sometimes a psychological reason develops as to the importance of planetary positions. On its own this could be reason enough for changes in market conditions.

Chp. 1 Page. 5

## SUMMARY OF IMPORTANT CYCLIC TIMES THAT COULD SIGNAL A CHANGE IN TREND

Astrological times of the year between the 20th and 22nd of each month when Earth passes into another star sign, these are possible times for a change. If these times coincide with other planetary phenomena they have a stronger significance for change. The impact of major lunar phases (new or full moon) occurring at these times appears to strengthen the possibilities. A solar eclipse or lunar eclipse would seem even more important to monitor. The march equinox always seems to signal a turn in some market each year.

It is not really important to know the reason why these dates or planetary configurations are significant for a change, only to be aware of their influence on human nature and that group of traders who believe in the importance of these times for new beginnings.

If a market is susceptible to the likely possibility of a change in trend it is more probable to occur at these times. We must recognize this possibility and seize the opportunity to trade should it be available.

As we progress it will be seen that we do not require anything but a basic knowledge of astrology. The main way we track these time relationships is by their very repetition.

*REPETITION OF THESE IMPORTANT TIMES WILL HOLD A MATHEMATICAL RELATIONSHIP TO THE PAST, DUE TO THE CYCLIC NATURE OF THE MARKETS. BY CONSTANTLY MONITORING CYCLES AND IMPORTANT ASTROLOGICAL DATES WE CAN ALWAYS BE AWARE OF IMPORTANT TIMES THAT GIVE US ADVANCE WARNINGS FOR AN IMPENDING CHANGE IN TREND IN THE MARKETS THAT WE FOLLOW.*

Research of the past will show how consistently the astrological time periods through the year mark major turning points in most markets. These times may only be a coincidence but from a technical level they are very important to watch.

Some of the many tools I use for monitoring future markets and researching the past are these natural times of the annual cycle.

By graphically illustrating the earthly progressions in degrees on a circle of one year below a price chart, one can quickly judge the effectiveness of these time periods.

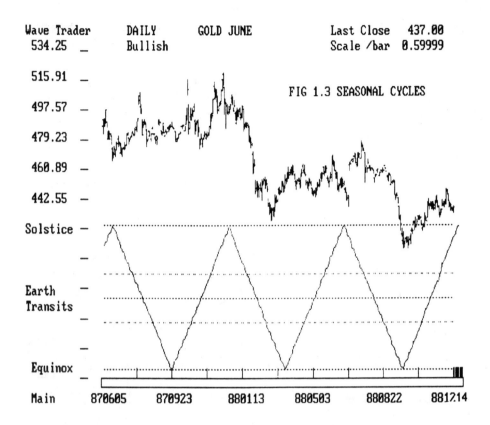

**FIG 1.3    ILLUSTRATES THE CYCLES FROM EQUINOX TO EQUINOX.** The center dash line indicates the 45 degree mid points between equinox and solstice. star sign progressions are signaled at the 1/3 level bars as the range of each oscillation is 90 degrees.

Since the velocity of earth in its orbit around the sun varies it is necessary to plot each day to find the actual location in the orbit.

Velocity reaches a peak around the 5th January each year as earth reaches its closest distance to the sun (perigee). July 5th, thereabouts, is when earth is furtherest from the sun and traveling at its slowest (apogee).

NATURAL TIME CYCLES

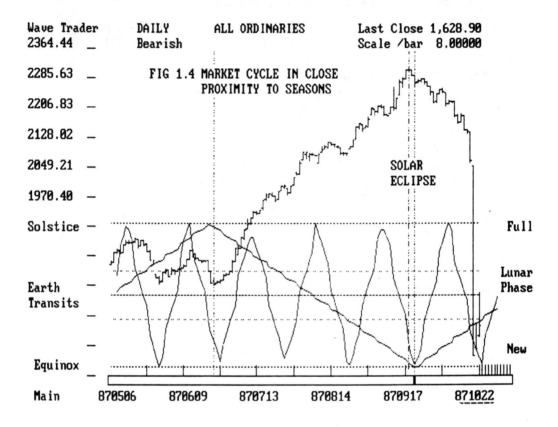

**FIG 1.4   ILLUSTRATES  IMPORTANT  SEASONAL TIME CYCLES**

And how I monitor them. If I had more than two signals coming together at the same time I would place greater emphasis on that signal. Generally I will plot these in advance and pencil the dates in my dairy. A full or new moon occurring on an equinox is a particularly strong signal.  A lunar or solar eclipse  occurring at the same time adds even more strength.  A solar eclipse date is one of the most important cycle points to monitor, solar eclipses fall in regular cycles on the square of 89, ie., approximately every 177 days.

The reason that the lunar oscillator fails to peak sometimes is due to a new or full moon falling over a non trading day.

# ANCIENT GEOMETRY

**PYTHAGORAS delivered the MATHEMATICAL TRUTHS OF THE LAW OF CYCLES to his spiritual community at Crotona, Italy in the sixth century B.C. All of the cosmos, he taught, is comprehensible through numbers because the material universe is born from their very essence.** By knowing the secret of the numbers behind cosmic cycles, the initiate could approach a powerful understanding of the workings of the universe. So vast were the implications of this knowledge that the Pythagoreans kept it in strictest silence.

## ANCIENT GEOMETRY

The basic geometric forms are :- SQUARE - CUBE - CIRCLE - TRIANGLE - RECTANGLE

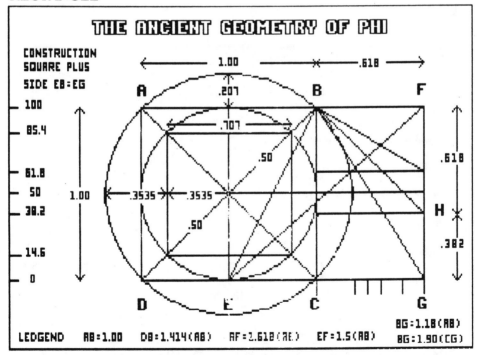

Sacred mathematical ratios have been enshrined in such great works as the Parthenon of Greece and the Great pyramids of Egypt.

# A SQUARE

If we use a square as our starting point we can then draw a circle, a triangle and a rectangle and prove that strict relationships exist. These relationships will never vary, they are an exact science.

If a geometric form is a square then each side will be equal to the other sides.

When a square is divided by a diagonal line to form two triangular halves, the length of the diagonal can be calculated using the Pythagorean theorem for right angle triangles.

If the sides of a square are equal to 1 unit then the diagonal of a square will be equal to the square root of 2. The diagonal of a square will be 1.41421 times the value of the side.

The first set of ratios that we see as important once we study a square divided by a diagonal are:- **Root 2 = 1.414** and **Root 5 = 2.236**. These are the sacred roots. The reciprocals of these roots are just as important, ie., **0.707 and 0.447**.

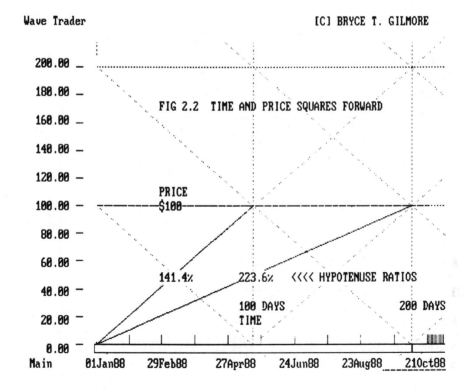

ANCIENT GEOMETRY

## A CIRCLE

The circumference (distance around the 360 degree arc) is measured using the ratio of Pi. Pi = 3.141593 + sometimes expressed as 22/7 and represented as π.

The formulae for measuring the circumference and area of a circle are :-

**Circumference = Pi times DIAMETER,   Area = Pi times radius(half diameter)$^2$**

There is a strict inter-relationship between Pi (3.142) and Phi (1.618). This relationship is demonstrated in the structure of the Pyramid of Giza. The Pyramid of Giza demonstrates the "squaring of the circle", ie., the perimeter of the base is equal to the circumference of a circle drawn using the height as the radius. The height is equal to 1.272 times half the base (root 1.618). When the base equals 2.000 the height equals 1.272. Then perimeter = 2.000*4 or 8.000 and a circle with a radius of 1.272 has a circumference of 1.272*2*3.142 or 8.000.

The relationship between the first square and the inner circle, the outer circle and the circle with a radius of 2 is the **SACRED CUT. 1:1.4142 = 1.4142:2.000**

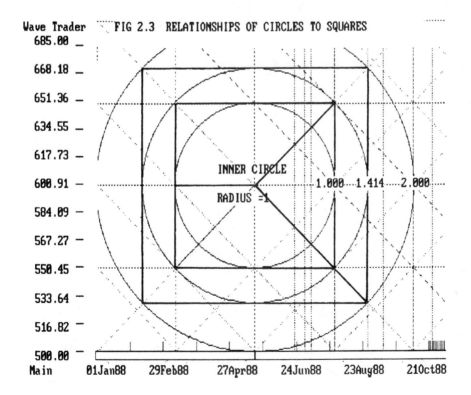

FIG 2.3 RELATIONSHIPS OF CIRCLES TO SQUARES

## A TRIANGLE

The simplest triangle can be formed by dividing a square in half with a diagonal line from opposing corners. The length of this diagonal can be measured using the Pythagorean theorem. The length of the HYPOTENUSE in any right angle triangle will be equal to the square root of the sum of the squares of the other two sides.

A diagonal of a triangle formed by dividing a square into half will be 1.41421 times the side of the square. Root 2 (1.414) times the side.

The diagonal of a triangle formed by dividing a square into quarters will have a value in relationship to half the square root of five (2.23606). If the side is equal to 1 then the hypotenuse will equal 1.11803, if the side of the square is equal to 2.000 the hypotenuse of two squares divided will be equal to root 5 (2.236).

We can see from this illustration that we have a binding relationship between root 2 (1.414) and root 5 (2.236), ie., one grows out of the other.

If we wish to compare the unequal sides they are 2:1 and 2.236:1.414

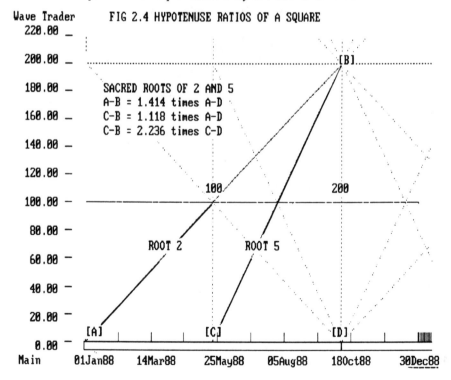

# A GOLDEN RECTANGLE

A Golden rectangle is a rectangle where the length of the longest side is 1.618034 times the length of the shorter side. A Golden Rectangle is formed from a square and has a direct relationship with a square. To form a Golden rectangle the length of a diagonal line drawn from one corner of a square to the center of an opposing side forms a triangle that divides off one quarter of that square. This diagonal is added to half the base of the square to form the base of the golden rectangle.

The value PHI or Ø = 1.618034 and is represented by the Greek letter theta.

The irrational number 1.61803+ or Ø has several remarkable properties. Its square, for example, is equal to itself plus 1.000 (2.61803+), while its reciprocal equals itself less 1.000 (0.61803+). The square root of 0.618 equals the reciprocal of the square root of 1.618 (1.272), ie., root Phi = 1.272, 1 divided by 1.272 = 0.786, $0.618^2$ = 0.786

The Geometry of Markets® spiral expands in direct factors to the root of PHI, ie., **1.000, 1.272, 1.618, 2.058, 2.618, 3.330, 4.236, 5.39** et cetera.

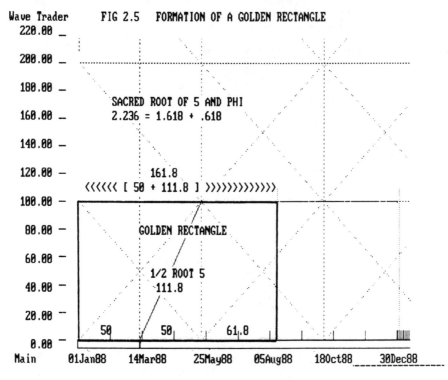

ANCIENT GEOMETRY

## A GOLDEN TRIANGLE

A Golden triangle is formed by drawing a diagonal line to divide a Golden rectangle in half. The length of the base of the triangle is 1.618034 times the height of the triangle.

The diagonal side of the Golden Triangle is 1.902113 times the shortest side.

1.902113 divided by 1.618034 = 1.17557

1.17557 ≈ the diagonal of a right angled triangle with base 0.618 and height 1.000

The reciprocal of 1.902 = 0.526 and reciprocal of 1.17557 ≈ 0.854

1.902 is the relationship of the length in the four outer slopping edges of the pyramid of GIZA to half its base.   VERY SIGNIFICANT!

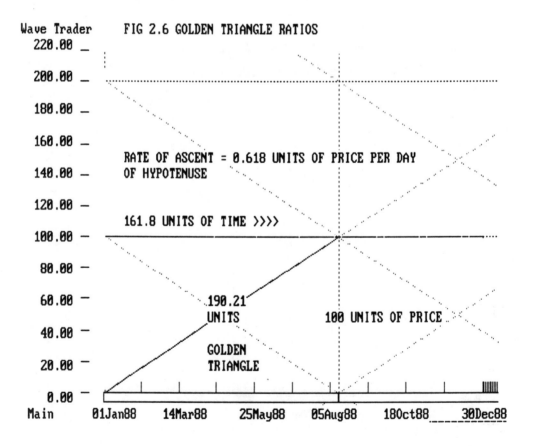

FIG 2.6 GOLDEN TRIANGLE RATIOS

ANCIENT GEOMETRY

# THE GREAT PYRAMID OF GIZA

The **Great Pyramid of GIZA** has encoded in its structure all of the ancient relationships that bind the sacred root of 2 and 5 and the irrational ratios of PHI Ø and PI $\pi$ together. Its design is a monument to the revelations of the ancient philosophers. From this base originated the science of mathematics. The encoded secret of the universe was not invented by man, only revealed to him. It is extremely difficult to place a time on the original building of this structure. Modern scholars are still debating whether it is 4000 or 16000 years old.

From Pythagoras to Plato, every ounce of their mathematical knowledge can be evidenced in the measurements of the pyramid. Just the same it is enlightening when you can prove how the architect came up with the design. Pythagoras is said to be the originator of mathematics. I contend he only learnt from an older source.

The pyramid is a representation of the natural forces in the universe. It cannot be anything else.

The relationship of the height to the base "squares the circle". The relationship of the slope to the height represents the logarithmic spiral. The divisions in the diagonals represent the golden rectangle. The bottom line is that the pyramid is a perfect structure that represents the exact measurements of the earth and the moon placed adjacent to each other and the cardinal points are joined together.

The radius of the moon is 1080 miles; the radius of the earth is 3920 miles. The total radius is 5040 miles; Plato's mystical number. When you form a right angled triangle with a height of 5040 and a base of 3960 you get a diagonal of 6409. 6409:3960 as 1.618:1.000 and 6409:5040 as 1.272:1.000. When you draw a square around the earth the perimeter is equal to the circumference of the circle with a radius of (3960+1080), ie., 3960*8 = $2\pi$*5040 or 31680:31680

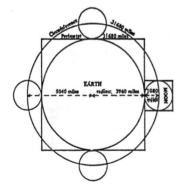 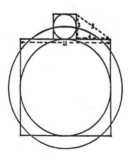 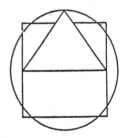

## PYTHAGORAS & PLATO

Pythagoras came first, Plato was a scholar who perpetuated the works of Pythagoras. The Pythagorean students were taught ancient geometry to awaken their powers of intuition. Pythagoras taught, that man cannot learn anything, until he has experienced its truth for himself. Pythagorean teaching set about formulating rules or laws for its followers to learn. These no doubt are the rules and laws that we wish to re-discover.

Pythagoras taught that all was arranged according number. Number and ratio were the key to the universe. It's such a shame to see today that the education system has forgotten its origins.

The Pythagoreans learnt the art of music by number, they studied philosophy by number. The origins of which were revealed originally by the inate constuction of the universe.

Nothing has changed since the days of Plato and Pythagoras. The secrets they protected are still basically secrets. Except for those students who source out the information (decendants perhaps).

Even this work will have little effect in the education of non-believers, not that I am trying to force my opinion on the world. My purpose for revealing my knowledge is to help others, who are willing to search; I know only those who wish to learn will take the trouble. I deliberately left the last page as it was, so students would make the effort to draw out the relationships; perhaps they might even go to the trouble of buying a book on the pyramid. If they don't, they might as well forget reading any further. Not that they won't learn anything, just that they won't experience its truth.

There's an old proverb that goes like this, "If you learn something valuable and keep it to yourself, it is worthless." at the same time you could say that, "something received for nothing is also treated as worthless."

Maybe my style is off at a tangent right now; but I must warn the novice that there is no point in proceeding any further, until you have grasped the concepts so far.

The understanding of ancient geometry holds the key to your successful application of my theories.

# ANCIENT NUMEROLOGY

From the ancient geometry revealed so far the ancient philosophers divised a sacred canon. The science of numerology, relating number to geometry, is an interesting one. Geometry and ancient numerology was used in finding parallels between the inherent structure of number and all types of form and motion. John Michell in his book, "Dimensions of Paradise", states, "The special regard paid to mathematical studies in the ancient world arose from the understanding that number is the mean term in the progression from divine reason to its imperfect reflection in humanity".

Gann said that all was revealed in the bible. This maybe so, but ancient numerology has also been preserved for antiquity in the structures of ancient religious groups. The Stonehenge, Plato's cosmic temple of the New Jerusalem and the great pyramid are only a few that I can mention. The similarities between these three provide ample evidence for our purposes.

**The master number** appears to be **Plato's mystical number 5040** (the combined radii of the earth and the moon). In days this is **720 weeks**. In fact this number is divisible by 2520 (2), 1680 (3), **1260 (4)**, **1008 (5)**, 840 (6), **720 (7)**, **630 (8)**, 504 (9), **420 (12)**, **360 (14)**, **336 (15)**, **315 (16)**, **280 (18)**, **252 (20)**, **240 (21)**, **210 (24)**, **180 (28)**, **168 (30)**, **144 (35)**, **140 (36)**, **126 (40)**, **120 (42)**, 112 **(45)**, 105 **(48)**, **90 (56)**, 84 (60), 80 (63), **72 (70)**, **70 (72)**, now that we have hit the balance point the number in the brackets will revert to the other side of the denominator.

There are two reasons why I have highlighted many of these numbers, the first is because many of them have been mentioned by W.D. Gann and others as being important. The other reason is that I have experienced these numbers signalling the termination of a trend on many more than three occasions.

**SYMBOLIC NUMBERS**

864 the foundation number (6x144)

1008 (7x144) relates to Pi 22/7 where 22 = 3168 and 7 = 1008

3168 the perimeter of the New Jerusalem (22x144)

1224 the number of Paradise

1080 the lunar number

666 the solar number, and the number of the beast.

1746 the number of fusion (1080 + 666)  666 = 0.382 and 1080 = 0.618.

These numbers should be treated with the utmost respect.

# FIBONACCI NUMBER SERIES

For those not familiar with the Fibonacci series, the series begins at 1 and generates new numbers in the series with an increase in value of approximately 61.8%  It would not commonly be known how Leonardo Fibonacci arrived at his famous series, but it would be fair to assume that it was as a result of his observations of the Great Pyramids of Egypt.

Leonardo Fibonacci, was reputed to be the greatest mathematician of the middle ages.  His published works include *LIBER ABACI* year 1202, *PRACTICA GEOMETRIAE* year 1220 and *LIBER QUADRATORUM*.

The famous series takes on the sequence  1, 1, 2, 3, 5, 8, 13, 21, 34, 55, 89, 144 and so on into infinity.  As the numbers advance they become closer in ratio to PHI the ancient ratio of 1.618034

As an example the number 144 is 1.618034 times the value of 89.

To further understand the importance of PHI in mathematics one needs to study the geometric formation of a logarithmic spiral derived from the Golden Rectangle.

I would like to offer the following explanation on how Fibonacci derived this famous series.

If we take the Golden Rectangle as a starting point and draw a diagonal line to divide the Rectangle in half, we then have two right angle triangles each with adjacent sides of length 1 and 1.618034 , This is a GOLDEN TRIANGLE. To find the length of this diagonal line we use the Pythagorean Theorem.

In any right angle triangle the length of the Hypotenuse is equal to the square root of the sum of the squares of the other two sides. As a mathematical formulae this equates to :-

The Diagonal = Square root [ (1x1) + (1.618034x1.618034) ]

= Square root [ 1 + 2.618034 ]

= Square root [ 3.618034 ]

= 1.90211

In the pure mathematical sense we should be aware that the number 2 in the Fibonacci series is a rounding of this value.

To obtain the next value in the series we need to expand the Golden rectangle to its next perfect degree. This is easily demonstrated by increasing each side by the value of PHI 1.618034 ie SIDE 1 x 1.618034 and SIDE 1.618034 x 1.618034

We now have a rectangle with sides 1.618034 and 2.618034 if we apply the same mathematics, demonstrated just now, to find the length of the diagonal of the first Golden Rectangle, we can prove that this new diagonal has increased in value by PHI 1.618034

New Diagonal = Square root [( 1.618034 x 1.618034 ) + ( 2.618034 x 2.618034 )]

= Square root [ 9.472136 ]

= 3.07768

The relationship of the new diagonal to the first is illustrated as:-

New Diagonal divided by Original Diagonal :-

1.90211 into 3.07768 equals 1.618034

This then proves that all future diagonals will increase by 1.618034 should we expand the sides of the golden rectangle in powers of phi. The relationship of phi now holds an intriguing significance to the science of mathematics.

If we were to continue this expansion of the golden rectangle then we would arrive at a series of values representing the increasing values of the diagonals in an expanding golden triangle.

1.90211, 3.07768, 4.97979, 8.05747, 13.03726, 21.09473, 34.13199, 55.22673, 89.35872, 144.5854

When rounded these values are the same as the fibonacci series.

1,1,2,   3, 5, 8, 13, 21, 34, 55, 89, 144, 233, 377, 610, 987, 1597, 2584, 4180, 6763, 10943, 17706, 28648

Each higher number in the series is approximately 1.618034 times the value of the previous number.

## LUCAS NUMBER SERIES

This number series is derived by taking one as the origin and increasing each successive number by PHI 1.618034

1, 1.618, 2.618, 4.236, 6.854, 11.09, 17.95, 29, 47, 76, 123, 199

322, 521, 843, 1364, 2207, 3571, 5778, 9348, 15125, 24473.

From 29 on I have rounded off each value. This series is popularly known as the LUCAS series of numbers. Each number also holds a fixed relationship to the Fibonacci series of numbers. If you multiply a Fibonacci number by 1.382 it will equal the next Lucas number that falls between the Fibonacci series.

When this series is reversed to project a contraction we get the values :- 1 divided by PHI 1.618034 then the result divided by PHI and so forth.

1, .618, .382, .236, .146

These ratios are natural divisions of PHI and hold an extremely important place in the methods of analysis to follow.

Phi expanded by a factor of Phi

1.618*1.618 = 2.618

2.618*1.618 = 4.236    [1.618*1.618*1.618]

4.236*1.618 = 6.854    [1.618*1.618*1.618*1.618]

Phi contracted by a factor of Phi

1.618/1.618 = 1.000

1.000/1.618 = 0.618

0.618/1.618 = 0.382    [0.618*0.618]

0.382/1.618 = 0.236    [0.618*0.618*0.618]

# ANCIENT GEOMETRY & NUMEROLOGY

These expansions and contractions hold the secret to the natural progressions of the golden logarithmic spiral. Between each of these ratios is another on the progression of 1.272 (root 1.618).

$$1.000 * 1.272 = 1.272$$
$$1.272 * 1.272 = \mathbf{1.618}$$
$$1.618 * 1.272 = 2.058$$
$$2.058 * 1.272 = \mathbf{2.618}$$
$$2.618 * 1.272 = 3.330$$
$$3.330 * 1.272 = \mathbf{4.236}$$
$$4.236 * 1.272 = 5.388$$

et cetera.

## POWERS OF NUMBERS

Besides the Fibonacci and Lucas series of numbers we have natural squarings of numbers. The most important are squarings of prime numbers. Often these squarings will form common numbers calculated from other base numbers. These numbers are more significant as they can be derived from several sources. Without covering every number under the Sun one should place emphasis on the following numbers.

**Powers of 3, 5, 7, 9 and 12 are very important numbers to watch.**
powers of 3   =   3, 9, 27, 81, **243**, 729, 2187
powers of 5   =   5, 25, 125, **625**, 3125
powers of 7   =   7, 49, **343**, 2401
powers of 9   =   9, 81, **729**, 6561
powers of 12  =   12, **144**, **1728**, 20736

**SQUARES OF FIBONACCI NUMBERS**
$13^2$   =   169
$21^2$   =   441
$34^2$   =   1156
$55^2$   =   3025

**Multiples of numbers can be important.**
For instance   144      144, 288, 432, 576, 720, 864, 1008, 1152, 1296, 1440 etc.,
                90       90, 180, 270, 360, 450, 540, 630, 720

**Gann's square of $90^0$ in the circle of the year.**

## DIVISIONS OF ONE OR MORE YEARS ON THE SACRED RATIOS

My favorite static time counts to watch for are in ratios of 1 year.

53, 86, 110, 140, 177, 225, 287, 365, 465, 516, 544, 590, 632, 730, 752, 816, 956, 1216 and 1547.

## IN SUMMARY

All of the time and price squaring procedures used in modern charting rely on the geometric relationships of the ancient canon. These relationships are an exact science that has been passed down through the ages. Mathematics is not some modern day fad or invention but a form for measuring precise relationships.

The science of mathematics is common the world over, it does not matter if you are a Russian, Chinese, Japanese or Indian, the same principles apply.

One strong arguement to explain why these formulae are so useful is the fact that they form a common bond throughout the modern world and the ancient world. These principles have stood the test of time.

Markets can expand or contract in time and price relationships covered in this chapter and find solid resistance or support at precise levels. To use these methods to advantage it is simply a matter of recognizing their significance and acting accordingly, should other important criteria exist at the time.

**In nature, especially music, certain vibrations are pleasing to the ear. These vibrations when explained using mathematical terms relate directly to ancient geometry. The sacred roots of 1, 1.618, 2, 3, 4 and 5 can be found to exist in all things. My research work using these same ratios in markets has enlightened me to an approach of analysis that has such accurate predictive qualities, it is second to none.**

It is very important that you memorize the relationships found in the ancient geometry that binds together the square, circle and golden rectangle. Time is a wheel (circle), as time unfolds it can be squared to the past in ancient geometric ratios to make accurate predictions for future important time areas. These cycle periods could indicate an opportunity to profit.

# IMPORTANT STATIC TIME ELEMENTS CAN SIGNAL A CHANGE IN TREND

## USING MATHEMATICAL TIME ELEMENTS

Technical analysis is the title given to the mathematical study of human behavior in markets. If we accept the fact that market trend is precipitated by human endeavour and weigh up the facts, we can see repetitive time price elements for trend changes in markets. Often these become habit forming.

By measuring the **DURATION OF A TREND IN TIME FROM ITS ORIGIN** we can expect a change in trend to occur when a move has been in progress for **13, 21, 34, 55, 89, 144, 233, 377, 610, 987 trading or calendar days.**

To a lesser degree but still very important time zones are **29, 47, 76, 123, 199, 322, 521 trading or calendar days.**

It is important to realize that if we are charting a commodity using only business days and allowing gaps for public holidays we will have 262 bars per year. 262 is an expansion of PHI. [PHI SQUARED (1.618034 X 1.618034 = 2.618034)]. Important times to watch for a change in trend in trading days elapsed will be signaled at **61, 101, 161, 262 bars** from the beginning of a major move. 61 trading days is approx. 89 calendar days, 101 trading days is approx. 144 calendar days. 161 trading days is approx. 233 calendar days, a higher degree Fibonacci series number. A review of past markets will highlight this fact.

The use of these times by chartists and analysts for timing trading entries and exits has a profound effect on market action. ON LONG TERM WEEKLY AND MONTHLY CHARTS THESE NUMBERS ALSO REPRESENT IMPORTANT AREAS FOR A CHANGE IN TREND TO OCCUR. 144 WEEKS IS NEARLY 34 MONTHS AND WILL OFTEN SIGNAL A MAJOR TREND CHANGE. AS YOU BECOME FAMILIAR WITH THESE RATIOS IT WILL PAY TO INVESTIGATE THE VARIOUS COMBINATIONS OF MULTIPLES AND SQUARES AS THEY INTER RELATE TO TIME IN WEEKS AND MONTHS.

For instance 3025 calendar days ($55^2$) is the equilavent of 432 weeks (3x144). 729 calendar days ($9^3$) is equal to two years. 61.8 weeks is 432 days.

## SEASONAL CARDINAL POINTS

Always be prepared for a change in trend occurring at the strong astrological cardinal points. **0, 90, 180, 270 DEGREES. MARCH 21ST, JUNE 21ST, SEPTEMBER 21ST and DECEMBER 21ST. (EQUINOXES and SOLSTICES)**

If a current trend has been entrenched for **34, 55, 89, 144, 233, 288, 343, 377, 432 days** etc., or maybe **90, 180, 240, 270 or 360 degrees** and multiples of these counts from previous market swing highs or lows fall on the above dates, a counter trend reaction is almost certain to occur. The degree still needs to be determined by other factors.

One could possibly become rich following these signals alone.

## CLUSTERS OF TIME

Working time forward from previous swing highs and lows in trading days, calendar days, weeks and months will pinpoint clusters of time ratios that adhere to the numbers listed in chapter 2. When obvious clusters of important time elements exist around future dates we should investigate market performance closely to evaluate the possibility of a trend change coinciding with these clusters.

The following was extracted from my first book written in 1987....

Just recently the Australian all ordinaries index completed the fifth intermediate wave of primary wave five on the 21st september 1987, the exact time for intermediate wave five from the intermediate fourth wave low was 89 calendar days. **September 21st** was a day prior to the equinox and also the 56 year (7x8) anniversary from the major low of 1931. The last wave up not only expanded **33%** in value but also advanced **573** points (just short of 4 times 144). This was also the exact rise in points in the cycle bull market expansion from the 1974 bear market low to the 1980 high, a correction of 40% in value followed and the new bear market endured into 1982.

The time from the intermediate wave 3 high was 89 trading days, the total time from the beginning of the final advance (primary wave 4) was 293 trading days from low to high. in just a little over 1 month the crash had retraced 1160 (8x144) points for a loss of 50.1% in value from the 2312 high.

## DIVISIONS OF A YEAR

Measure the time elapsed from major turning points in divisions and multiples of a year. **ANNIVERSARIES AND DIVISIONS of one year are very strong forces for a change in trend. 53 days (0.146), 86 days (0.236), 90 days (0.25), 122 days (0.333), 182 days half a year, 225 days 61.8% (time of a VENUS planetary year) of a year, 244 days (0.666), 287 days (0.786), 465 days (1.272), 516 days (1.414), 544 days (1.50), 590 days 161.8% of a year, 609 days (1.666), 632 days (1.732), 730 days (2.00), 816 days (2.236), 956 days (2.618).**

The above times are very strong for signalling a change to trend. You can use them in two ways, count the time as a cycle ie., TOP to TOP or BOTTOM to BOTTOM or as a half cycle TOP to BOTTOM or BOTTOM to TOP.

**Minor trend changes are likely to occur at intervals of 30, 60, 90, 120, 150, 210, 240, 270, 300, 330 Calendar Days/ degrees.** These divisions mark 1/12ths of a year. Once a pattern of turning points in a market is identified adhering to these times the future becomes far more predictive. Be sure to make allowances for long periods over running a little. The reason for this is that the degrees of a year, ie., 360 as opposed to 365 days allow some latitude. If you want to be particularly precise you can count off the static divisions of a year in degrees. This will require either a planetary calendar or an ephemeris. Wave Trader is programmed to make these calculations easier to monitor in absolute terms.

## EXAMPLES OF TIME AT MAJOR TREND CHANGES

DECEMBER GOLD HIGH SEPTEMBER 22nd 1986

**In 1986 on September the 22nd (September 21st was a Sunday) the Gold market made an expected high. (equinox 180 degrees)**

This date coincided with the square of the June low of $287 (287x2 = 574).

September 22nd 1986 was exactly 574 calendar days from the major low February 25th 1985.

574 was also very close to (4x144 = 576).

The December contract high on September 22nd 1986 was $446. The low in 1985 on December gold was $301.50 and the market had risen $446-$301.50 = $144.50 (Fibonacci number 144)

## STATIC TIME

The market had a fast fall over the next few days as traders sold off long positions. By October the 6th the market had climbed back to $445 and was testing the previous top.

On October 8th on its fourth attempt to penetrate the double top of September 22nd the market continued a retracement that lasted 60 days and reduced the December price $70 down to $376.50.

**October 8th 1986 was exactly 1.618 years (590 days) from the major low on February 25th 1985.**

The newspapers probably gave some fundamental reason for this decline but I am positive that it occurred purely by way of the natural actions of traders as price and time squared in the natural sense to these vibrations. By using both price and time squaring methods the dedicated analyst can make his fortune by patiently awaiting signals of this dimension and entering the market at the precise time and price for a change in trend.

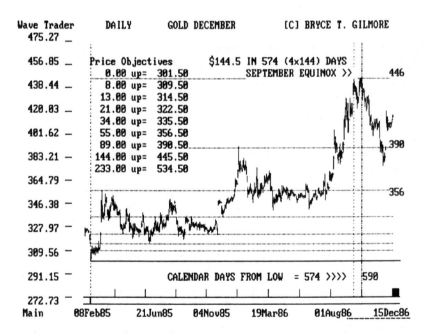

**FIG 3.1      CONTINUOUS COMEX GOLD DECEMBER FUTURES.**

STATIC TIME

## JAPANESE YEN HIGH DECEMBER 31st 1987

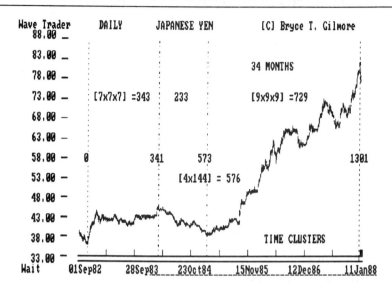

FIG 3.2    FINAL WAVE 34 MONTHS AND 729 (9 CUBED) TRADING DAYS.

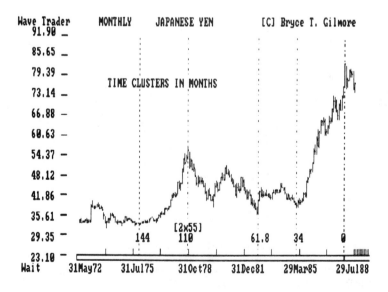

FIG 3.3    FINAL WAVE TOP SQUARED TIME WITH MOST MAJOR SWINGS.

STATIC TIME

# COMEX GOLD HIGH DECEMBER 14th 1987

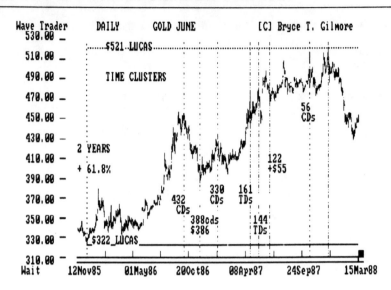

FIG 3.4    SOME TIME VIBRATIONS AT THE DECEMBER 1987 HIGH.

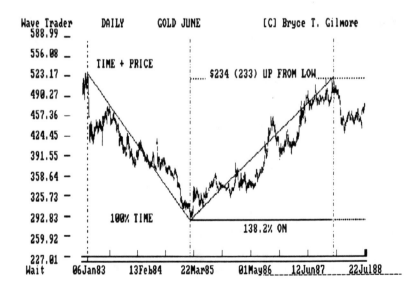

FIG 3.5    WAVE VIBRATION AT THE DECEMBER 1987 HIGH.

STATIC TIME

# ALL ORDINARIES INDEX - HIGH 21st September 1987

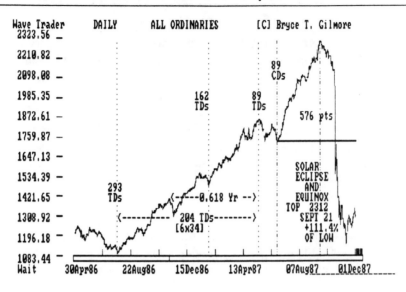

FIG 3.6     SHARE INDEX TIME VIBRATIONS

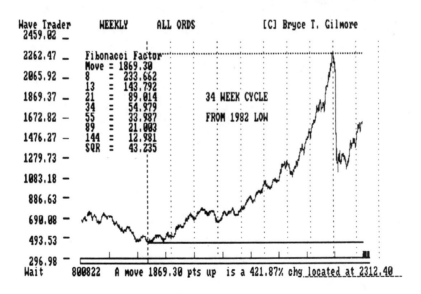

FIG 3.7     SHARE INDEX TIME CYCLES

## SUMMARY

There are many other important time elements to be considered for a change in trend, but these are not common numbers and require dynamic calculations to be made over past data. These are fully detailed in the pages ahead.

Free trading markets are heavily influenced by the power of technical traders. Technical traders are speculators who use mathematical concepts to guide their decision making. At times when the signals are clearly strong enough they combine as a force to turn even the strongest apparent trend. When these actions coincide with the natural vibrations a market will react violently allowing excellent opportunity from which to profit.

In practice, the best use of these time periods can be achieved by measuring off time from major and minor swing points, look to locate CLUSTERS of time zones that adhere to important numbers, be they daily, weekly or monthly periods.

Carefully watch the 90, 120, 180, 240, 270 and 360 degree points of a year, beginning from the March equinox, for major trend reversals. These are the 1/4, 1/3, 1/2, 2/3, 3/4 and 1 year periods.

Always monitor time periods of 53-55, 89-90, 122, 140-147, 177-182, 225, 238, 244, 287, 321, 365, 385, 432, 465, 516, 544, 576, 590, 610, 632, 730, 816, 956 and 1096 days from any major high or low, especially when a TREND appears to be in its final stages.

# STATIC PRICE INCREMENTS AND LEVELS FOR SUPPORT & RESISTANCE AREAS

## PRICE ELEMENTS

The perspective of markets is clearly identified when charted. Charts have two axis. These axes are the time scale and the price scale. In the geometry of markets each axis is as important as the other. In the previous chapter we covered static time elements that can signal a change in investor sentiment that leads to a change in the apparent trend. To confirm our views on time we use price. The term that I will use will be *time and price "squaring"*. Squarings of time and price balance a third element known in technical terms as space. (a later chapter is devoted to time, price and space)

PRICE is the most common measurement used by technical traders in determining support and resistance areas in markets. Few traders really appreciate the value of measuring time, yet most have a knowledge of calculating price objectives.

If we refer to chapter 2 and the ancient geometry that gives us a basis of natural numbers we can apply these to increments of price movement as well as time.

## FIBONACCI DEGREE PRICE RISES AND DECLINES

The first series of numbers to watch are price moves in ratios of the Fibonacci series. If we investigate past markets we will find that trend changes regularly occur in markets after a rise or fall in points coinciding with the Fibonacci series, ie 13, 21, 34, 55, 89, 144, 233, 377, 610 et cetera.

The way we monitor these levels is to extend price values in Fibonacci degree up from lows and down from highs. Clusters of price support and resistance levels will be clearly identified.

On page 28, FIG 3.5 the lower chart demonstrates a price move of $233 from the Gold low in February 1985 to the high of December 1987.

STATIC PRICE

FIG 4.1      FIBONACCI PRICE LEVELS FROM A MAJOR LOW.

## PRICE LEVELS IN FIBONACCI DEGREE

The power of these natural numbers seems to play an important part in the subconscious actions of traders therefore it is important to watch for reversals of trend that coincide with exact price levels on these numbers, ie., a trend could terminate at levels of **55** points, **89** points, **144** points, **233** points, **377** points, et cetera, in actual **PRICE VALUE**.

The December gold chart above terminated its bull trend on the September 1986 **EQUINOX** after rising **$144** from the 1985 low. On the same day the 1st month futures chart had risen exactly **$161.80** from its 1985 low. I will never forget this high as it cost us a $500,000 account and some pride. The fund had allocated $25000 to see if we could trade our techniques. The gold high swing was $446 so I purchased 100 Dec $400 puts with the $25000 and $5000 worth on my own account without thinking. The puts expired worthless on the 8th November, 13 days later the low of $376.50 (**377**) was registered. If I had bought more time my decision would have been very profitable. I never take option positions now unless I buy 90 days worth of time. As Gann said, "I can teach you the rules but you will have to overcome your own weaknesses to profit by them".

# STATIC PRICE

**FIG 4.2**

This chart of the December contract demonstrates a price rise of **$199** from the 25th February 1985 low $301.50 to the 27th April 1987 high $501.00.

## LUCAS DEGREE PRICE RANGES AND LEVELS

The LUCAS series of numbers, ie., **11, 18, 29, 47, 76, 123, 199, 322, 521, 843**, et cetera, can be used in the same way as the Fibonacci series. These numbers relate geometrically with the Fibonacci series.

On page 28, the upper chart FIG 3.4 of June Gold demonstrates a geometric price move in Lucas degree from the low of **$322**.5 on 11th December 1985 to the high **$521** on 14th December 1987 (two years, 720 degrees) and an increase of **$199 (61.8%** rise in value). This top was also **$233**.5 (Fibonacci) from the 1985 low of $287 **(2x144)**.

FIG 3.4 clearly demonstrates the value of these LUCAS numbers, two very significant reversals in trend occurred at exact Lucas price levels, ie $322 and $521. When the time factors, the percentage factors and signals from other ranges and market squarings were taken into account, the technical picture was outstanding.

STATIC PRICE

## SQUARE OF 144

144 is psychologically one of the most important numbers to watch when working with relationships of time and price. 144 relates to the harmonic of the speed of light. See *ANTI-GRAVITY AND THE WORLD GRID*. Published by Adventures Unlimited Press, Box 22, Stelle, Illinois, USA. Price moves of 72 (half 144) points, 144 points, 288 (2x144) points, 432 (3x144) points, 576 (4x144) points, 720 (5x144 and 2x360) points.

5 is a natural harmonic cycle and multiples thereof are equally as important, ie., 10x144 = 1440, 15x 144 = 2160, 20x144 = 2880.

Price and time multiples of 144 in calendar days, degrees of a year, trading days, weeks and months should be measured off important swing highs and lows in markets for a possible guide to a future trend reversal. Price levels in multiples of 144 points, ie., $288, $432 et cetera, should be monitored as possible natural support and resistance areas in markets. 144 is of prime importance. Not only is it a Fibonacci number but also the square of 12 (12x12 = 144). 360 divided by 2.5 (half a harmonic cycle) equals 144. 5 times 144 = 720 the master number, two revolutions of the circle.

**Squares of 144 to monitor are :-**

**144 ($12^2$), 288 ($17^2$ = 289), 432, 576 ($24^2$), 720, 864, 1008, 1152, 1296 ($36^2$), 1440, 1584, 1728 ($12^3$), 1872, 2016, 2160, 2304 ($48^2$), 2448, 2592, 2736, 2880, 3024(55x55), 3168 (Plato), 3312 and 3600 ($60^2$).**

The more important SQUARES are the ones divisable by 90, 180, 360 and 720 and the ones which are natural squares or cubes of other numbers.

Other important divisions of 144 are :-

161 = 144 x 1.118 (PHI)

183 = 144 x 1.272 (half year in days)

204 = 144 x 1.414 (6x34)

233 = 144 x 1.618 (Fibonacci)

249 = 144 x 1.732

296 = 144 x 2.058

322 = 144 x 2.236 (Lucas) and 377 = 144 x 2.618 (Fibonacci)

STATIC PRICE

## SIMPLE SQUARINGS OF TIME AND PRICE

Time and price will square when, say, a market moves 90 points in 90 days or 144 points in 144 days. Both of these examples would be exactly square as units of price equal units of time. In Gann terms you could join the start and finish with a 1x1 angle.

**FIG 4.3**

The following chart demonstates a major move in the Platinum market that **squared a $432 rise in 432 days.**

## COMPLEX SQUARINGS OF PRICE IN TIME

Squarings of price in time often occur in a more complex relationship. For instance a valid squaring could fall on any ratio that is related to the Golden Rectangle, Square or Circle. Relationships of time that could balance price could be a 0.618 relationship, a 1.414 (root 2) relationship or even a 1.272 (root Phi) relationship. For instance the 1st month futures gold rose from $281.20 in 1985 to $443 on 8th October, 1986; this was a rise of $161.80 in 1.618 years. December gold rose $144 ($12^2$) and June gold rose $169 ($13^2$).

## STATIC PRICE

At the moment it is important to realize that a move of 89 points in 144 days would signal a price move of 0.618 units of price to 1.00 unit of time. Similarly a price move of 144 points in 89 days would signal a 1.618 relationship of price to time. $233 in 34 weeks could signal a valid squaring of price in time. In fact the June Comex Gold contract made a complex bear market rally from June 1982 until February 1983 that terminated on this exact ratio.

When price terminates a move on clusters of Fibonacci or Lucas numbers, even on squares or multiples of these numbers, a valid price level has been attained. Should the important time elements mentioned in chapter 3 coincide with this price level then a genuine "squaring" of time and price has normally been witnessed.

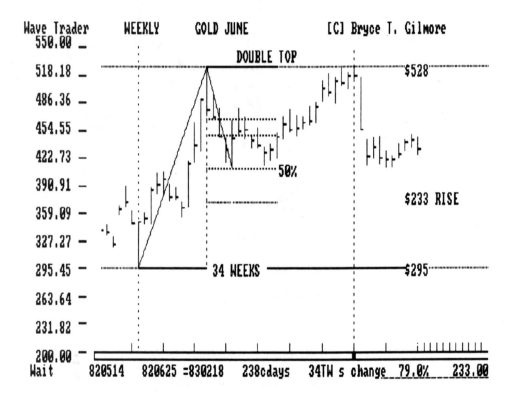

**FIG 4.4**    **GOLD 1982-1983 BEAR MARKET RALLY**

**PRICE ROSE   $233   PER OUNCE IN   34   WEEKS ON THE JUNE CONTINUOUS FUTURES CONTRACT.**

## USING STATIC PRICE ELEMENTS

The Gold market is one area that I have found to be very reliable in its reversal signals often generated via the above methods. Some heavily traded stocks often move in these relationships. The criteria for using these signals for trade timing should be that the market is free trading (that means it must be free of governmental subsidies or interference). The more diversified the participants and the greater the activity of traders the more reliable these methods become.

Generally any free trading market be it a currency option, stock or commodity will lend itself to these technical measurements. When analysising a bond index or a share price index consider these relationships in percentage change. In fact as far as everything is concerned always consider percentage change in important static divisions.

Important price expansions or contractions should be measured up from any low of importance and down from any high of importance. Clusters where multiple price calculations are falling on similar price levels should be given priority as strong probable areas of support and resistance. When time clusters of importance, ie., clusters of time measured forward in the degrees mentioned earlier - fall due from previous swing highs and lows, the market will be in a position where price in time can square out.

Even though this chapter is not directed to time it is important to realize that as the future unfolds time will be balanced by price. Sometimes trend changes will seem vague in their relationships, but later on some relationship will unfold to confirm what has passed. By this statement I mean that it could happen that a bottom or top in a market is reached prior to say 144 days or 233 days from an approaching Equinox, Solstice, Apogee or Perigee.*

By working backwards from the important cardinal points in a year other time elements will be present at major price levels using static elements. An example comes to mind on the All ordinaries index this year. February 10th, 1988 was a low point (price bottomed at 1169.6) that signaled the lift off for the latest rally which has so far seen a high of 1642. This was just 142 calendar days from the all time high of 1987 also 72 calendar days (half 144) and 47 trading days from a minor correction to the great crash. February 10th /12th is also 144 days prior to the July 5th, 1988 Apogee (position of Earth in its annual orbit when velocity is at its slowest and it is at its most greatest distance from the Sun), February 11th was also 233 days from the June 1987 Solstice.

* CHAPTER 16 WILL GIVE A MORE DETAILED EXPLANATION about THIS PLANETARY PHENOMENA.

STATIC PRICE

# BE ALERT TO THE NATURE OF MARKETS

As one learns more about the cycles of nature that manifest themselves in markets, the ratios and numbers produced from the square, cube, circle, and the golden rectangle will take on an importance not formally recognized.

Research of past markets will confirm the regularity of trend changes occurring at strict numerological price in time squarings, in the ratios of ancient geometry.

To succeed in using these techniques one has to develop a sense for working forward of the market; whilst at the same time keeping an open mind to the nature of markets.

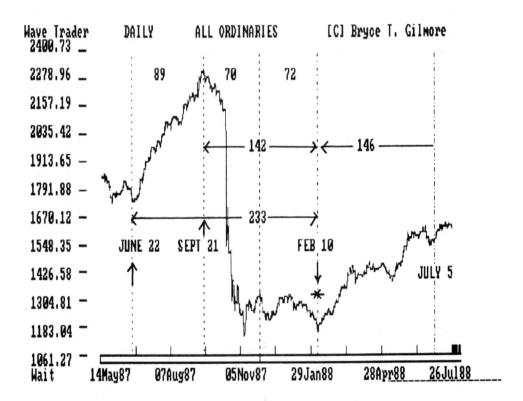

**FIG 4.5** TIME FORWARD AND TIME BACKWARDS - 10/12 February, 1988

**DEMONSTRATES THAT STATIC RATIOS IN TIME ARE VERY IMPORTANT TECHNICAL METHODS TO MONITOR.**

# DYNAMIC PRICE LEVELS FOR MARKET SUPPORT AND RESISTANCE

This section covers the **natural price barriers** that markets encounter when in either an uptrend or downtrend. The reason I have headed these supports and resistances as DYNAMIC is because they are forces generated from previous market action. To measure these forces requires making calculations based on the value of previous market highs and lows.

The most natural area of resistance or support encountered in price movement is at the double or half way levels of a previous major swing low or high. If a market were to rise in value 100% most traders would recognize it was expensive and become reluctant purchasers, even to the extent some would become willing sellers. Should a market fall in value by 50% it would seem inexpensive at half the price, the new value would attract buying.

Investor sentiment plays the major role in determining the price levels to which a trend will go before reversing. The psychology of traders follows a mathematical pattern. The important ratios of the sacred canon handed down through the ages are the ratios found in the **CUBE, CIRCLE & THE GOLDEN MEAN.**

Resistance levels that could halt a market trend are percentage change to price in INCREASES of 33.3%, 38.2%, 50%, 61.8%, 66.6%, 70.7%, 78.6%, 100%, 141.8%, 161.8%, 173.2% and 200%. These can be seen from studies of past markets. At times in the future these levels will continue to be reliable.

In the case of a bear trend, support will be reached when a market has declined to represent value. These levels could be at a discount to previous high prices by discounts of 16.6%, 20%, 23.6%, 25%, 29.3%, 33.3%, 38.2%, 50%, 57.7%, 61.8% and 66.6%.

Dependent on the cause the effect will vary in relative degree. The larger the dimension of the trend the greater the price rise or decline. Market psychology will be your guide in these circumstances.

The best use of these technical tools comes from experience and your ability to read the market sentiment. A trend won't just cease because it hits one of these values. The sentiment must be right and so must the time factors.

## DYNAMIC PRICE LEVELS

## DOUBLE TOPS AND BOTTOMS

Two of the most important levels of resistance and support to become familiar with are past market price levels. These levels are easily visible when charted. If one maintains long term price charts for a commodity or stock these previous high and low points can be easily monitored.

As a market approaches previous high points investor psychology changes, they fear that prices have gone too high and stocks or commodities are no longer worth holding, this precipitates selling. The further the distance between double tops the stronger the psychological effect. Traders learn from the past and remember what happens when markets rise too high in too short a time. When a market declines to a previous low point the natural subconscious alerts investors to the possible value of buying. This action supports any further decline.

If time dictates a change in trend and the market is overbought or oversold at these levels then a reaction to trend will be more certain.

FIG 5.1          COPPER DOUBLE TOPS 1980-1987

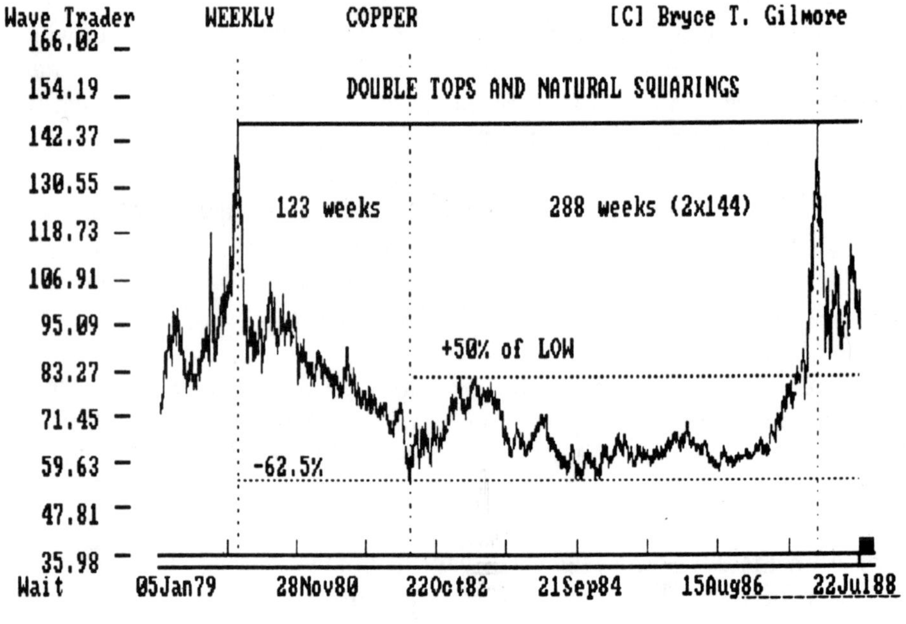

The first chart above is the Copper cycle between the high of 1980 and the high of 1987. The bear market decline was a fall of 62.5% in value in 123 weeks (LUCAS). The initial reaction to this fall was a rise of 50% in value before declining once again to test the lower end of the range.

A double bottom was formed and a new bull market was underway. After a dramatic rise in prices throughout 1987 the bull market expired exactly on the 288 week time frame (2x144) from the low of 1982 forming a double top with the 1980 high. The level reached in 1980 was $1.47 per pound, in 1987 price terminated at $1.46 per pound. At the time market expectation was for much higher prices to come. As you can see from the chart this did not eventuate and the correction to the rise was swift and devastating.

Just recently the Sugar market went into a meteoric rise. This next chart shows the geometric chart of NCSCE MARCH SUGAR #11 and how time and price were balanced in Fibonacci degree at the double top of July 14th, 1988. The double top formed was within 0.08 of a cent of the 1983 high. Top tick was 14.39 cents per pound, 1 tick off 10 times 144 and the time between the two tops was 267 weeks (3x89) another Fibonacci relationship. The other time frame of interest shown is the relationship of the first advance from 1985 to the double bottom before the final advance resumed. These two periods balanced out at exactly 383 trading days. (maybe it's a coincidence but 383 ties in with the 38.2 ratio from PHI). The price at the double bottom was 5.77 cents (4x144) which means that the rise up to 14.39 cents was 6 times 144, this was also another technical factor present at the 1988 high.

FIG 5.2         MARCH SUGAR DOUBLE TOPS 1983-1988

# DYNAMIC PRICE LEVELS

## 100% MULTIPLE RISE IN VALUE FROM A LOW PRICE

This, in Gann terms, is the 1st square of the low price, one of the most significant areas for a reaction to trend. It may not necessarily mean that the trend will not continue on at a later date but in the short term these areas are a logical psychological force to be overcome before further advances can be made. Once breached, these 100% levels can act as support. I have included a chart of an Australian stock MOUNT ISA MINES to demonstrate this characteristic of markets. A major low was formed at 99 cents in July 1986. The third wave advance from this low terminated at $2.98, exactly 200% up and on the 2nd square of resistance from the low. A 50% retracement of the total rise from 99 cents came quickly. This coincided with the 100% square of the low price. The market then resumed its upward trend which terminated at $3.80. The previous highest high on MOUNT ISA had been at $3.78 back in 1980. A double top ended any further advances in that cycle. The bear market decline terminated at the 66.6% discount level to the new high. Two time elements are shown on this weekly chart, others will be shown in later chapters as more confirming methods of market geometry are demonstrated.

FIG 5.3     MOUNT ISA 3rd WAVE TOP = 200% SQUARE OF LOW.

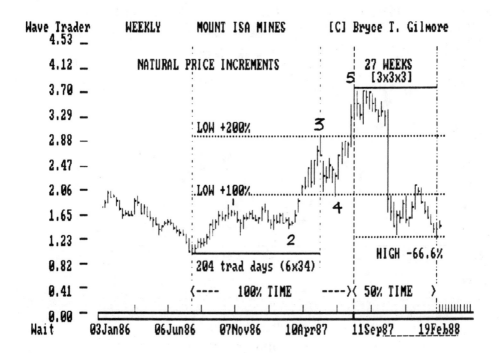

## 50% DECLINE IN VALUE FROM A HIGH PRICE

In Gann terms this level marks the half square of the high, the mid point between the high price and zero value. Once a market declines to a level of 50% of its highest price a reaction will be almost certain, depending on the fundamental reasons for the decline and the duration. Often a violent reaction will ensue as investors scramble to pick up the newly identified bargain. The more psychologically oversold a market is the greater the upward reaction. Again, this may only signal an intermediate interruption to the bearish longer term trend.

All Ordinaries Index CRASH OF 1987 - Support was met at the 50% level of the all time high. From a high of 2312 on the 21st September 1987 the market declined down to 1149.2 on the 11th November 1987, a fall of 1163 points. 2312 less 50% equals 1156. 1156 divided by 144 equals 8. On the day of the low of 1149.2 the market sentiment was one of complete despair, investor confidence was in tatters. On the evening of November 11th, 1987 I attended a meeting of about 30 technical traders. When it was my time to speak I outlined all of the reasons I had for buying the market that day just prior to the close, not one other person in the room had bought that day on his own analysis. Had it not been for my knowledge of investor psychology and market geometry I am certain I would have lacked the confidence to act against the prevailing trend.

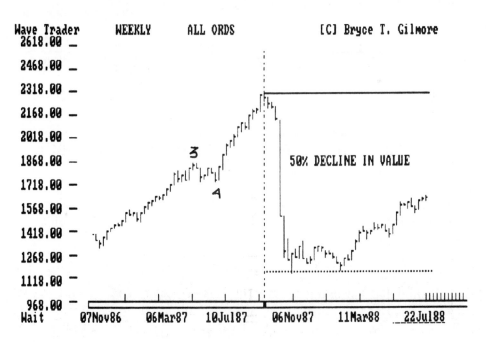

FIG 5.4   AUSTRALIAN ALL ORDINARIES - 50% SQUARE OF HIGH.

Another example of a 50% decline in value of the previous highest level attained is demonstrated by this chart of the Swiss Franc against the US$. This decline unfolded over a seven year period and was a major bear market decline, nevertheless support was reached within points of the 50% value of the 1978 high.

FIG 5.5         SWISS FRANC 1985 LOW WAS 50% SQUARE OF THE 1978 HIGH.

## 61.8% to 66.6% DECLINE IN VALUE FROM A HIGH PRICE

This area is the most significant support for the termination of a major long term bear market. I am including numerous examples of this phenomena to demonstrate the importance of these levels.

The first example is the chart of the Australian dollar versus the US$. The Australian dollar began a decline in 1974 from a high of $1.495 to the US$. In 1986 some 12 years (144 months) later a bottom was made at $0.572 to the US$. $1.495 less 61.8% equals $0.571 another amazing example of the ratio of PHI at work in the geometry of markets.

If this chart had been plotted as a reciprocal ie., with the A$ expressed as a factor of the US$ then the value in 1974 of a US$ in AUD$ would have been $0.668, in 1986 at the low it would have required $1.748 to buy one US$. $0.668 increased in value by 1.618 (phi) equals $1.748.

FIG 5.6    AUSTRALIAN DOLLAR SQUARING 1974 HIGH BY 61.8%.

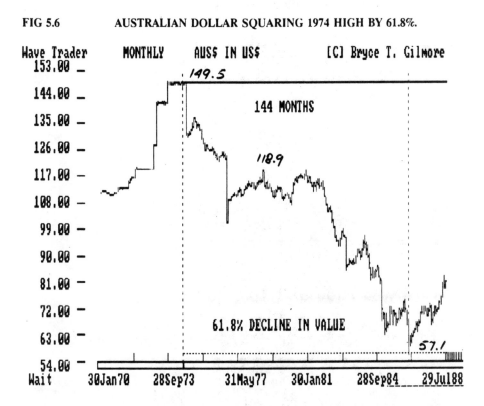

This currency moves in fibonacci ratios of all types. For instance, the decline from the 1978 high of 118.9 to the history low at 57.1 in 1986 was a fall of exactly 61.8 cents.

A rise in value of 61.8% from the low of 57.1 would give a target of 92.38 cents, also a 61.8% retracement of the 1974-1986 range (149.5 - 57.1) [61.8% of 92.4 equals 57.1] lies at 114.2, a 38.2% retracement [38.2% of 92.4 equals 35.3] and lies at 92.4 cents.

At the low of 57.1 one US dollar bought AUD$ 1.75, on the 8th December 1988, 864 calendar days [6 times 144] from the 1986 low the market made an intermediate reversal after trading to a high of 88.33. That high represented US$ 1.00 to AUD$ 1.132 or 61.8 cents less than AUD$ 1.75 at its 1986 high point.

# DYNAMIC PRICE LEVELS

The next example is the major Australian share market decline of 1970 to 1974, The adjusted All Ordinaries index made a high of 448 in 1970. By the low of September 30th, 1974 the price had reduced itself to 173.5 points. 448 less 61.8% equals 171.14 points. This is another incidence of PHI relationships and the geometry of markets at work.

**FIG 5.7**     1970-1974 AUST SHARE INDEX

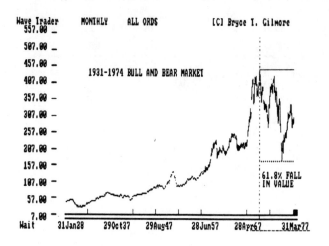

**FIG 5.8**     1972-1985 IMM BP.

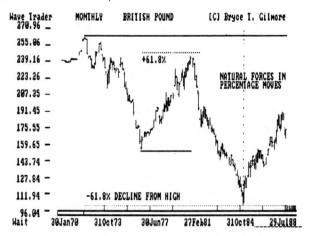

This chart of the British Pound versus the US$ shows two occurrences of PHI ratios in major market moves. The major decline from 1972 in the pound terminated at the 61.8% discount level in 1985. A primary rally in the midst of the decline rallied 61.8% in value along the way.

Comex Gold chart of the continuous December contract prices.

FIG 5.9 - Shows two time and price levels easily recognized from the methods discussed so far. The main example here is the support zone in the area of the 66.6% discount to the all time high. Time itself, and other methods that follow, will show how it was possible to locate the 1985 low support within $1.00 per ounce.

FIG 5.9    COMEX GOLD DECEMBER FUTURES

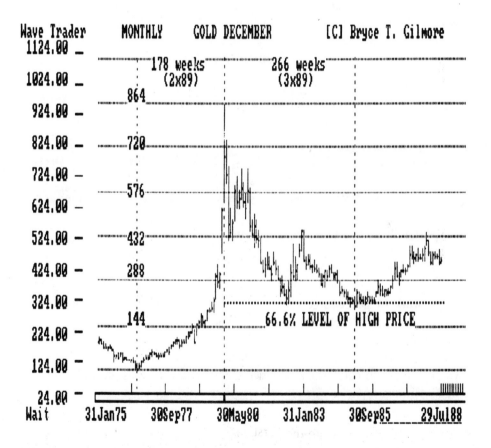

## SUMMARY OF DYNAMIC PRICE LEVELS

The important message in this chapter is to learn about and remember the **PRIMARY** technical areas for major support and resistance. When a market is approaching these areas you will normally be in a state of flux, just as the other market players are. Don't abandon technical methods, especially when the crowd are totally weighted in one direction. Markets will turn on the technical levels, the greater the overbalance between buyers and sellers, being observed, then the greater the probability. I can vouch for this as I have experienced that many now and I still get nervous when a new one comes along. One must remember that the final high in a bull market or the final low in a bear market is the pendulum point where everybody holds a similar view. Or if they don't no one is prepared to create liquidity, which boils down to the same thing.

The first advance in any new trend occurs from the action of the sellers or buyers trying to take profits in a vacuum. Not because all of a sudden everyone became smart and identified the bear market low or the bull market top. Sheer power of numbers retained total control, not the individual traders.

**KEEP A WATCH FOR THESE SET UPS:-**

**Double tops and bottoms** that occur over long periods of time.

Levels of **50%, 61.8% and 66.6% declines in value** from an all time high.

**100% SQUARES OF LOWS** as major price resistance.

**Always think in percentage terms** when looking for a major support or resistance level that will echo in a reversal and mark the beginning of a new long term trend.

If you can learn to catch the long term trends you can relax once you have established positions.

# 6. SQUARING PRICE FOR LOCATION OF FUTURE SUPPORT AND RESISTANCE ZONES

The Gann technique for squaring price adopts three approaches :-

      1. SQUARING A PRICE RANGE

      2. SQUARING A LOW PRICE

      3. SQUARING A HIGH PRICE

## SQUARING PRICE

The term squaring relates to calculating percentage increases of a price by values of half or 100% increments. Increments of each square in 1/8th values as well as 1/3rds are important for minor divisions. Fibonacci degree increments are also important. The major levels are 50% and 100%.

As an example the squares of 144 are :-

| | | | |
|---|---|---|---|
| 1st Square | = 288  | (144 + 144)     |
| 2nd Square | = 432  | (144 + [2*144]) |
| 3rd Square | = 576  | (144 + [3*144]) |
| 4th Square | = 720  | (144 + [4*144]) |
| 5th Square | = 864  | (144 + [5*144]) |
| 6th Square | = 1008 | (144 + [6*144]) |
| 7th Square | = 1152 | (144 + [7*144]) |
| 8th Square | = 1296 | (144 + [8*144]) |

and so forth

## Square divisions from zero of 144 would be :-

| | | |
|---|---|---|
| 1/8 Square | = 18 | (144*1/8) |
| 1/4 Square | = 36 | (144*1/4) |
| 1/3 Square | = 48 | (144*1/3) |
| 3/8 Square | = 54 | (144*3/8) |
| 1/2 Square | = 72 | (144*1/2) |
| 5/8 Square | = 90 | (144*5/8) |
| 2/3 Square | = 96 | (144*2/3) |
| 3/4 Square | = 108 | (144*3/4) |
| 7/8 Square | = 126 | (144*7/8) |
| 1st Square | = 144 | |

## IMPORTANT DIVISIONS OF SQUARES FROM ZERO OF 144

IN PHI (1.618) RATIO, ROOT 2 (1.414) and ROOT 5 (2.236) INCREMENTS

| | | |
|---|---|---|
| .146 | Square | = 21 |
| .236 | Square | = 34 |
| .382 | Square | = 55 |
| .618 | Square | = 89 |
| .707 | Square | = 102 |
| .786 | Square | = 113 |
| 1.00 | Square | = 144 |
| 1.414 | Square | = 204 |
| 1.618 | Square | = 233 |
| 2.00 | Square | = 288 |
| 2.236 | Square | = 322 |
| 2.618 | Square | = 377 |
| 5.00 | Square | = 720 |
| 8.00 | Square | = 1152 |

## SQUARING A PRICE RANGE

**The term squaring refers to divisions of 100%** of something, in the case of price squaring we divide the price to be squared into naturally square divisions. The main level of resistance or support will be reached when a move either progresses another 100% or falls 100%.

To square out a range we first have to define that range.

The first thing we need to find out for any stock or commodity option is the **HISTORY HIGH AND THE HISTORY LOW. THIS IS THE PRIMARY RANGE TO BE SQUARED.**

**THE SQUARE OF THE HISTORY RANGE AND THE DIVISIONS OF THAT SQUARE WILL BE THE NATURAL LEVELS FOR FUTURE SUPPORT AND RESISTANCE.**

The history high and history low will provide the means to calculate these levels most clearly. Any future price action that contains itself within this range will be subject to these technical levels of support and resistance.

The purpose of squaring a range is to find the mathematical levels of previous price movements that will cause a natural resistance or support to current price action.

To appreciate why range squaring is so important in market analysis it helps to understand the mentality of traders. In any bull move many participants will be caught buying right at the top; as prices decline in a bear move professional traders will buy more to average out the price of their holdings. When a new uptrend or correction reaches the level of their averaged out price they will liquidate part of their holdings. This action will increase selling pressure and temporarily halt any future gains.

Markets move in four phases, accumulation, advance, distribution, decline. Accumulation occurs before any sustained advance. Distribution occurs before any sustained decline.

Accumulation and distribution phases occur when the smart money players have a shift in sentiment about the future direction of prices. Advances come when demand overbalances supply, declines naturally occur because of oversupply.

## EXAMPLE OF RANGE SQUARING USING SOYBEANS

The history high so far registered by the July beans was 1290 cents per bushel, trading there on the 5th June 1973. The known low price is 44 cents per bushel registered on the 28th December 1932.

Using this historic range we can calculate the natural levels that technical traders should use in the future to locate possible support and resistance zones.

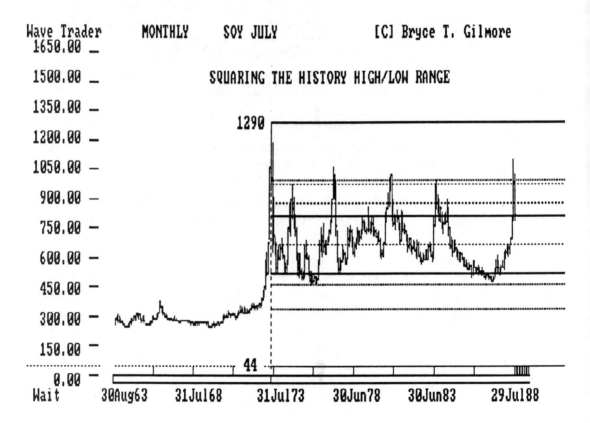

FIG 6.1  DIVISIONS OF A RANGE DETERMINE NATURAL PRICE SUPPORTS

## SOYBEAN RANGE LEVELS OF EXTREME IMPORTANCE

| | | |
|---|---|---|
| 1290 | HISTORY HIGH | 100% |
| 1134 | 7/8ths | 87.5% |
| 978 | 3/4 | 75% |
| 874 | 2/3rds | 66.6% |
| 667 | support levels | 50% |
| 459 | 1/3rd | 33.3% |
| 355 | 1/4 | 25% |
| 200 | 1/8 | 12.5% |
| 44 | HISTORY LOW | 0% |

If at a future time the price rises above the HISTORY HIGH of 1290 cents we can make projections for future resistance based on this range, by simply expanding the range upwards in square divisions.

The following calculations would be applicable :-
The range is 1246 (1290 less 44)

25% of 1246 = 311.5............................ ADDED TO THE HIGH 1290 = 1601.5
33% of 1246 = 411.2............................ ADDED TO THE HIGH 1290 = 1701.2
50% of 1246 = 623.0............................ ADDED TO THE HIGH 1290 = 1913.0

and so forth (66.6%, 75%, 100% et cetera) .....

Square divisions of a range that will offer price resistance or support do not necessarily only rely on the history high and history low. Shorter term support and resistances may be established using more recent extremes in range. **In fact from an everyday trading point of view these are the levels that are most useful.** It pays to always watch the longer term range levels when they are close to the price action in an extended move of a long bull or bear campaign.

**DOUBLE AND TRIPLE TOPS** These levels are 100% levels of a previous range, the further apart in time that they occur the more important is the technical significance.

**SHORT TERM DOUBLE TOPS OR BOTTOMS** often form prior to a major trend change. The market first makes a high or low point, then it will make a fast correction. An advance or decline in a very short time period back to the previous high or low price that fails to penetrate these shorter term levels will form a double top or bottom. If a time period coincides with this type of exhaustion phase, then a major turning point in trend is indicated. Always be on your guard for double tops or bottoms as these are one of the best entry points for trading purposes. The most significant technical indication is for a market to penetrate or fail on it's 4th attempt to rise above or fall below a previous turning point. Here is a point to trade off because if a market penetrates a triple top or bottom you can be sure of a good move..

## MARKET CORRECTIONS

Corrections to major and minor moves often retrace previous ranges in square degree or Phi degree exactly to the tick. For instance, common retracements in a correction are 38.2%, 50%, 61.8%, 66.6% of the preceding range. A more detailed study of retracements and projections of range is covered in a later chapter.

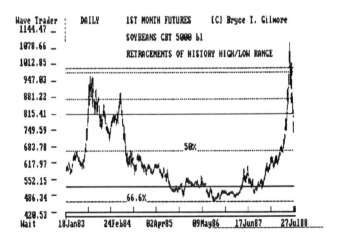

FIG 6.2 ENLARGEMENT OF THE HISTORY RANGE RETRACEMENT LEVELS.

# SQUARING PRICE

## SQUARING A LOW PRICE

As previously mentioned a square of a price is a 100% increase or decrease. In the case of a low this extends to future squares of the original low, ie 100% 200% 300% 400% 500% etc,.

First we start with the history low of any particular stock or commodity option. For our example we will use Soybeans once again.

The square of the low price, 44 cents, will offer resistance to future rises in the following increments.

| | | |
|---|---|---|
| 44 increased by | 25% | = 55 |
| 44 increased by | 33% | = 58.5 |
| 44 increased by | 50% | = 66 |
| 44 increased by | 66% | = 73 |
| 44 increased by | 75% | = 77 |
| 44-1st Square | 100% | = 88 |
| 44-2nd Square | 200% | = 132 |
| 44-3rd Square | 300% | = 176 |
| 44-4th Square | 400% | = 220 |
| 44-5th Square | 500% | = 264 |
| 44-10th Square | 1000% | = 484 |
| 44-12th Square | 1200% | = 572 |
| 44-21st Square | 2100% | = 968 |
| 44-24th Square | 2400% | = 1100 |

These values demonstrate how to square a low price.

**FIG 6.3 SQUARES OF 44 FROM ZERO.** The low of February 1987 on the July contract was 477 which gave the last bull market a range of 622.5 cents (7x89 = 623). Coincidently this was exactly 50% of the history range 44-1290 = 1246 (14x89).

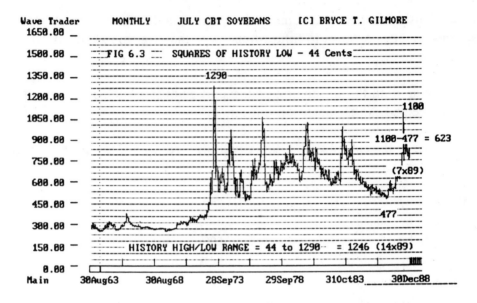

**FIG 6.4 1983 AND 1987 MARKET HIGHS.** The last two bull market highs in Soybeans for the spot futures contract fell on squares of 44. In 1983 a high of 968 on the November contract ended a dramatic rise in prices. In 1988 on June 23rd, 1099.5 cents was the high of the July contract. .

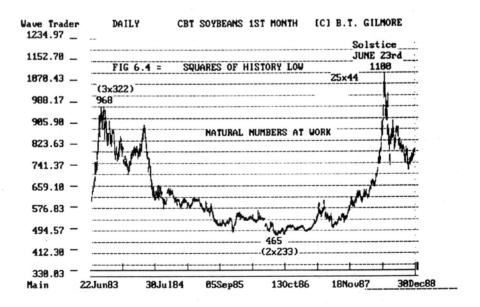

## SQUARING A HIGH PRICE

Squaring a high price to find support levels is a common practice. I have found that on occasions it pays to look at squares of previous highs expanded vertically when finding resistance levels for markets traveling upwards into previously uncharted territory.

If we square a high price down then we can only use one square, if a price were to fall 100% then it would be worthless, this would be a very rare occurrence.

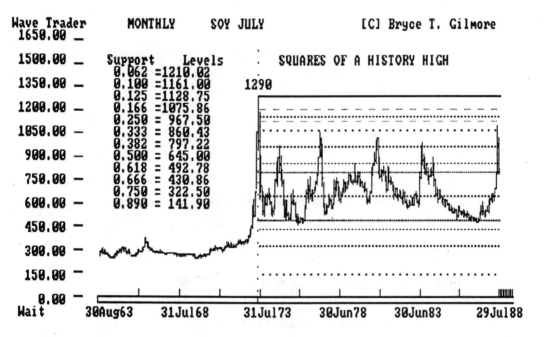

FIG 6.5 Using the history high of Soybeans once again, 1290 cents, we can examine the percentage levels that should naturally create support and resistance whilst trading beneath this price.

| 1290 | less 25%   | = | 967.5  |
|------|------------|---|--------|
| 1290 | less 33.3% | = | 860.4  |
| 1290 | less 37.5% | = | 806.25 |
| 1290 | less 50%   | = | 645    |
| 1290 | less 62.5% | = | 483.75 |

SQUARING PRICE

| | | | |
|---|---|---|---|
| 1290 | less 66.6% | = | 431 |
| 1290 | less 75% | = | 322.5 |
| 1290 | less 87.5% | = | 161.25 |

**Squaring a high price is a very simple exercise as you can see.** Oddly enough as we approach the lower end of this squaring we find a link between 144 and the values.

## ANY MAJOR TURNING POINT

**It will always pay to square all recent major lows and highs as a guide to future support and resistance levels. These levels, depending upon their significance will act as future support or resistance in the eyes of technical traders. If any other strong technical influences apply at a time the market trades at these levels, then a reversal in trend is highly likely.**

## MAJOR PRICE SUPPORT AND RESISTANCE ZONES

**SQUARE RANGES IN THE FOLLOWING ORDER :-**

**HISTORY HIGH TO HISTORY LOW**

**PRIMARY HIGH TO PRIMARY LOW**

**INTERMEDIATE HIGH TO INTERMEDIATE LOW**

**MINOR HIGH TO MINOR LOW**

next keep up the price levels generated by percentages of :-

**HIGHS OF MAJOR AND PRIMARY DEGREE.**

**LOWS OF MAJOR AND PRIMARY DEGREE.**

THESE ARE THE MOST SIGNIFICANT AREAS FOR A LIKELY CHANGE IN TREND.

# 7. DYNAMIC TIME SUPPORTS AND RESISTANCES

This section covers the natural time barriers exerted by previous market action. The time axis for any commodity or stock is even more important to market analysis than the price axis. The measurements we use to calculate these dynamic forces are again the ratios found in the SQUARE, CIRCLE, GOLDEN RECTANGLE and the GREAT PYRAMID of GIZA.

## PREVIOUS MAJOR RANGE TIMES

The most natural area for a change in trend is when a previous major range time has been balanced in time. It is fairly simple to understand that the trend forces at work in markets take time to dissipate. In science we are taught that for every action there is an equal and opposite reaction. Any shock to a market will generate a force that compels the participants to act in a certain way. Depending upon the mass psychology of traders, price will often trend in an upward or downward direction for long periods of time. Along the way there will be corrections to this trend as minor forces interact to the current long term force in motion. The further away in time we go from a major shock then, theoretically, the less force it has as time has allowed the traders room to erase this past from their memory. In practice, however, the mass psychology that drives prices up and down in varying cycles has some natural basis. Natural forces in markets can be measured, and the accuracy of these measurements is often amazingly precise for predicting days on which a future change to the current trend will occur.

The most important range time to start measuring future vibrations off is the last major trend. The term vibrations has been selected to cover the varying measurements one can use to calculate future areas where a change in trend will be most likely. If one studies price movement, one will see that in each major trend a series of market movements go together to form the complete move. Ralph Elliott earlier this century discovered that bull markets generally expand in five wave movements and bear markets unfold in threes. Elliott states in his theory that waves of price action will be related in both time amplitude and price amplitude. Another discovery made by students of the Elliott wave theory was that bull markets generally last 1.618 (PHI) times the duration of bear markets. This means that bear markets are generally 61.8% of the time amplitude of bull markets. A bull market as a general rule is not complete until it has formed five waves, three impulse waves in the upward direction of the trend each separated by a corrective phase before the next advance. The original principle applies to each of the impulse waves, they will also unfold in five wave movements. Corrections in a bull market will form three waves, each minor wave will form three waves. In a bear market the three waves will be two down broken by a corrective phase. The two impulse waves down will contain five waves and the correction will contain three waves.

For our purposes if we use the basic tenets of the Elliott wave theory to identify important wave movements in markets we have a sound basis from which to measure time.

## The most important ranges from which to measure time will be :-

1. A completed bull and bear phase.

2. A completed bull phase.

3. A completed bear phase.

The **major time vibrations** for a newcomer to this theory too watch for counter trend reactions are the **38.2%, 50%, 61.8%, 100% and 161.8%** as these are the strongest forces at work in the natural sense.

Other vibration ratios and how to use them are detailed later but first let us look at a few examples of time forward from previous market cycles in the NYCSE MARCH SUGAR contract. Below is a table of swing highs and lows going back from more recent times to the major cycle highs and lows of years past. The following table is an example of the detailed information that I keep to monitor vibrations forward from previous cycles.

## DYNAMIC TIME VIBRATIONS

### NYCSE MARCH SUGAR #11 - FACT FILE

| ATE | SWING POINT | | TIME | RANGE | IMPORTANT NOTES |
|---|---|---|---|---|---|
| 20621 | 61 | LOW | 0 | 61 | HISTORY LOW |
| 70103 | 123 | LOW | 12614 | 62 | 1802 WEEKS-414.4 MTHS MAJOR LOW |
| 41121 | 6600 | HIGH | 2880 | 6539 | HISTORY HIGH- super cycle |
| 70106 | 743 | LOW | 777 | 5857 | 1st Bear Market Low |
| 70422 | 1106 | HIGH | 883 | 363 | [A] |
| 80725 | 655 | LOW | 1342 | 5945 | [B] |
| 01105 | 4550 | HIGH | 1293 | 3895 | CYCLE [B] |
| 30131 | 605 | LOW | 817 | 3945 | PRIMARY [A] |
| 30531 | 1448 | HIGH | 937 | 3102 | PRIMARY [B] or INTERMEDIATE (A) |
| 50620 | 334 | LOW | 3864 | 6266 | CYCLE [C] or INTERMEDIATE (B) |
| 60410 | 964 | HIGH | 294 | 630 | INTERMEDIATE (A) |
| 60430 | 967 | HIGH | 314 | 633 | b |
| 61002 | 575 | LOW | 155 | 392 | A |
| 61104 | 730 | HIGH | 33 | 155 | a |
| 870107 | 577 | LOW | 97 | 153 | b |
| 870304 | 885 | HIGH | 153 | 310 | B |
| 870826 | 639 | LOW | 175 | 246 | INTERMEDIATE (B) |
| 880125 | 1083 | HIGH | 152 | 444 | A OF (C) |
| 880226 | 756 | LOW | 184 | 327 | B OF (C) |
| 880714 | 1439 | HIGH | 1120 | 1105 | PRIMARY [A] |

## COMPLETED BULL AND BEAR CYCLES

A completed market cycle is the bull and bear phase. Over the years a series of these cycles will join together to form larger cycles. The time vibrations forward from lesser degree cycles and larger degree cycles will relate in mathematicly degree. When vibrations from a series of cycles, be they long term or short term, fall together they can signal a natural area for a trend reversal.

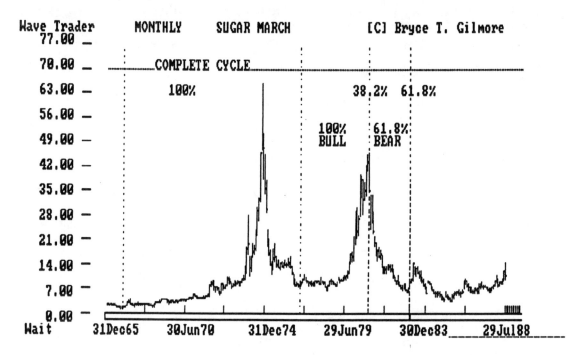

FIG 7.1 THE LONG TERM MONTHLY CHART OF MARCH NYCSE SUGAR #11. This shows how time of the major cycle LOW to LOW, (which included an amazing bull market lifting price from a low of 1.23 cents to a high of 66 cents per pound then back to 7 cents over a period of 10 years), set in motion a vibration that clearly signaled two future highs and lows. The second bull market range time adhered to the Elliott wave theory teachings as it was 1.618 times the length of the next major bear market phase. As an aside it is interesting to note that the low price of 1.23 cents was 100% square of the all time history low for sugar registered on the 21st June 1932 at 0.61 of a cent. Also the time in days from the 1.23 cent low of January 3rd, 1967 to the high 66 cents, November 21st, 1974 was exactly 2880 days (20 times the square of 144).

## BULL MARKET CYCLE

A bull market cycle could be defined as any market cycle when prices trend upwards to higher values over long durations of time. To measure the time vibrations of a bull market phase it is simply a matter of measuring ratios of time forward from the conclusion of the bull market phase.

The chart below (FIG 7.2) of March Sugar shows graphically how to do this. One should not become over anxious that each vibration forward will cause a violent reaction to trend. Sometimes the market will be in a state of equilibrium and little volatility will result. Obviously when the market has been in a volatile medium greater reactions can be expected. Another problem arises when we inspect this chart and that is forecasting whether to expect a high or low on future time vibrations. From past experience I have found great difficulty predicting highs and lows too far distant into the future. However, with a thorough understanding of how to combine all of the time and price methods to form an analysis this problem is alleviated to some degree. Be careful not to go out on a limb in your expectations, just remember that a counter trend reaction often occurs on these important vibration times.

FIG 7.2 VIBRATIONS OF A RANGE - NYSCE MARCH SUGAR #11

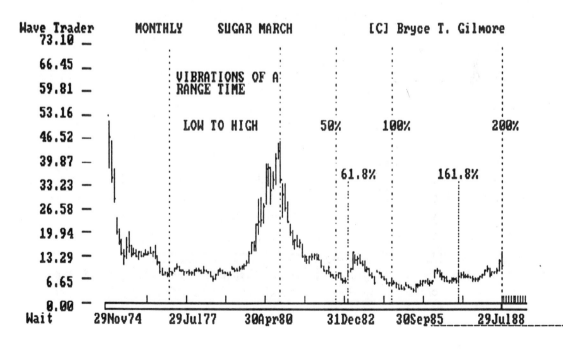

## BEAR MARKET CYCLE

Vibrations of a bear market cycle are measured forward in time in the same ratios as demonstrated above. This chart (FIG 7.3) of March Sugar shows two reactions to trend on the 50% and 61.8% vibration markers. In this particular instance the bull market that followed this bear market was 61.8% in time duration of the previous bear market. In Elliott wave terms this bull market could be construed as a bear market rally since the time duration was less than the underlying forces that dragged the market down from its previous high price. In the grand cycle of events this bull market was merely a corrective phase to the previous major cycle, under Elliott wave theory this bull market could be called a B wave cycle.

FIG 7.3  VIBRATIONS OF A RANGE - NYSCE MARCH #11

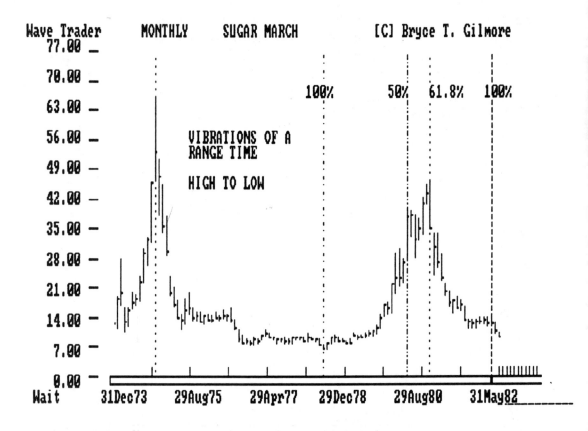

# DYNAMIC TIME VIBRATIONS

## USING RANGE VIBRATION TIMES FOR TRADING SIGNALS

Range vibrations of cycles, half cycles, one and one half cycles can be extended forward in the major ratios 38.2%, 50%, 61.8%, 100% and 161.8%. The important areas for counter trend reactions will be highlighted by clusters of time vibrations falling together. These areas are the natural vibration elements that abound in all free trading markets. Carry forward vibration times of selected ranges on monthly, weekly and daily charts. Follow the basic tenets of the Elliott wave theory of markets as a guide to the type of counter trend reaction to expect on the time clusters. If a major price squaring occurs on these time elements then both time and price amplitude has been satisfied and a major change in trend is indicated.

The high on March Sugar of 45.50 cents in November 1980 occurred on two major cycle vibrations mentioned above. At the same time a range retracement of 66% price of the previous bear market decline was fulfilled. Another time period of importance was 72 months (half 144) from the all time high of 66 cents when the double top was formed and the next bear market got underway. This top was also 165 months (3x55) from the low of 1.23 cents. You can clearly count five waves up from the low which further helps confirm ones suspicions that a major change in trend would be forthcoming.

FIG 7.4 NYSCE MARCH SUGAR #11

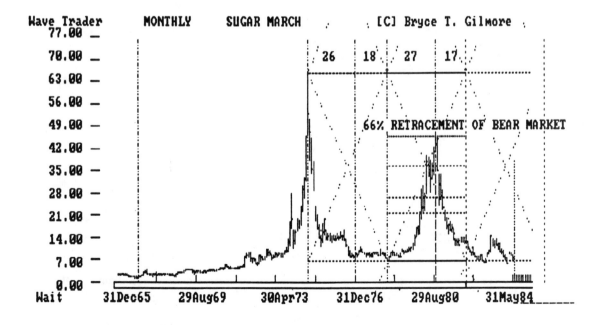

DYNAMIC TIME VIBRATIONS

## RANGE VIBRATIONS IN INTERMEDIATE WAVES

Once all primary cycle vibrations have been calculated and extended forward for future recognition we can move down a wave degree and plot intermediate wave vibrations in the same manner as with primary cycles.

The same mathematical ratios apply throughout the complete process for establishing vibration time clusters of previous cycles and half cycles. Measurements are taken from previous intermediate swing highs and lows, high to high, low to low and low to high. When more than two intermediate time vibrations cluster on a future date a reaction to trend is indicated for this time. Once again to confirm a price and time squaring is taking place a price objective should be obvious, ie a retracement or projection of a previous market move of primary or intermediate degree should be present to signal a counter trend reaction. Price retracements or projections in the same wave ratio as time offer the most convincing squarings, yet is is not mandatory that time and price actually fall in the same identical ratios only that they fall on the common ratios put forward in this text.

FIG 7.5 WEEKLY March Sugar NYCSE #11 example of an intermediate WAVE time vibration. VIBRATIONS OF 38.2% AND 61.8% forward pinpoint a high and low swing point.

## DAILY CHART FOR ACCURACY OF TIME MEASUREMENT

DAILY March Sugar NYCSE #11 (FIG 7.6) is an example of the same vibrations 38.2% and 61.8% in trading days. The time of the range being projected forward was 518 trading days (3 days less than 521 Lucas). The 61.8% vibration calculated at 518*61.8% equals 320 (322 = Lucas) trading days. Exactly 320 trading days forward of the June 1985 low a support in the market was reached as the chart shows. This was the low of 2nd October 1986 at 5.75 cents (4x144).

The vibration of 38.2% of the same range signaled the high of 10th April 1986 at 9.64 cents. This was 1 day off the required calculation 518*38.2% equals 198 trading days as the high fell 199 (Lucas) trading days from the June 1985 low of 3.34 cents.

FIG 7.6 NYSCE MARCH SUGAR #11

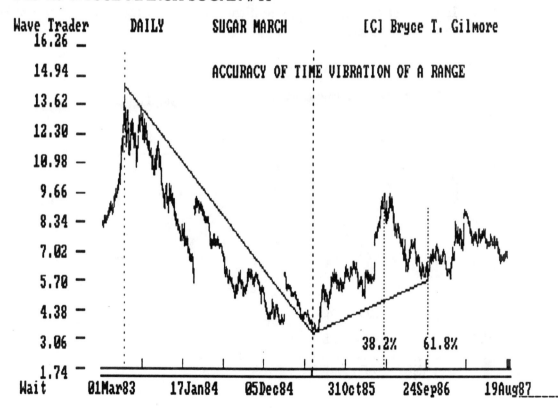

## CONFIRMING ORIGINAL FINDINGS

RANGE FROM APRIL 30th, 1986 HIGH 9.67 cents TO LOW OCTOBER 2nd, 1986 5.75 cents.

Time squared on a 50% vibration of the previous intermediate bull market range, namely the time from the 20th June 1985 low of 3.34 to the high 9.67 on 30th April 1986 which was 213 trading days. Time in trading days down to 5.75 was 107. As seen above there were now two important vibrations that squared out on the same day, 2nd October 1986.

In terms of price retracement of the previous upmove from 3.34 to 9.67, which equaled 633 ticks, a 61.8% price decline of this range calculated out to 633*61.8% equals 391 ticks. 9.67 less 3.91 equals 5.76, the low made on the dual time vibration was 5.75 which I would consider close enough to confirm my belief in the geometry of markets as a science rather than an art.

FIG 7.7 NYSCE MARCH SUGAR #11 - 1985-86 RANGE SQUARED

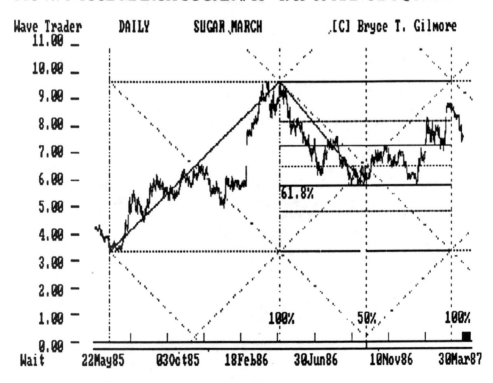

## ALTERNATIVE CONFIRMATIONS OF TIME SQUARINGS

The last chart (FIG 7.8), to conclude this section, is further proof of the geometry of time vibration. The time in trading days from the May 1983 high of 14.48 cents to the top of 30th April 1986 was 731. Incidentally this was the day of the Chenoble disaster news being released and one would have expected prices to rise rather than decline on the fundamental news.   [ 731 * .618 * .618 * .618 * .618] equals 107. 0.618 raised to the fourth power equals 0.146. 107 divided by 731 equals a 0.146 time vibration.

The low of 2nd October, 1986 at 5.75 cents basis March futures came in on the 107th trading day measured from the April 30th high.

FIG 7.8 NYSCE MARCH SUGAR #11 - Shows the relationship of ratios in reverse should we project time backwards for more confirmation of unfolding cyclic events. [6.85 = 1.618 to the 4th power]

## THE BOTTOM LINE ON RANGE VIBRATION

The bottom line of this section is to leave one in no doubt as to the value of time vibration in markets. The technical signals using these methods to pinpoint the 2nd October 1986 low at 5.75 cents are too overwhelming simply to be a **random** coincidence. One can only conclude that a natural force is at work in the subconscious minds of traders. These forces dictate market patterns that once set in motion will reverberate well into the future. Until some major shock overrides their strength and new patterns begin to evolve from the new factors present, in the particular market being followed.

**The clearest indication to trade these signals is when both time and price relate geometrically; the market can be seen to be overbought or oversold and volatility dictates good risk reward ratios. Fortune will favor the astute analyst who is prepared to put his money up against the prevailing opinion that usually abounds at such turning points in trend.**

Extreme importance should be placed on vibrations of 38.2%, 50%, 61.8%, 100% and 161.8% in both time and price.

Vibrations of 127.3% (root Phi), 141.4% (root 2), 173.2% (root 3), 200% (root 4) and 223.6% (root 5) are also extremely important.

Begin by tracking the first group and then see how many cross confirmations you can relate to the second group.

**At every major swing high or low relationships will exist in the primary waves, intermediate waves, the minor degree waves and the very short term waves.**

# 8. CHART SCALING OF TIME AND PRICE

This chapter deals with the complexities of chart scaling. It is quite important that chart scales are understood prior to explaining Gann techniques for squaring price to time and Gann support and resistance angles.

Geometric charting implies what it means, the price scale must relate to the time scale in a ratio of the square, circle or golden rectangle if we are to transpose one axis to the other and expect measurements to hold a strict relationship.

## 1 UNIT OF PRICE EQUALS 1 UNIT OF TIME SCALE

FIG 8.1 Is an example of a daily 1 by 1 chart scaling using the Comex Gold market as an example.

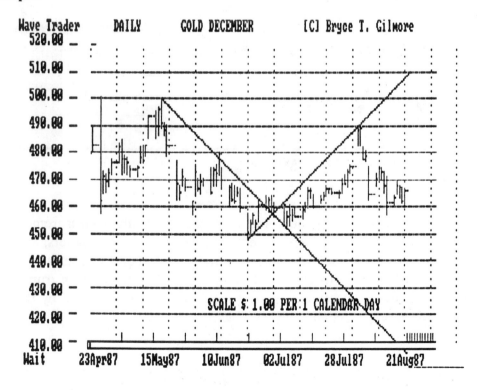

Time is the axis that is fixed. Time is uniform, we can plot 1 hour, 1 day, 1 trading day, 1 week, 1 month or even 1 year. Nothing arbitrary, time is a fact of life. Price on the other hand sometimes causes a dilemma. Before we look at various forms of squaring price scales to time scales we should understand that the correct scale of price to time can only be 1 unit of time to 1 unit of price. This means we must plot 1 unit of price to 1 hour, 1 day, 1 trading day, 1 week, 1 month or 1 year if we are to work in SQUARE ratios.

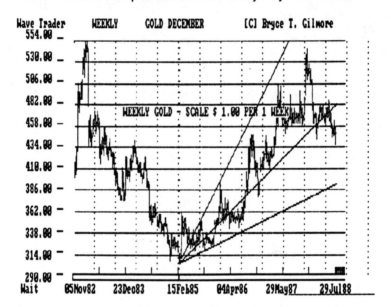

FIG 8.2  Comex Gold price series on a weekly 1 by 1 chart scale.

## ALTERNATIVE PRICE TO TIME SCALES

Throughout the ages man has endeavored to introduce standard measurement scales to all things. Land areas have been scaled in square feet, square meters, acres, hectares, square miles and square kilometers. Produce has been measured in ounces, pounds, kilograms, tonnes, tons, bushels and so forth. Financial instruments are measured in rates of change to a contract specification. Time is fixed by the movement of the Sun yet price is completely variable.

# GEOMETRIC CHARTS AND ANGLES

Each commodity has its own psychological price unit that balances units of time. Over years these units can change as inflation and deflation of price unfolds with economic developments.

As a guide I am going to detail in this section the scales of price to time that I have found useful for a base value of 1 unit of price to 1 day of time. These relationships could change in the future yet at the moment they are appropriate to this subject.

## RECOMMENDED GANN SCALES PRICE-DAY FOR US FUTURES CONTRACTS.

| | |
|---|---|
| GOLD COMEX | US$ 1.00 per ounce |
| SILVER COMEX | US$ 0.01 per ounce |
| SOYBEANS CBT | US$ 0.01 per bushel |
| CORN CBT | US$ 0.01 per bushel |
| WHEAT CBT | US$ 0.01 per bushel |
| SUGAR NYCSE | US$ 0.0001 per pound |
| COTTON NYCE | US$ 0.01 per pound |
| COPPER COMEX | US$ 0.10 per pound |
| US TREASURY BILLS - IMM | 1/100th of 1% |
| US TREASURY BONDS - IMM | 1/100th of 1% |
| BRITISH POUND - IMM | 1/10th of 1 cent |
| DEUTSCHE MARK - IMM | .05 ticks |
| JAPANESE YEN - IMM | .05 ticks |
| SWISS FRANC - IMM | .05 ticks |

### AUSTRALIAN STOCKS

| | |
|---|---|
| BHP | $0.02 per day |
| | $0.05 per week |
| BHP GOLD | $0.01 per day |
| | $0.05 per week |
| MOUNT ISA MINES | $0.01 per day |
| | $0.05 per week |

These are purely a guide, see the next section for a general approach.

# GEOMETRIC CHARTS AND ANGLES

FIG 8.3 Deutsche Mark IMM futures daily on a scale of 1/20th point to 1 trading day.

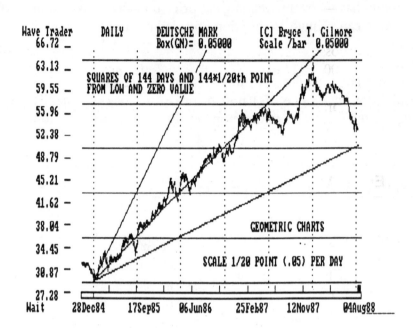

## STOCKS AND SHARES SCALING

Depending upon the trading value of each individual stock or share we can experiment with the base value to associate with time.

>Stocks trading below $ 5.00 should use 1 cent per day.

>Stocks trading between $ 5.00 and $ 10.00 should use 2 cents per day.

>Stocks trading between $ 10.00 and $25.00 should use 5 cents per day.

>Stocks trading between $ 25.00 and $50.00 should use 10 cents per day.

>Stocks trading between $ 50.00 and $100.00 should use 20 cents per day.

As price value increases so does the theoretical psychological unit of measurement that controls volatility. Personal experimentation with individual stocks, based on volatility, will help guide you to the correct value for your analysis. Price scale is an arbitrary value, from time to time certain markets will require changes. It is better to understand this fact beforehand so that disasters in judgment can be avoided.

GEOMETRIC CHARTS AND ANGLES

## BEST ADVICE ON SCALING

At all times where possible select a base unit that is a round number psychologically, ie., .01, .10, 1, 10, 100, 1000 et cetera. ONE UNIT will always perform better than variations of this theme although at times it is necessary to expand scales. A later chapter on commodity vibration will certainly alleviate the major problems one has wrestling with this dilemma.

## DAILY, WEEKLY AND MONTHLY CHARTS

The practice of scaling each different time frame back to a base price unit of ONE is a strict prerequisite in geometric charting. At times the scale will be far too small for the plotted price series, when this occurs instead of increasing the base unit to an arbitrary figure we can increase the base unit used on the daily chart by square ratios so that price remains in perspective.

If a unit price used on a daily chart causes the weekly chart to become unmanageable, ie., price scale is far to sensitive to time scale, then a ratio in square degree should be used on the weekly and vice versa the monthly price series. By this I mean that assuming a scale of say $ 1.00 per day is being used as a base price to time scale on a daily chart then ratios of $1.00 x2 = $2.00 or $1.00 x4 = $4.00 or $1.00 x8 = $8.00 should be used for price to time on the weekly or monthly charts so that price scales remain square.

You may not appreciate the reason for this at this moment yet once we have discussed geometric angles used by Gann traders and technicians it will become quite clear. The same principle applies when we have longer periods of data to plot and it is physically impossible to maintain the base scale due to vertical limitations of our worksheet.

## GEOMETRIC ANGLES OF SUPPORT AND RESISTANCE

FIG 8.4 COMEX DECEMBER GOLD ON A SCALE OF $ 8.00 per month.

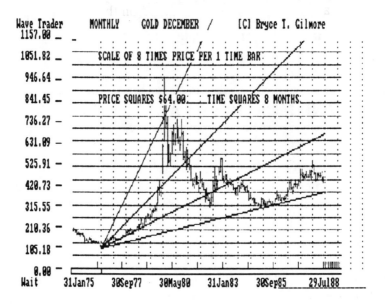

Once a suitable scale of price to time is found for a commodity or stock we can use geometric angles to monitor time and price squarings in the ratios of the square, circle and golden rectangle.

Geometric angles take on the following form when drawn on a 1 unit to 1 day chart.

A 1 unit of price to one unit of time is a 45 degree angle (1/8 of the circle of 360 degrees).

A 2 units per day angle is an angle of 63.5 degrees, this angle will square price to time in a ratio of 2 to 1. Eg, a move of 288 points in the angle will take 144 days.

A half unit of price to 1 day angle is approximately 26.5 degrees, this angle will square price to time in a ratio of 1 to 2. eg, a move of 72 points will take 144 days.

The Gann philosophy of markets assumes that the 1 by 1 angle is the strongest guide to trend strength or weakness. Correctly drawn on a geometric chart this is the 45 degree angle. When a 45 degree angle is drawn down from a major swing high and the market trades below this resistance it is said to be in a weak state. Conversely a 1 by 1 or 45 degree angle drawn up from a major swing low will signal the state of the trend.

If the market is trading above this angle it is said to be in a strong state, if below this angle then it is in a weak state. At times reversals to trend will be signaled at points along these angles. These reversals are generally at times when significant time periods from swing highs or lows elapse, ie., at say 144 points in 144 days, 89 points in 89 days. Often an angle may appear confusing as price will trade above and below it, then when time and price are square a reversal will be signalled on the angle.

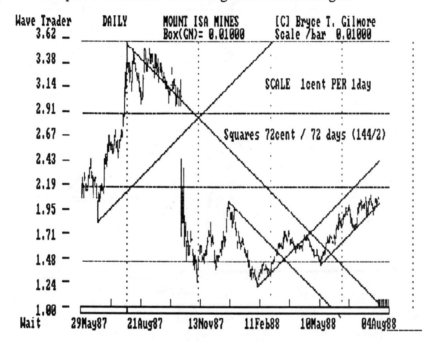

FIG 8.5 MOUNT ISA MINES scale 1 cent per day. Examples of the 1x1 or 45 degree angles of support and resistance.

## ANGLE INTERSECTIONS AND TIME SQUARING

If the 1x1, 2x1 and 1x2 angles are drawn geometrically down from swing highs and up from swing lows they will square time at their crossings. One Gann practice for measuring time forward for a trend reaction area is this principle.

If each swing high and low of major degree on a geometric chart is related in some strict mathematical degree, and the chart scaling reflects this, then it would be true that intersections of these angles would signal a third dimensional squaring. This practice is known as the squaring of space. These intersections of angles do not necessarily need to coincide with price, yet their crossings are an important area in time as they form triangular relationships with the past at these points.

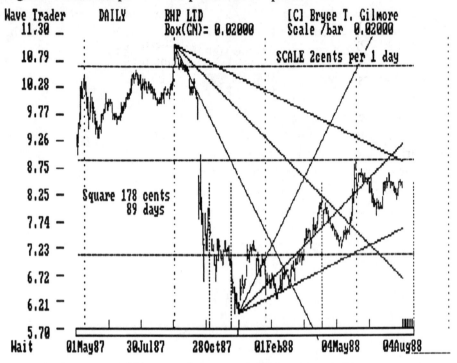

FIG 8.6 BROKEN HILL PROPRIETORY LIMITED scaled at 2 cents per trading day demonstrates some relationships that can be found in markets using geometric angles.

## MY BEST GUIDE TO THE USE OF GEOMETRIC ANGLES

The 1x1, 2x1 and 1x2 angles are best used as a guide to trend strength. Occasionally they will pinpoint a turn in trend by forming a support or resistance on the actual high or low point reached before the trend reversal. This will only occur should an exact squaring take place in the ratios of a square. More often than not time and price squarings will be made in other degrees, ie., price 61.8% and time 50%, price 50% and time 38.2% et cetera.

Third dimensional squarings of space seem to be one of the best uses for these angles so it is important to keep up your geometric angles from major swing points and be aware of their specific use in your analysis. As you become proficient at utilizing all of the various geometric techniques in this text you will understand how each technique is also a variation of another method.

## ALTERNATIVE ANGLES USED BY TECHNICIANS

Students of time and price squaring have devised many alternatives to the original theories passed down by the masters of geometrical charting over this century. Angles of 1.5 units of price to time are considered important technical ratios to monitor, 1 unit of price to 1.5 units of time is also considered a strong geometric relationship.

**FIG 8.7** of the GOLD chart below gives a quick pictorial view of the angles that can be used by chartists to determine strength of trend. One must bear in mind that with the volatility of markets today there is an increased need to find levels of price that are within daily ranges to gauge support and resistance zones.

**FIG 8.7**  1x1.5, 1x1, 1x0.666 GEOMETRIC ANGLES.

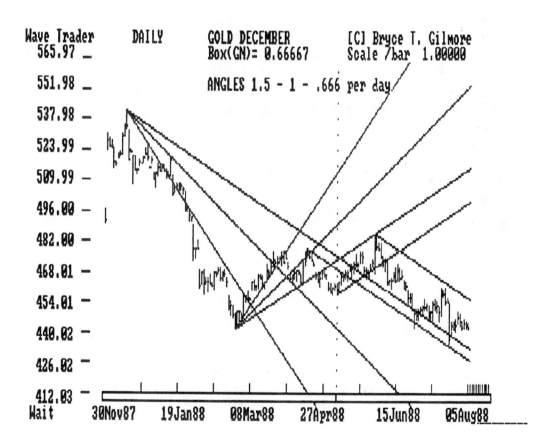

## 1.618 AND 0.618 ANGLES OF PRICE TO TIME

Technicians that work in Fibonacci degree also use 1.618 x 1 price to time, 0.618 x 1 price to time angles. These angles are in the ratios of the Golden rectangle. On occasions, as price and time vibrations revolve through the geometric circle, these angles pinpoint ratios of price moves in Fibonacci degree. For example, a 1.618 price to time angle will measure units of price such as 144 points travelled in 89 days, a 0.618 angle will measure the reverse such as 89 points travelled in 144 days. Any angle drawn in strict mathematical degree to the square, circle and golden rectangle is important from a technicians point of view. If price squares time in an ancient geometric relationship it is important. Angles are purely a way of stating the obvious. If we wish to keep one step ahead of the unfolding price patterns we need to be aware of all the techniques that we can employ.

FIG 8.8 Shows the same swing highs and lows of the December Gold chart using angles of 1.618 per day and 0.618 per day to measure future moves for support and resistance.

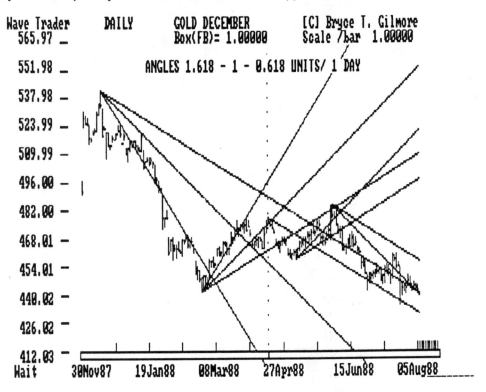

## PERCENTAGE OF A PRICE SQUARING TO TIME

As an adjunct to this method of measuring price to time squarings it would not be fair to dismiss percentage price moves from a high price or low price as insignificant. In some commodity and stock indices, averages are used to determine the value for the index. In cases such as these it is fair to assume that averages of previous price could be just as important to geometric relationships as points moved. In effect this means that some price series can be geometrically charted in percentages. This would at first seem totally impossible, yet we do not need to concern ourselves with the problems of day to day entries that do not reflect the true exchange value given out. All we need to do is monitor price rises and declines in percentage increments of previous important swing highs and lows. Examples of major bear markets terminating at 50%, 61.8 and 66.6% decreases in value to their highs has been demonstrated in an earlier chapter. What was not demonstrated was the relationship of price decline per day, week or month in percentage terms.

To begin with this type of analysis one should use an index of a group of stocks or a group of commodities.

For my purpose of demonstration I am going to cite a major move in the ALL ORDINARIES INDEX (The Australian equivalent to the American Standard and Poors 500 stock index) over the past two years.

Firstly the ALL ORDINARIES made a low on 28th JULY 1986 at 1094.1 points. In Elliott wave terms now that we have experienced the crash of 1987 we can safely label this low as a primary wave 4. This means that from an analysis viewpoint any time squarings emanating from this low are strictly written in stone. On 21st September 1987 the ALL ORDINARIES index made its final high prior to the October crash at 2312.4 this was exactly 293 trading days and 420 calendar days from this low. The rise in points from 1094.1 was (2312.4 less 1094.1) 1218.3 points. In percentage terms the rise from 1094.1 to 2312.4 fulfilled a mathematical ratio often overlooked by students of this science, 1.118 (the section of the square that goes to make the golden rectangle, ie., 0.5 plus 1.118 equals 1.618). 1094.1 increased in value by 111.8% equals 2317.3, The exact rise in the ALL ORDINARIES was 111.4% very close indeed. Another factor that should not be overlooked was the 2 x 610 (Fibonacci multiple) present at the completed primary wave 5 advance. The price rise fell only 1.7 points short. The 5th intermediate wave fell 2 points short of 576 points (4x144) taking 89 calendar days and terminated on the September equinox at the time of a solar eclipse.

From a time perspective the move up from 1094.1 to 2312.4 was 293 trading days (144 * root 2 plus 89). If we divide 111.8% by 293 we get an average rise of 0.38157% per day.

This means that an angle drawn up from the 1094.1 low at 0.38157 % of 1094.1 per day intersected the high price made on the 21st September 1987 at 2312.4. Obviously to follow these particular calculations requires some thinking, I would rather think than suffer when it comes to market analysis and trading decisions. IN CASE ANYONE HAS MISSED THE POINT 0.382 IS $0.618^2$.

Of course before arriving at this brilliant deduction one would have looked at numerous other methods to pick the top of the bull market. I have detailed many other relationships that squared price and time at the 2312.4 top in other sections of this text.

How do we plot angles off swing highs and lows in percentage degree? This is easy as 1% substitutes for $1.00, 1 point et cetera. In this instance 1094.1 reduced to 1% equals 10.941 points per day. By emitting our Fibonacci angles up and extending our times forward we would have been prepared to recognize a geometric squaring of price and time at the 2312.4 top.

FIG 8.9

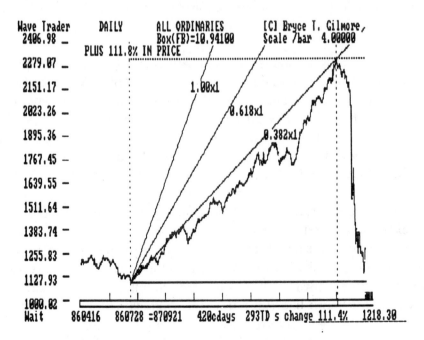

# 9. FUTURE TIME SQUARINGS OF PRICE

**SQUARING PRICE UNITS FORWARD IN TIME** FOR FUTURE AREAS LIKELY TO SIGNAL A COUNTER TREND REACTION **IS A METHODOLOGY DEVELOPED** AND TAUGHT **BY** THE GRAND MASTER OF GEOMETRIC ANALYSIS **W.D. GANN.**

There are three techniques used for this methodology:-

SQUARING A LOW PRICE IN TIME TO THE FUTURE

SQUARING A HIGH PRICE IN TIME TO THE FUTURE

SQUARING A PRICE RANGE IN TIME TO THE FUTURE

Since it is possible to transpose price units to future time units it is also possible to reverse the procedure and transpose time units back into future price. An example of this technique is demonstrated at the end of this chapter. (See FIG 9.6)

SQUARING A RANGE TIME TO FUTURE PRICE

## SQUARING A LOW PRICE IN TIME

On a chart scaled at 1 unit of price to 1 unit of time, if we were to draw a square starting with a vertical line up from zero to the low price to be squared, then horizontally forward the identical units of time, then vertically back down to zero a square will be formed. The forward vertical line will measure the first square of time of the low price.

A low price of $ 100 will square out in time 100 days forward from the date of the low. On a weekly chart it will be 100 weeks on a monthly chart 100 months.

These squares of time to price are very important areas for Gann theory traders to look for and expect a counter trend reaction to price movement.    It does not stop here, as depending upon the significance of the low (Major, History or Minor), their influence can predominate over many future squares as well as divisions of squares.

**The strongest points to watch are at the 50% and 100% levels.**

Next watch 33.3%, 66.6%, then 25%, 75%. Minor divisions such as one eighth could be of importance. 141.4%, 161.8% and 223.6% of major squarings should also be noted.

These technical methods are particularly useful for agricultural products such as Soybeans, Wheat and Corn. They also help to confirm time squarings within the Gold complex.

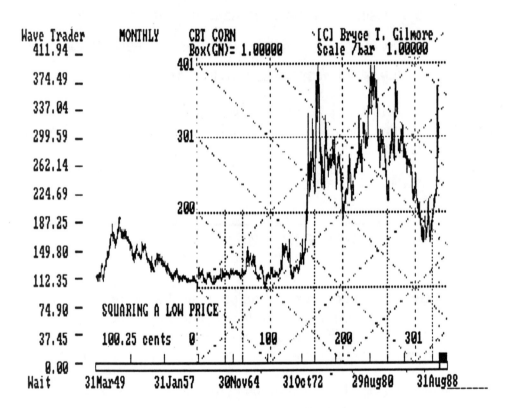

FIG 9.1 CBT CORN DECEMBER DELIVERY - This chart demonstrates the low of 100.25 cents squared forward in both price and time. One can see by careful study of this price series how significant some of the future 100% levels in both price and time turned out to be.

GANN TIME SQUARINGS OF PRICE

## SQUARE OF THE 1982 LOW IN THE STANDARD & POORS 500

This weekly chart (FIG 9.2) is an example of Gann at work. The low of 102.41 registered on the S&P 500 cash back in 1982, worked forward, signaled many a significant trend reversal on this weekly chart. Of course research will show that other relevant technical information coincided with the major turning points. Squaring of major lows in both time and price has proven to be a powerful technical tool for the students of geometric charting.

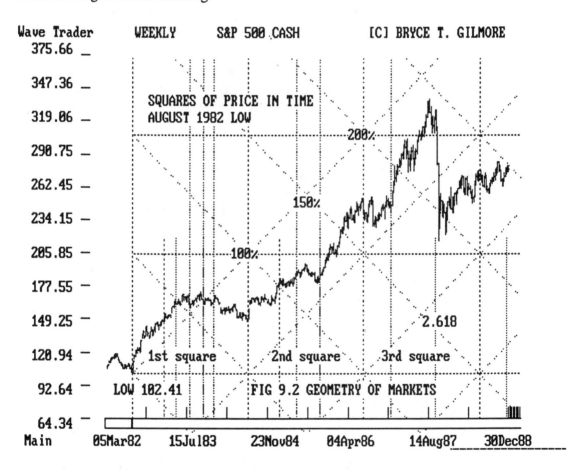

FIG 9.2  S & P 500 CASH INDEX - MAJOR LOW IN 1982 OF 102.41 SQUARED IN TIME AND PRICE.

Chp. 9   Page. 85

# GANN TIME SQUARINGS OF PRICE

## SQUARING A HIGH PRICE IN TIME

On a chart scaled at 1 unit of price to 1 unit of time if we were to draw a square starting with a vertical line up from zero to the high price to be squared, then horizontally forward the identical units of time, then vertically back down to zero, a square will be formed. The forward vertical line will measure the first square in time units of the high price.

A high price of $ 144 would square out time 144 days forward from the date of the high. On a weekly chart it will be 144 weeks, on a monthly chart 144 months.

The strongest levels are at 25%, 33.3%, 38.2%, 50%, 61.8%, 66.6%, 75%, 100%, 141.4% 150%, 161.8%, 200% and 223.6% divisions of a high price squared forward in time.

FIG 9.3 CHART OF CBT DECEMBER CORN

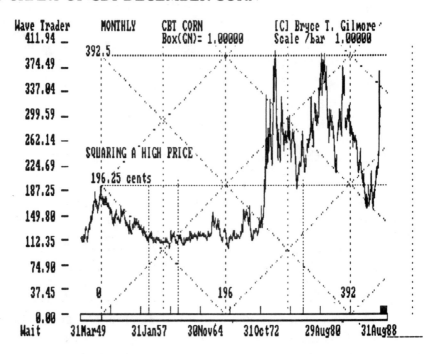

The high price of 196.25 registered in December 1951 has been squared forward in both price and time. Time divisions of this square marked several turning areas of trend, although the first chart of the low in November 1960 of 100.25 cents squared the high to the cent. (see Fig 9.1)

Chp. 9   Page. 86

GANN TIME SQUARINGS OF PRICE

## SQUARING A PRICE RANGE IN TIME

When squaring lows and highs in time we measure forward in units of price translated to time units. We do the same when squaring a price range in time. First we measure the units moved from either a low to a high or a high to a low and then we calculate forward from the turning point of that range, squares of that previous move.

FIG 9.4 CBT CORN DECEMBER DELIVERY

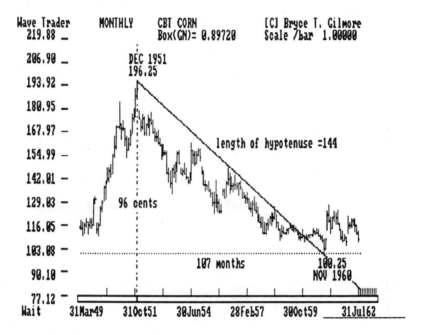

For this example I have used the price range from the high 196.25 and low 100.25 used in the first two examples of squaring a low and a high price. The geometric relationship formed from the high to the low is a right angled triangle. The vertical axis is price. In this case 96 cents (196.25 less 100.25). The horizontal axis is time, in this case 107 months. The hypotenuse of the triangle formed by this range is 144 units if we are using a 1x1 scale of price to time.

You may already be thinking that I have made liberal use of the number 144 in the text so far. The obvious reason is that I consider 144 the strongest static number one can relate to market action. In fact if you were to only trade when a vibration squared in 144 relationships you would make a fortune. Any geometric vibration in a market that contains 144 is confirming the existence of natural law at work. 96 by the way is exactly 66.66% of 144, 108 is 75% of 144.

The two price measurements that are transposed to time and measured forward into the future are the vertical range 96 cents and the hypotenuse calculation 144. On this example I have only used 100% squares for ease of explanation. I also included the 100% anniversaries of the time of the range 107 months to show how each method of squaring range can be worked forward.

FIG 9.5 This chart of Corn also demonstrates the price squarings in 100% increments of each axis of the triangle formed by the geometric range.

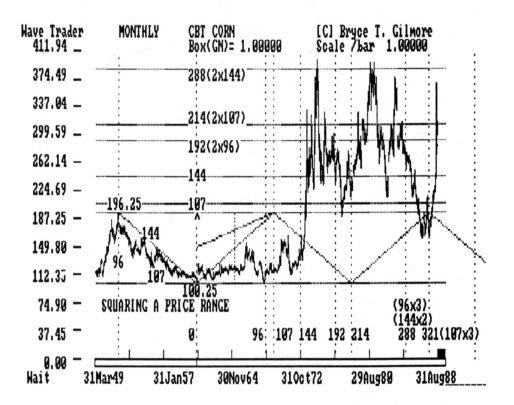

Just for the record, the all time high on this Corn contract was 400 cents which was reached in October 1974. From the methods of price squaring discussed to date this high fell on the 300% square of the low 100.25 cents (100.25 plus 3x100.25 equals 401 cents). Another geometric relationship with the previous bear market range of 96 cents was evident ( 96 by PI (3.141593 x 96 equals 301.5)). If you were to add 301.5 to the low of 100.25 where the 96 cent bear market decline terminated you would square price to the 400 cent all time high.

## SQUARING A RANGE TIME TO A FUTURE PRICE

If a move from a high to low or a low to high of major degree has occurred, then to square out the time duration to future price we translate time units to price units and add or subtract the value to the last turning price of the range.

The NYCSE SUGAR example below shows a range in time of 155 days converted to 155 tics and added to the low price to calculate squarings in this fashion. It is important to realize that these relationships can repeat whilst time is still working out the first square. I feel happier using these methods when they coincide with other calculations such as vibration angles and retracement levels. This sugar chart nevertheless shows an accuracy for this technique that defies explanation using "standard" charting methods.

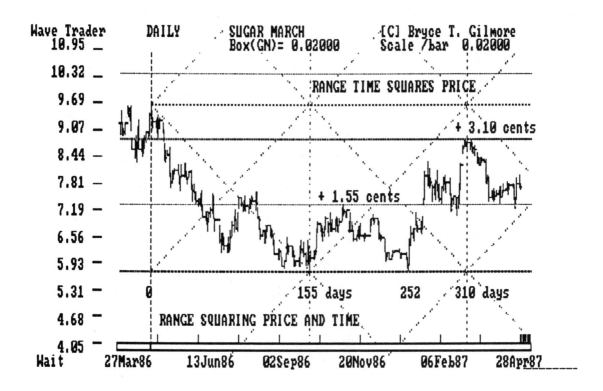

FIG 9.6   SQUARING A RANGE TIME TO FUTURE PRICE EXAMPLE.

## USE OF THESE METHODS

As a guide to the effective use of these methods it will pay only to use highs or lows that are higher or lower than the current wave of prices. Major market turning points have an enduring effect on markets whilst the price is contained within that range. Some knowledge of the Elliott Wave Principle will help define ranges into Cycle, Primary, Intermediate and Minor degree and give a good guide to the influence that specific turning points may have in the future.

**A combination of time clusters coming from numerous squarings of lows and highs at a future time will signal a stronger geometric influence for a change to the current trend.**

# 10. RATIO ANALYSIS OF PRICE RETRACEMENTS AND PRICE PROJECTIONS

In this chapter we will cover the most important price range projection and retracement levels needed to be monitored for market support and resistance. This section only deals with the price axis and is a more detailed explanation of range squaring covered in chapter 6.

**When price is plotted geometrically on a two dimensional chart it will be seen to move in waves. As these waves unfold they are telling us a story. We know from experience that the driving force behind any market is the balance between buyers and sellers. When nobody is prepared to sell prices will rise and when everybody wishes to sell prices will fall. Under normal trading conditions price will move in four stages, accumulation, advance, distribution, decline. At times the advances and declines will overreact to the generally held view of what the fair price should be. These periods of extreme are naturally caused by the mass psychological habits of market participants and are commonly referred to as periods of fear and greed. Human nature, being what it is, tries in many ways to justify why a market price is at a certain level yet in the end supply and demand rules the day as prices retrace previous advances or declines looking for support or resistance levels where the market can once again find a logical balance.**

Changes in economic patterns can produce extended moves in price, both up and down in value. These periods are referred to as bull and bear markets. In a bull market prices will advance and decline from a stable area in stages; as a bull move progresses the retracements to advances will diminish in degree. A detailed description to this phenomena can be found in the works of R.N. Elliott. A fully fledged bull market will normally contain three major advances interrupted by two adjustment periods where prices retrace part of the previous advance wave. Retracements to advances can be measured with a great degree of accuracy as they are working to some natural law. As a guide the first wave of a new bull market will normally be retraced at least 50% and often 61.8% for a wave two. The third wave, which is often the longest in a bull market, extends above the high price of the first wave and terminates at a level in relationship to the first wave advance. Several common levels for a third wave top are 61.8% of the first wave advance added to the high of the first wave, 100% of wave one added to the wave one high and 161.8% of wave one added to the wave one high. As the third wave reaches its peak distribution begins as the players who gained from the long advance start to take profits. Generally the mood is still optimistic and declines are usually limited to between 14.6% and 38.2% of the third wave advance. Fourth wave adjustments often unfold as triangles and the pattern of price adjustments on a chart can give one a guide as to the extent of the fifth wave that has yet to unfold. In a bull market third wave, new buyers are progressively entering the market and volume is increasing. During a fourth wave the late comers see the adjustment as good value compared to the established trend. By the time the fifth wave begins to unfold old buyers, who were smart enough to have participated in the bull market so far, have distributed their stocks to the latecomers and the market forces are being driven by greedy uneducated traders. Fifth waves can have two characteristics, they can be wild affairs that take the market to new extremes and cause even the most rational traders to re-enter as buyers close to the top, or they can be very short lived upmoves that rise only slightly above the third wave top. Bull markets generally terminate at levels that relate to previous major low prices (see chapter 4) or projection squares of earlier major ranges. Price levels for a resistance top can be easily calculated in advance. As we approach these areas we monitor the risk, if the risk is real we take evasive action.

## PRICE PROJECTION EXAMPLES IN BULL MARKETS

FIG 10.1 SYDNEY SHARE PRICE INDEX

Although this chart is of the last bull market advance from July 1986 to September 1987 of a 5 year bull market the wave tops terminated extremely close to ideal ratios of the first wave price advance. The wave top labeled (1) reached a high of 1385 after advancing from a low of 1058 (1385 less 1058 equals 327). 327 points was incidentally only 5 points greater than the Lucas ratio 322. The wave top labeled (3) terminated at 1906 for a net increase from the low 1058 of 848. 848 less 327 was 521 (Another Lucas number exactly) the net advance above the wave (1) high, 521, is precisely 1.618 times 322 which means that the wave (3) high terminated at roughly a projection of 1.618 times the wave (1) advance. Observation of this chart also shows a correction between the wave (1) high and the wave (3) high occurring when the advance reached the 61.8% projection level of wave (1).

The correction from the wave (3) high terminated very close to the 100% projection level of wave (1).

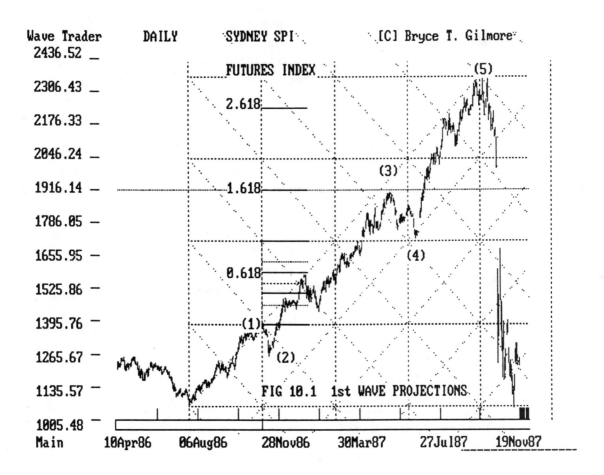

FIG 10.1 - SYDNEY SHARE PRICE INDEX - FINAL ADVANCE BEFORE THE 1987 CRASH.

If projection levels of waves from lows to highs can be used to anticipate new highs it must follow that, if retracements to these price advances fall in precise mathematical degree to natural law, then projections from lows to lows can be used to project future highs.

## FIG 10.2   SYDNEY SHARE PRICE INDEX

This chart is of the same time period as Fig 10.1. The all time high on this index fell at 2387.5 on October 2nd, 1987. From a base of 1058 the overall rise was 1330 points. The wave labeled (4) terminated at 1723 a drop of 183 points from the wave (3) high of 1906 (earlier I demonstrated that 183 was a root PHI relationship of 144 ie 144 * 1.272 equals 183 and is very important). The net ground gained from the 1058 low to the 1723 wave (4) low was 665 points (666 is the number of man and holds an important meaning in the study of numerology). Forgetting numerology for a minute and sticking with basic mathematics, the advance from the wave (4) low traced out a 100% price advance to the high of 2387.5 to terminate wave (5) and end this amazing bull market.

Wave (1) related to wave (3), wave (4) related to wave (5), the overall advance from the low 1058 traced out a geometric pattern based on the square and the golden rectangle.

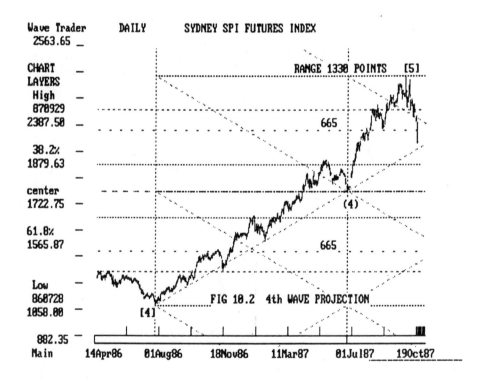

FIG 10.2  Wave [4]-(4) equals wave (4)-[5] in price.

# PRICE RETRACEMENTS AND PROJECTIONS

If one approaches market analysis with **a clear understanding of the psychological factors that motivate price movement** then it is not such a difficult task to anticipate turning points in trend when the geometry unfolds in such precise ratios as demonstrated in this text.

## FIG 10.3   COMEX GOLD DECEMBER DELIVERY

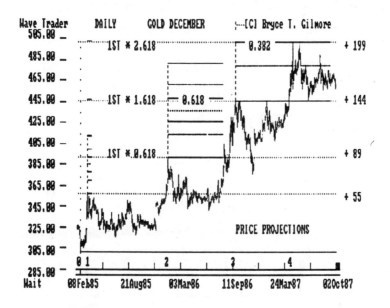

This chart graphically illustrates the relationships that can unfold in a long protracted price advance. Across the lower scale wave points are labeled 0, 1, 2, 3, 4. The price at 0 was $301.50, tops 1 ($357.00), 2 ($392.00), 3 ($446.00) and 4 ($501.00). The first advance terminated at $357 a move of $55.50.

$55.50 by 0.618 added to $357.00 equaled $390.30

$55.50 by 1.618 added to $357.00 equaled $446.80

$55.50 by 2.618 added to $357.00 equaled $502.30

All of these price levels were met within $2.00 before subsequent reversals in trend. Naturally projections taken from each advance top related in lesser degree ratios of Phi as the expansion continued. One would have to seriously question the random walk theory in markets after reviewing this price action. As it turned out, the expansion also followed the Fibonacci and Lucas series in dollar value which made it even more convincing.

## COMPLEX RETRACEMENTS AND PROJECTIONS IN MINOR WAVES

To continue with this section I am going to work through the Comex Gold December contract from the low of $301.50 on January 25th, 1985 to the low of $447.70 on June 22nd, 1987, using only the known information prior to each turning point.

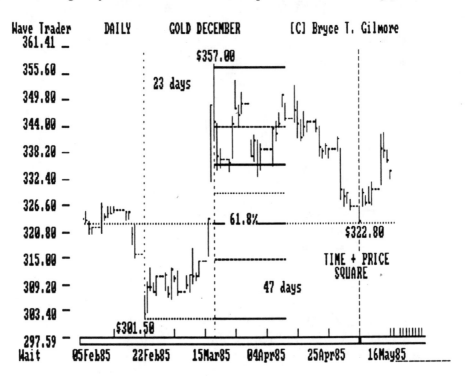

FIG 10.4 GOLD LOW OF $322.80 MAY 6TH 1985

The wave advance from $301.50 to $357 was $55.50 in 23 days. The high was made on the equinox of March 20th. The first decline was exactly $23 in five days which squared the range time. A counter trend rally of $20 over two days failed to get back to the high. Over the next seven days a further decline of $21 broke just below the first correction indicating lower prices to come. After rallying back another $20 over the next 12 days the market failed to go above the first reaction high indicating once again lower prices to come. The next low at $322.80 squared time in two ways (1); 47 days is a Lucas ratio, (2); 47 days was twice (200%) the time of the 23 day wave in the first advance. MAY 6th is also 45 degrees on the circle of 1 year from the March equinox. Price squared a 61.8% retracement of the advance from $301.5 to $357. The fall in price was $34.20 a Fibonacci multiple. The market then rallied $19.50 over the next 8 days. Recognizing this opportunity would have been worth a tidy profit.

FIG 10.5 $342.30 HIGH 14th May 1985

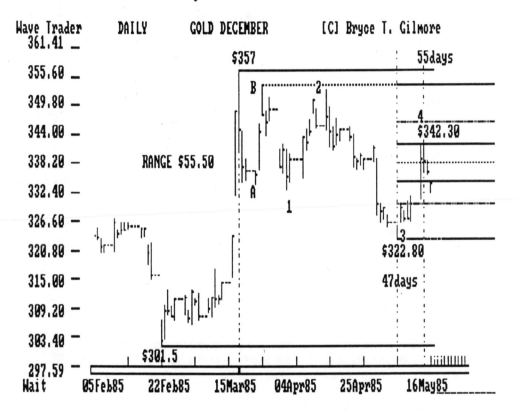

In this chart I have used some Elliott wave labels to identify the corrective phases from the $357 high. The price decline from the B wave high down to 3 was $31.20, 61.8% of this is $19.30, $342.30 less $322.80 is $19.50 giving the wave 3-4 a 61.8% relationship with B-3.

The high of $342.30 was made exactly 55 days from the $357 high giving a Fibonacci ratio and a squaring of the price range from $301.50 to $357.

**FIG 10.6   WAVES C OF (2), D of (2) and E of (2) [D-(2)]**

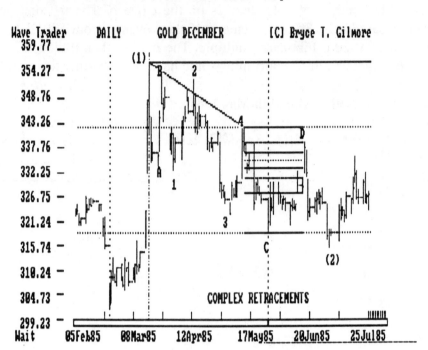

FIG 10.6 COMPLEX RETRACEMENTS IN CORRECTIONS.

Wave C = $319 MAY 28th, 1985

Wave C of (2) on this chart was 69 days from the $357 top labeled (1), this was a 3 times multiple of the 23 days rise. The ratio of price (1) to 4 was 38.2% of the decline from (1) to C. The decline from 4 to C was $23.30, 30 cents greater than (1) to A. Time of B to C was 62 days and a decline of $35.

Wave D = $339 JUNE 18th, 1985

Wave D rose $20 in 21 days. This wave alternated with wave B which also was $20. Wave D terminated 90 days from the $357 wave (1) high, both 89 and 90 are important ratios of time.

Wave E for (2) = $315.50 JULY 2nd, 1985

Wave E fell $23.50 to complete a 75% retracement of the rise from $301.50 to $357 [Wave (1)].

Wave (2) contained 9 minor waves for a total decline of $41.50 in 104 days. Three waves equaled each other at $23 to $23.50, five waves equaled each other at $19.50 to $21. The longest wave of $30.20 was the 3rd wave of C, as expected under Elliott wave rules.

## PRICE RETRACEMENTS AND PROJECTIONS

### FIG 10.7 WAVE STRUCTURE UP TO $392 HIGH 16th JANUARY 1986

The main technical feature here was the expansion of wave (1) by 61.8% to arrive at the $392 target price. Time in days from the start at $301.50 was 325 days (a few days off 322 Lucas). The correction that immediately followed this high retraced 50% of the rise from $301.50 before halting. You will notice that this correction unfolded in five waves, a very bearish scenario. The third wave as usual was the longest and strongest wave. Time between the $357 high and the $350.20 high was balanced at the $392 high. Another interesting relationship between the high of $357 to the $315.50 low ($41.50) and the high of $350.20 to the high of $392 ($41.80) becomes apparent with a little exploration. Everywhere we look we keep finding repetitive ratios in the total wave structure so far. Will this continue in the future?

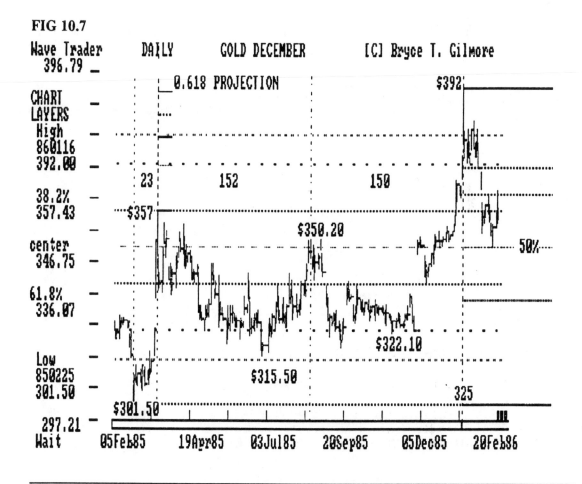

Chp. 10 Page. 99

## PRICE RETRACEMENTS AND PROJECTIONS

### FIG 10.8  CORRECTION FROM $392 HIGH

This chart is a good example of how time overrides price in many instances. After the first two minor waves from the $392 high unfolded in perfect ratios of time and price a consolidation period set in that followed time rather than price for the next several counter trend reactions. Time ratios in degrees of Phi of the first corrective wave projected forward signaled numerous swing points during the consolidation phase.

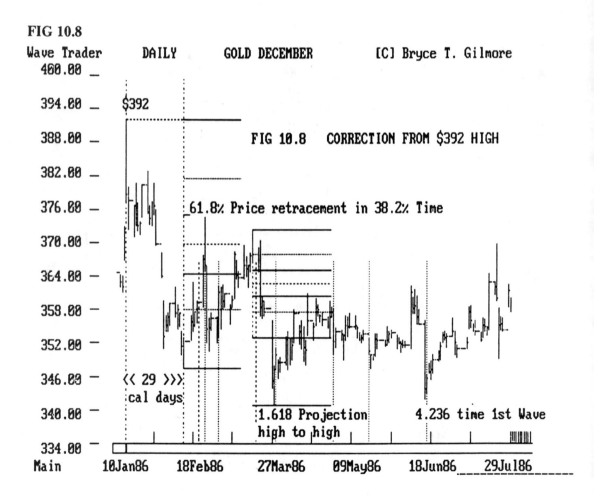

# PRICE RETRACEMENTS AND PROJECTIONS

### FIG 10.9   WAVE STRUCTURE $301.50 TO $447.70

This chart should reinforce the concept of price relationships in wave structures. Most of the major ratios have already been detailed, the only one I wish to point out here is the retracement from the $446.50 high back to $376.50 ($70.00). The price advance up to $446.50 from $301.50 expanded $145, as a ratio of the overall advance $70 did not appear to satisfy a satisfactory level although $70 is [ $55 * 1.272 (root Phi)]. $55 as a ratio of $144 is 38.2% therefore $70 interlinks somehow. As it turned out the total ground gained from $301.50 to the low of $376.50 was $75. $75 * 1.666 equals $125, $376.50 plus $125 equals $501.50 which was near enough the high of April 27th, 1987 at $501.

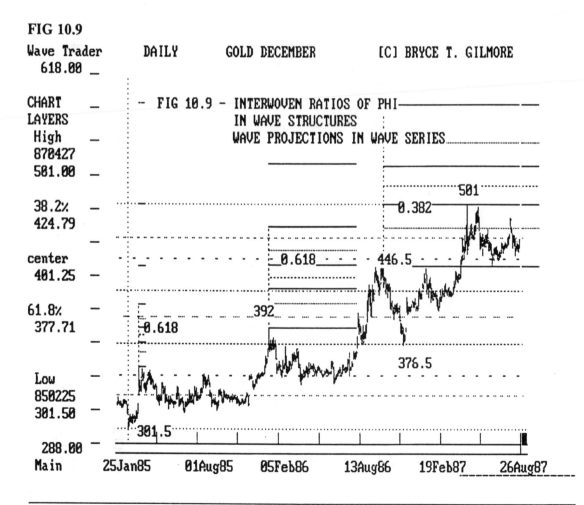

Chp. 10 Page. 101

PRICE RETRACEMENTS AND PROJECTIONS

## 61.8% EXAMPLE RETRACEMENT IN BEAR MARKETS

### FIG 10.10    SILVER BEAR MARKET RALLY 1986-1987

One only needs to look at this chart to be convinced of the accuracy of these measurements. The high at 61.8% retracement fell on a time of 343 calendar days (7x7x7) from the 1986 low. There were also a number of other time elements at this high but the important aspect I wish to illustrate is the runaway market coming to a halt exactly at the 61.8% retracement level. The subsequent market action that followed may help prove that this was no fluke.

FIG 10.10

# PRICE RETRACEMENTS AND PROJECTIONS

## FIG 10.11   SILVER CORRECTION AFTER 1987 HIGH

This chart speaks for itself. Here two successive intermediate wave turning points fell within a cent of the ratios we have been discussing throughout this chapter.

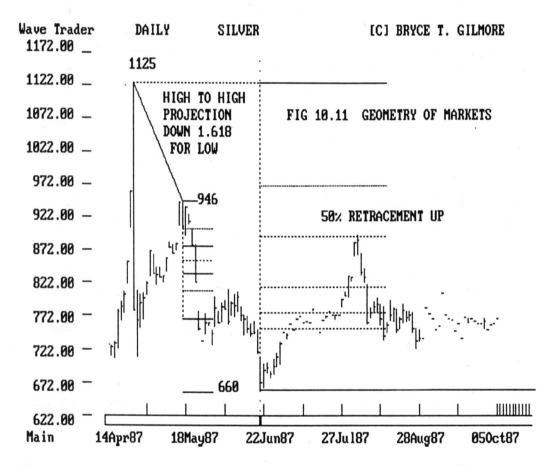

FIG 10.11

Using projections and retracements of previous ranges to gauge support and resistance levels in geometric markets is quite simple. If a market turns at these levels and an important time ratio of some other wave structure concurs, a change in the current trend should last for a while. Depending on the severity of the price and time signals and the prevailing psychological factors present at the time, an astute experienced analyst can evaluate profit making strategies.

## PRICE RETRACEMENTS AND PROJECTIONS

### The most important future range levels to consistently monitor are :-

**RETRACEMENTS OF**   33.3% 38.2%, 50%, 61.8% and 66.6%

**PROJECTIONS OF**   38.2% 61.8% 100% 161.8% and 261.8%

### Following range retracement and projection levels

To remain abreast of important price retracement and projection levels of previous ranges one should maintain long term weekly charts and mark out the important price levels that could square price in the future.

Start with the history high to history low range.

Then the latest primary high to primary low range.

Next use the latest intermediate high to low range as this is normally the most important unless a major change of trend has occurred.

In minor waves follow the equality of waves and how they relate to the overall structure.

Watch for triangular formations as these could signal trading opportunities. Triangles generally form in fourth waves, this means one more impulse wave then a complete change in trend.

## 11. GEOMETRIC VIBRATION ANGLES

This chapter should clear up any misunderstandings regarding the geometric ratios used to find technical support and resistance put forward in this text to date.

## VIBRATION

Vibration is the key to the universe, all matter emits a vibration. Even though we cannot see it, it is there. The human heart vibrates at around 70 beats per minute, if excited these vibrations increase, as things settle down to normal the vibration decreases, when we sleep the heart rate reduces. Each vibration fulfills a cycle and then adjusts its momentum into another phase. This phenomena continues unabated throughout our lives and follows a natural pattern. Markets vibrate up and down in the same manner, continually increasing and decreasing their vibration rate. These vibrations are a function of ever changing factors to do with supply, demand and speculator interest.

W.D. Gann used an arbitrary value of 1 to 1 to measure the vibration of price against time. This is merely a guide to the overall concept of vibration as vibration is not static in markets. Vibration of markets is a function of the players. These players fight a battle with each other and a markets vibration rate either increases or decreases depending upon the intensity of interest.

As a trend in a market progresses the vibration rate should increase until such time as the driving force exhausts itself, once this occurs a counter trend move will evolve, generally at the same vibration or intensity that led it into the situation of exhaustion. Nature adjusts to its excesses in an unforgiving way.

## DISCOVERING MARKET VIBRATION

When I first began squaring price and time I would draw my daily gold chart on a box scale of 10 cents per day. After some time it was becoming unmanageable and I had to change the scale to gain any perspective of the price movement against time. The

# VIBRATION OF PRICE AND TIME

scales being used by Gann traders went through an upheaval after the 1980 bull market. Some years ago I asked my friend Steve Barrett how he coped with the scaling on his daily, weekly and monthly charts, his answer was a little vague, so I realized he was wrestling with this same problem. Each chart had its own specific problem: **WHAT WAS THE CORRECT VIBRATION RATE TO USE FOR THE 45 degree angle?** This was even more of a problem when plotting the All Ordinaries Index which now had a range of 800 points and was rising.

## COMMODITY VIBRATION

Commodity vibration is the term used to describe the rate of price increase or decrease per day, week or month between two extreme points.

Some analysts I have met talk of commodity vibration numbers; by deduction I see they are talking about specific cycles observed as being regular. These are not vibrations as they are static in value.

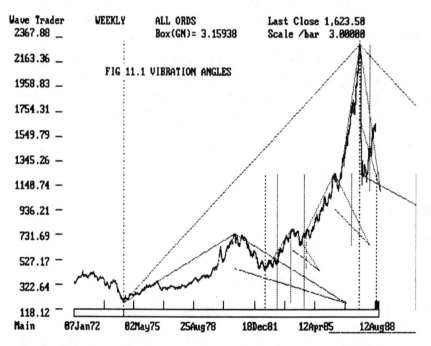

**FIG 11.1** DEMONSTRATES HOW EACH NEW WAVE IN AN ADVANCING MARKET GROWS IN ITS INTENSITY OF VIBRATION.

Extreme market turning points for measuring vibration could be a history high and history low, major bull market top to the next major low, minor top to next minor low etc.

If the vibration of a commodity was changing with each cycle then it seemed to me that I must change my 45 degree angles after each move if I wished to keep in tune with the market. This meant rescaling my charts after each major move. Taking this concept one step further meant adjusting angles to suit even the shorter term vibrations.

## CALCULATING A VIBRATION RATE

Geometric vibration angles are the true reflection of previous price ranges squared to time and price.

The vibration of a price move can be calculated by dividing the points travelled in that move by the time taken to complete that move.

An example of the calculation required when a price rise of say $144 occurs in a market trend over a period of say 233 days:

> 144 divided by 233 equals 0.618
>
> This means that the average vibration for the completed move was $0.618 per day.

In Fig 11.1 of the All Ordinaries Index, the vibration angle of the total move from the 1974 low to the 1987 high squared out at 3.15938 points per week, This can be read out from the Box(GN). This value holds a mathematical property often overlooked by students of geometric charting.

> Root 2 (1.414) multiplied by root 5 (2.236) equals 3.162
>
> Also PI which is 3.1416 came extremely close to this vibration.

**TIME OF THIS RANGE WAS 677 WEEKS - POINTS RISEN 1974-87 EQUALED 2138.9 (89 x 24 = 2136).**

## DISPLAYING A COMMODITY VIBRATION GEOMETRICALLY

Once the vibration of a trend is established we can then represent this vibration as the diagonal of a square, ie the vibration rate becomes the true 1x1 unit of price to time and the 45 degree angle of that square.

This 1x1 vibration angle can now be represented in degrees of the square, circle and golden rectangle as a guide to future market strength or weakness.

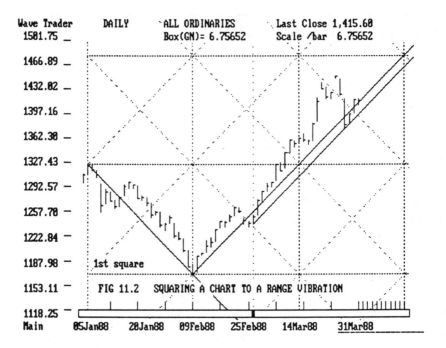

FIG 11.2 VIBRATION OF A MOVE REPRESENTED AS THE DIAGONAL OF A SQUARE

This chart is a little more descriptive of these methods. The corrective wave has been squared to price and time. The vibration of this move can be read off the scale/bar at 6.75652 units per day; hardly anything like 1 2 4 or 8 units per day that a standard geometric chart would use. This means that the 45 degree angle is vibrating at 6.75652 points per day. The next wave of similar degree needs to remain above the 45 degree angle if it is to signal strength. On this chart the bullish trend is in a touch and go position, the market is trading right on the primary 1x1 angle. There is good reason for this as at the last high both time and price were overbalanced by a larger degree vibration.

# VIBRATION OF PRICE AND TIME

If a trend is intact then the next impulse phase will increase its vibration, however, should the future vibration wain, then it will signal an end to the longer term trend in progress. This is generally a sign distribution is taking place.

1x1 vibration angles have a particular purpose for determining the future trend whilst prices remain in a counter trending move from the squared range.

The first square has the most relevance in both time and price. As prices move along they will form new important ranges that require new calculations to be made. Major market shocks will have a more enduring effect on the future as they take longer to erase from the memory.

**Range vibrations should be calculated for all important market moves. These originate from the range of the history high to the history low down to the most recent minor range of significance.**

An understanding of the Elliott Wave Principle is very important when it comes to selecting ranges for future vibration calculations, be they minor, intermediate, primary or cycle vibrations.

If we wish to represent a support or resistance angle of vibration that geometrically relates to both price and time of a past range in other degrees such as the golden rectangle, it is only a matter of manipulative mathematics. The 1x1 angle of the squared range is multiplied by the desired factor.

Using the same range illustrated in Fig 11.2, where the 1x1 angle was calculated at 6.7565 points per day, a quick calculation of the 1.618 vibration would be 6.7565 * 1.618 or 10.9352 points per day. Similarly a 0.618 vibration of the same 1x1 would be 6.7565 * 0.618 or 4.1755 points per day.

Strangely enough I can remember from an earlier chart presented on page 82 in chapter 8 where the vibration of the overall move from the 1986 low to the 1987 high of this same index had a similar vibration to the 0.618 angle ratio just calculated. This move lasted 293 days for a gain of 1218.3 points, a vibration of 4.158 points per day.

# VIBRATION OF PRICE AND TIME

**FIG 11.3** ILLUSTRATION OF 0.618 AND 1.618 VIBRATION ANGLES OF A RANGE

You will notice how easily one can view these angles once a chart has been presented geometrically.

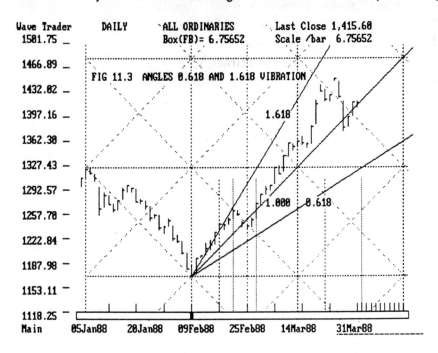

**FIG 11.4** VIBRATION IN THE LARGER DEGREE

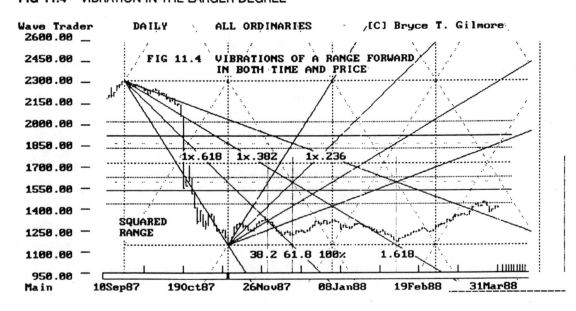

Careful observation of this chart (Fig 11.4) will explain the significance of vibration angles. Where they intersect they measure time. Markets vibrate on time and price relationships to the past. This market turned on cue at 61.8% time 100% time 161.8% time and 250% time. Look at the confusion during the first square. The last high of several days ago turned on the 25% retracement of price as well as the 250% of time vibration.

You may well be puzzled by Fig 11.4 as I did not square the chart range to the vibration value yet all of the angles have been drawn geometrically to represent their correct values. You can see that, just the same, they are all mathematically perfect. As long as one understands the underlying principle behind commodity range vibrations geometric angles can be represented on any chart time price scale.

## VIBRATIONS IN TRENDS

As a general rule the ratios of wave vibrations will hold a solid mathematical relationship throughout a complete trend in the market, this includes both a related bull market and bear market reaction.

**Once a trend is evident one should take readings from the first advance or decline and project these forward. Then vibrations of previous waves can be projected to confirm clusters where vibrations of price and time in past waves coincide with progressive vibrations as time and price move through an unfolding geometric series of waves.**

Whilst the market continues to unfold holding a pattern of past vibration tendencies we can be sure that the mass psychology of the participants is relatively unchanged and future trend will continue to advance or decline along the same relationships.

## FIG 11.5 - VIBRATIONS FORWARD OF A FIRST WAVE ADVANCE

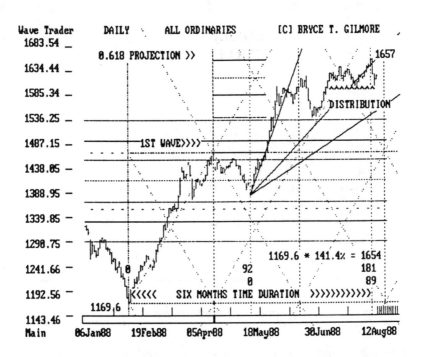

Vibration angles of 1.618, 0.618 and 0.382 times the first wave vibration drawn from the begining of the third wave. The first impulse follows the 1.618 angle indicating strength, after a correction the vibration then falls back to the 1x1 rate. Eventually as the distribution begins to take effect the market breaks below the 0.618 vibration indicating the conclusion of the move. From the chart low to the chart high the time elapsed was six months (Gann), the third wave beginning to the fifth wave ending took 89 days (Elliott). The fifth wave formed a diagonal triangle formation.

A diagonal triangle formation implies that the end is in sight. Even if this market were to stage one more advance I would not remain long after viewing this formation, a collapse could occur at any time, infact it did. (re-edited June 1989).

NOW THAT WE HAVE COVERED ALL OF THE GEOMETRIC CHARTING TECHNIQUES FOR SQUARING PRICE TO TIME WE CAN PROCEED IN THE ART OF USING THIS INFORMATION AS A GUIDE TO FUTURE FORECASTING OF MARKET TREND.

MARKETS UNFOLD IN A SYMMETRY OF MATHEMATICAL DEGREE TO THE PAST. RELATIONSHIPS BETWEEN PAST TRENDS AND FUTURE TRENDS WILL FALL INTO ONE OF THREE CATEGORIES; ARITHMETIC, GEOMETRIC OR HARMONIC VIBRATIONS. SOMETIMES MINOR MOVES ARE INTERRUPTED BY LONGER TERM VIBRATIONS. FUTURE VIBRATIONS COULD EMANATE FROM PREVIOUS INTERMEDIATE, PRIMARY OR CYCLE WAVES. SHOCKS ALONG THE WAY OFTEN PROVIDE NEW INGREDIENTS. OTHERWISE PERFECT SYMMETRY OF ALL MARKETS WOULD RESULT.

Arithmetic ratios are 33.3% 50% 66.6%

Geometric ratios are 38.2% 61.8% 161.8%

Harmonic ratios are 70.7% 141.4%

As analysts we must appreciate that we are only human and can get misled into believing, as others do, that all will work out as we now see it. Often because we are human we have neglected to keep up our technical calculations. Failure to recognize a trading opportunity mostly lies with this shortcoming, not the method.

# MARKET SYMMETRY

The main difference between using range vibration angles instead of standard geometric angles on daily, weekly and monthly charts is that an **equality with time and price is always maintained between each chart of a different time series.**

Some Gann analysts will no doubt be having great success using standard geometric angles and I would not in anyway discourage the use of these angles, they hold their rightful place in the art of time and price analysis.

Next I will illustrate vibration angles using Mount Isa Mines price data. I have included a chart (Fig 11.6), illustrating standard geometric angles on the weekly chart just so we can see their effective use. What I wish to point out is that this chart has just had price values adjusted for an issue. The 1x1 angle drawn at $0.025 per week would not have placed the angles in the same position relative to future time and price previous to three weeks ago.

**FIG 11.6** = MOUNT ISA MINES WEEKLY WITH STANDARD GEOMETRIC ANGLES AT 2.5 CENTS PER WEEK SCALE (2x1) (1x1) (1x2).

On the face of it they appear to be working quite well as an indicator of support and resistance. The only anomaly is that this price series was just adjusted 7% in value 3 weeks ago and prior to that these angles would have been positioned quite differently on the old price series. Whereas now the 1x1 vibration of the chart major low to high is 0.04981 per week (equal to a 2x1 angle of 0.025) before it would have been (99 cents to $ 3.80 in 53 weeks [ 380-99/53 equals 0.0530]).

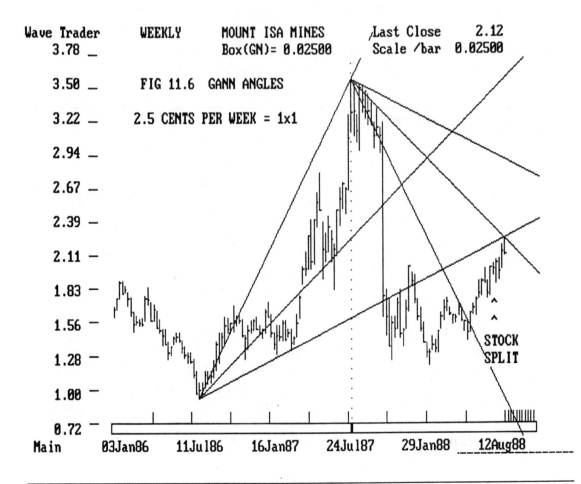

# VIBRATION OF PRICE AND TIME

**FIG 11.7 = MOUNT ISA MINES WEEKLY - VIBRATION SQUARING OF THE MAJOR RANGE.**

The power of geometric analysis is now in high gear, both price and time have been squared to the vibration of the chart low / high range and projected across the ensuing price series.

A geometric relationship of price to time exists at every level from either the horizontal price, vertical time or diagonal time price angles, intersections of the inner circle with diagonal angles form some strict relationship of the circle to the square. The main levels to watch are as stated earlier, the .382, .5, .618 and 100% areas as they are directly related to both the square and the golden rectangle. As one becomes proficient using these methods the relationships of the lesser degree vibrations will tie in as confirmations of the inter- relating range vibrations of multiple waves projected across the same data.

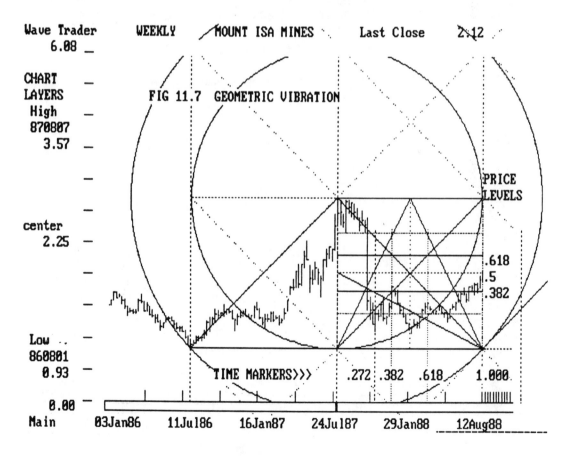

# FIG 11.8 = BULL RANGE VIBRATIONS OF THE SQUARE

In this chart I have endeavored to illustrate how accurately precise angle vibrations can act as support and resistance within absolute values of the progressing price patterns. In this chart an intermediate low and high of the market fell exactly on the 50% and 100% time levels of the previous range, the high on the 100% time level squared the 50% level of the previous range in price, this is a classic squaring of price and time in Gann degree. The low made at the 50% time vibration was a 66.6% decline in value from the high of the chart which also confirmed time and price intersecting at this point. This is better illustrated in Fig 11.12

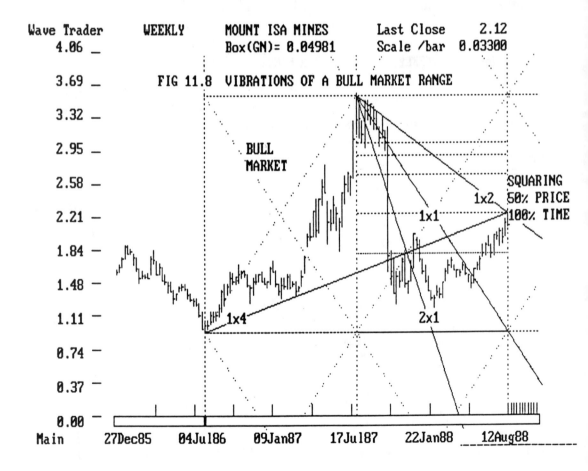

# VIBRATION OF PRICE AND TIME

## FIG 11.9 = VIBRATIONS OF BOTH THE BULL AND BEAR CYCLE FORWARD

The angles across this chart after the mid point of the square combine both the vibrations of the bull range as well as the vibrations of the bear range. The angles down from the high are in square ratios ie 50% and 100% vibration of the bull vibration and Fibonacci ratios of the bear range ie 38.2% and 61.8%, (these ratios I use when I start the angles from the beginning of the squared range). The angle up from the low is a 1x1 vibration of the bear range. The 1x1 up and the 0.618 down cross at the 0.618 time of the bull market square and intersect price at the exact reversal point. This time vibration of the bear market square is 0.236 (0.618*0.618*0.618).

The 0.382 angle down crosses the 1x1 angle up at exactly the mid point of the range of the bull square, the upper angle that squares the 100% time and 50% price intersection is the 1x2 angle of the bull market down from the high.

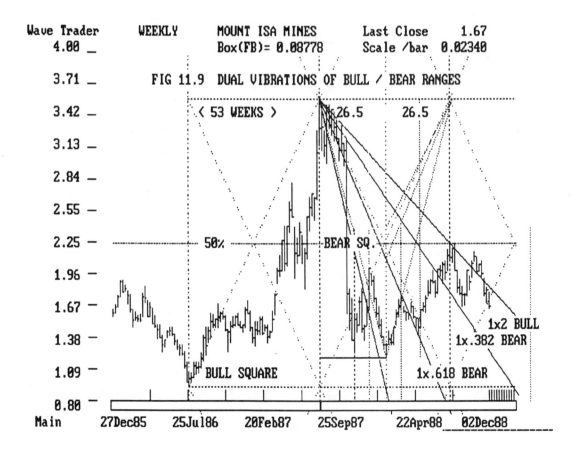

Chp. 11 Page. 117

# VIBRATION OF PRICE AND TIME

Just in case Fig 11.9 is a little complex to follow, the next few charts will help clear up the ratio examples presented.

**FIG 11.10 TIME VIBRATIONS OF THE BULL MARKET RANGE**

Time markers 27.2% 38.2% 50% 61.8% AND 100%.

On the previous chart you can reaffirm the crossing of the 1x1 and 0.618 angles of the bear range at the 61.8% time vibration and the subsequent reversal to trend.

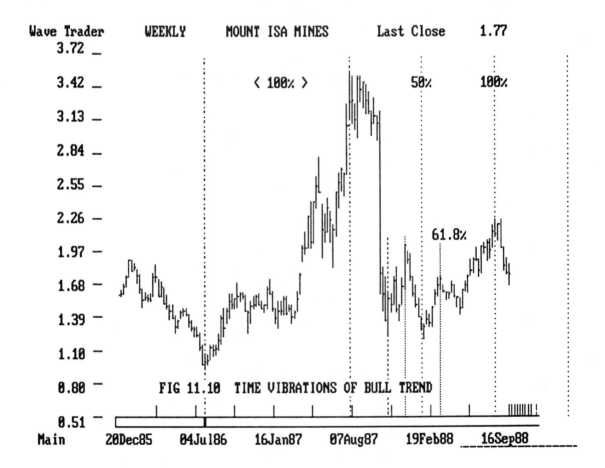

FIG 11.10 TIME VIBRATIONS OF BULL TREND

# VIBRATION OF PRICE AND TIME

## FIG 11.11 TIME VIBRATIONS OF THE BEAR MARKET RANGE

Time markers 23.6% 38.2% 50% 61.8% AND 100%.

Each timing period marked a counter trend reaction of some degree, the 50% level being the strongest signal for the continuation of the uptrend that began on the 50% time of the bull market square.

For those of you who are unfamiliar with the Mount Isa Mines stock. Mount Isa Mines is one of the oldest Australian mining companies, with interests in copper, silver, gold and coal. Mount Isa shares can be traded in Australia, London and now West Germany. A liquid put and call option market operates out of Sydney.

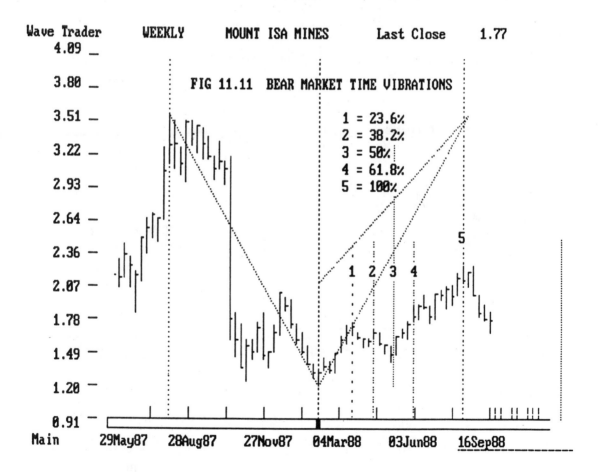

VIBRATION OF PRICE AND TIME

**FIG 11.12** BULL MARKET SQUARE SHOWING THE PRICE RELATIONSHIP WITH THE HIGH PRICE (66.6% DISCOUNT) AT THE 50% TIME PERIOD.

Another classic squaring of price and time. This particular ratio was discussed in an earlier chapter under dynamic price supports.

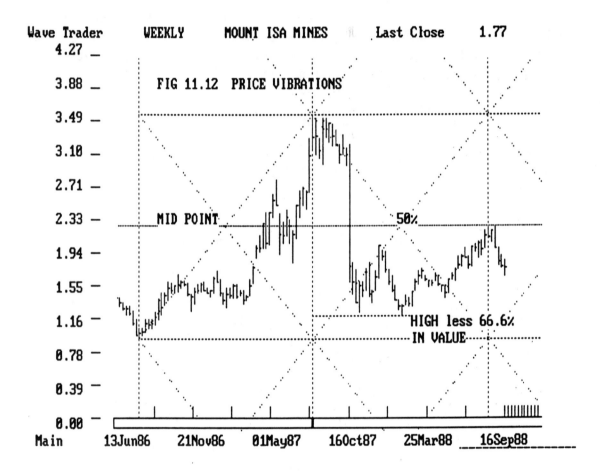

To further illustrate how the vibration angles hold form from daily charts to weekly charts the next two examples show the vibrations in the bear market square.

# VIBRATION OF PRICE AND TIME

**FIG 11.13 WEEKLY BEAR MARKET SQUARE FORWARD**

The angles drawn down from the high are at ratios of 0.618 and 0.382 of the bear range vibration. The angle up is the 1x1 vibration. The symmetry of this market is demonstrated by these mathematical techniques.

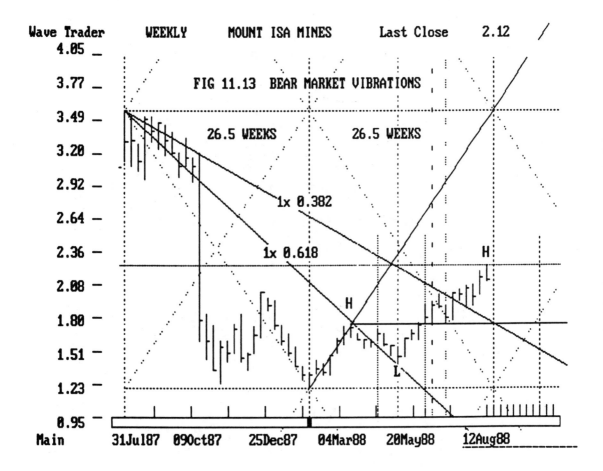

# VIBRATION OF PRICE AND TIME

## FIG 11.14 DAILY BEAR MARKET SQUARE FORWARD

The low made at the 66.6% discount to the high price fell 131 trading days from the high, this was in the 27th week forward of the high. The previous bull market range shown on the earlier charts was 259 trading days and 53 weeks. Time missed by two trading days but still fell in the right week for this low. The last high price at the end of the chart where the reversal occurred at the 50% price level of the bull market range was 256 trading days from the high and in the 53rd week, 371 calendar days forward of the high exactly 53 weeks. The bull market range was exactly 372 calendar days; the lesson here is that the major range of the bull market was overriding time of the bear market range, meaning that the greater the range the greater the future influence.

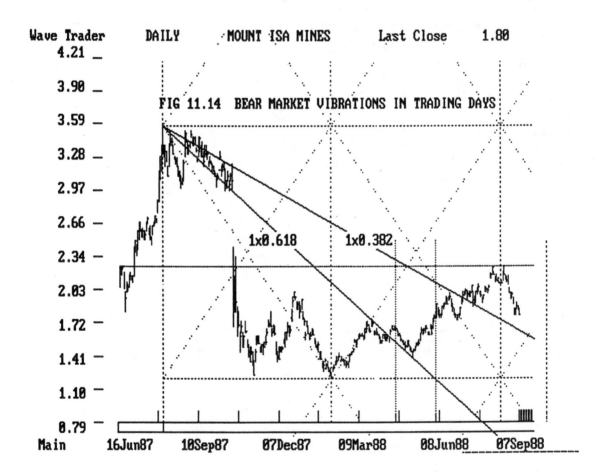

# VIBRATION OF PRICE AND TIME

**FIG 11.15 BULL MARKET RANGE SQUARED IN CALENDAR DAYS**

This chart bears out how accurately these methods can track the symmetry of markets over long periods of time.

When plotting vibration angles, do so by weeks, trading days and calendar days. You will find on occasions that time periods will balance out perfectly for all charts, these are the times we can be sure of our signals to the exact day. At other times when a slight variation is apparent revert to the Fibonacci and Lucas numbers as a guide to home in on the exact day. This means counting off time in days, weeks or months from previous swing highs and lows to find clusters of time around your more primary vibration signals.

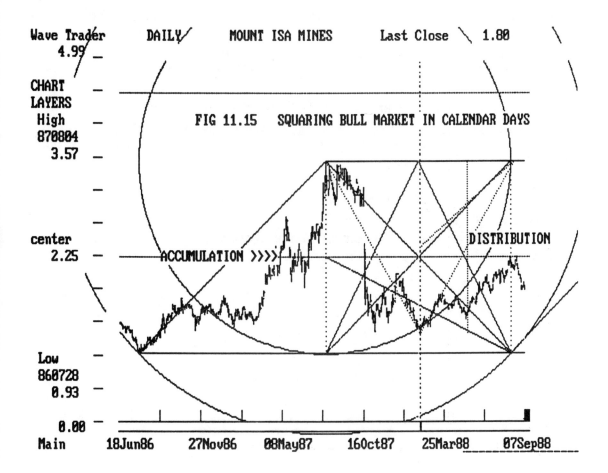

## Summary of important vibration ratios to monitor.

Watch the price levels reached at times when a market is squaring the time vibration of a range at 38.2% 50% 61.8% and 100%. Anytime a price vibration of 38.2% 50% 61.8% or 100% is achieved at the same time means that the symmetry is perfect and a counter trend reversal should follow.

These are exceptional areas from which to trade for fast profits. Remember there is no necessity to overtrade. An **educated trader** only needs four or five major trades per year to increase his trading account by 300% or more.

Throughout this chapter I have concentrated on the ratios 38.2%, 50%, 61.8% and 100%. These ratios, are the most common used by technical analysts familiar with these techniques. Before proceeding it would be wise to mention that 33.3% and 66.6% can be just as valid for a reversal in trend. Also 70.7%, half of root two is important if a trend continues unabated through both 61.8% and 66.6% ratios.

Ratios of lesser importance are 23.6%, 25%, 27.2%, 75%, 76.4%, 85.4% and 87.5%. Vibrations of past waves of lesser current significance often fall on these ratios at the same time a major squaring occurs in 38.2%, 50%, 61.8% or 100% adding extra confirmation to the unfolding pattern.

Strongest signals for a reversal of the current trend will be when vibrations of **PRIMARY WAVES, INTERMEDIATE WAVES and MINOR WAVES** square in a cluster around a future date. A combination of 50% and 61.8% or 100% and 161.8% or 50% and 100% are just a few to remember.

**Time, price and pattern will alert you when it is time to trade.** Experience is the best educator, in time you will gain more and more confidence as you see markets unfold.

# 12. ELLIOTT WAVE ANALYSIS

The most popularly known experts on this subject are Robert R. Prechter, Jr and A.J. Frost. There are two books by these authors which are mandatory study for any student of ratio analysis and Elliott wave, these are listed below.

"THE MAJOR WORKS OF R.N. ELLIOTT" Edited by Robert R. Prechter, Jr.
"ELLIOTT WAVE PRINCIPLE - Key to stock market profits" by Frost and Prechter.

There are a number of excellent books available by various other authors, since I have not read them I am at a loss to recommend their content. However Don Vodopich, David Weiss, Robert Beckman and Glenn A. Neely have written several books between them which must be considered essential reading.

Following is an outline of the important points that I have noted in my own use of the ELLIOTT wave theory.

## ELLIOTT WAVE STRUCTURES

To keep track of the stages that a bull or bear market moves through, Ralph Elliott developed a lettering system for keeping track of waves of similar degree.

Waves are broken down in stages from CYCLE - PRIMARY - INTERMEDIATE - MINOR - MINUTE.

The same principle applies in waves of minute degree as to waves of cycle degree. Impulse waves have a minimum 5 legs, sometimes 9, corrections have minimum 3 legs.

A *minute* wave structure when completed fulfills a completed stage of a *minor* wave. A *minor* wave when completed fulfills a completed *Intermediate* wave and so on, ie., 5 *minute impulse* waves will make up a *minor* impulse wave. 3 *minute* corrective waves will complete a *minor* corrective wave et cetera.

(i) (ii) (iii) (iv) (v) equals 1   (a) (b) (c) equals A and 1 2 3 4 5 equals (1)   A B C equals (A) et cetera.

## WAVE LABELING

CYCLE WAVES ....................................... I II III IV V
PRIMARY WAVES ................................. [1] [2] [3] [4] [5]   [A] [B] [C]
INTERMEDIATE WAVES ........................ (1) (2) (3) (4) (5)   (A) (B) (C)
MINOR WAVES ..................................... 1 2 3 4 5   A B C
MINUTE WAVES .................................... (i) (ii) (iii) (iv) (v)   (a) (b) (c)
MINUETTE WAVES ................................ i ii iii iv v   a b c

**FIG 12.1** - EXAMPLE OF INTERMEDIATE WAVES AND PRIMARY WAVES IN A CYCLE.

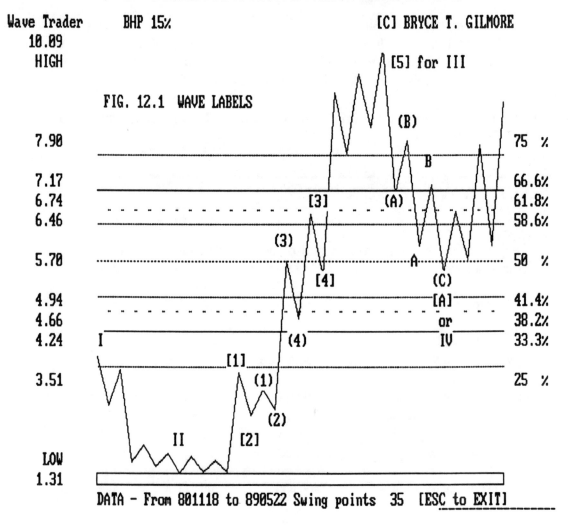

## WAVE PATTERNS FORMED ON A BAR CHART

Price movement in time, graphically illustrated in the form of a bar chart, leaves a pattern that characterises the market mood.

Pattern recognition is in my opinion the strongest analytical tool available to the astute technician.

A clear understanding on wave structures is required if one is to excell in the use of Elliott wave analysis. Understanding only comes with experience, following a number of diversified commodities and stocks daily for many years is how I learnt to interpret wave patterns.

Elliott wave analysis gives the technician a logical choice when it comes to anticipating future market action.

FIG 12.2 - PRICE PATTERNS
2nd edition update

## ELLIOTT WAVE STRICT RULES

As a general rule markets will advance in five waves and contract in three waves.

In an upward moving market there will be three major impulse waves and two corrective waves. The impulse waves will have a minimum of five minor waves and the corrective waves will have a minimum of three waves. Trend can be established by the direction of waves containing five wave sequences.

During corrective waves a decline in volume will signal a relief to selling pressure and possible trend reversal.

Corrective waves of a major nature in a five wave sequence will alternate. This means that a simple correction will be followed by a complex correction. A simple correction is an (a b c) three wave movement. A complex correction can contain 5 to 9 movements. Complex corrections form patterns of triangular appearance on a price chart.

**Triangles are far more common in fourth waves.**

The third wave in a five wave sequence is usually the longest wave, but never the shortest.

Wave four in a five wave sequence should not overlap wave one except within diagonal triangles.

Wave four corrections will most often than not terminate within the area of the previous wave four of lesser degree.

Extensions can only occur in impulse waves, and are very common, this will give an impulse wave seven to a maximum of nine waves.

Impulse waves always contain five waves minimum and up to nine waves with extensions.

Extensions in fifth waves are often retraced twice.

Cycle dimension bear markets retrace over 50% of the gains made in the bull market.

## MAJOR POINTS TO REMEMBER

**CORRECTIVE WAVES WILL RELATE TO IMPULSE WAVES IN BOTH TIME AMPLITUDE AND PRICE AMPLITUDE.**

**IMPULSE WAVES WILL RELATE TO IMPULSE WAVES IN BOTH TIME AND PRICE AMPLITUDE.**

**GROUND GAINED OR LOST IN MARKET ADVANCES OR CONTRACTIONS CAN BE ACCURATELY MEASURED, WAVE STRUCTURE IS A FUNCTION OF HUMAN EMOTION.**

**WHEN A MARKET MAKES A SIGNIFICANT HIGH, BULLISH CONSENSUS WILL BE AT A MAXIMUM.**

**AT IMPORTANT LOWS BEARISH CONSENSUS WILL BE AT ITS VERY WORST.**

## WAVE ANALYSIS

Wave analysis is the only means available for anticipating future probabilities in price movement.

Today is Sunday 4th June 1989 and I am editing this chapter to include more information where possible. Yesterday I attended a TAG seminar as the guest of Tim Slater from COMPUTRAC. I was amazed at one of the speakers comments in question time when an Elliott wave enthusiast asked the panel "What do you think of Gann analysis as a trading technique?". Jerrold Dickson from San Francisco replied "GARBAGE". This confirmed my suspicions, some traders just want to fly blind. Even though material is available some people will never bother to advance their knowledge. Here's a guy that has been trading the markets for over 10 years, by his own admission sometimes disasterously, yet has not bothered to seriously study the structure of markets. Jerry spent 2 hours dissertating on the use of RSI, DIRECTIONAL MOVEMENT, MACD and several different chart formations that occur over 4 to 5 day periods. What Jerry fails to realize, is the fact that he is using a form of wave analysis in his day to day approach to trade selection. Some traders may not understand what they are doing, but if they use charts, eventually the wave forms will create an intuitive sense which is reflected in their actions. This is the principle behind Gann and Elliott theory.

Every serious trader should study wave theory in finer detail, this way one can identify where they are making bad trading decisions.

# ELLIOTT WAVE CHARACTERISTICS

## WAVE ONE OF A NEW BULL MARKET

Wave one will be either a slow basing type movement as accumulation takes place from the previous downtrend, or a dynamic thrust caused by the large number of short traders covering positions in an oversold market.

When evaluating the price level potential for a wave one advance I find it better to use percentage increases of the bear market low. By squaring the low price to 25% 33.3% 50% 66.6% et cetera, will nearly always tell one where this first wave will find resistance. The reason is quite simple, a bear market terminates because prices have reached a level that even the bears consider cheap by previous standards. The low price becomes the new standard by which future prices are measured. It really depends on how far prices were decimated in the previous bear market as to the possibility and extent of a fast recovery. Any retracement in excess of 25% of the previous bear market is generally a sign that a new bull trend is in the making.

**THE BEGINNING OF WAVE ONE SHOULD COINCIDE WITH A MAJOR TIME AND PRICE SQUARING IN THE PREVIOUS BEAR MARKET.**

FIG 12.4   ILLUSTRATION OF FIVE MINOR WAVES FORMING AN INTERMEDIATE WAVE.

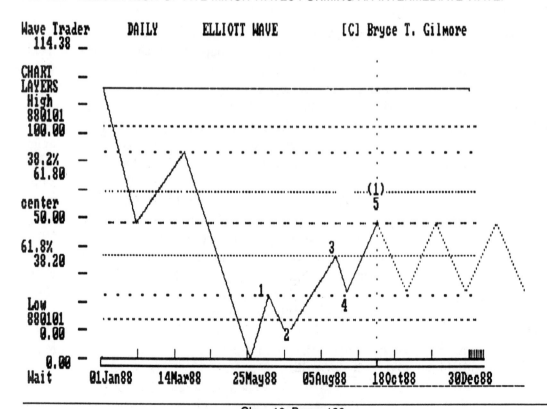

## WAVE TWO OF A NEW BULL MARKET

Second waves often appear to be part of the previous bear phase as they often retrace much if not all of the first wave up. They are not inspiring moves to create the atmosphere for a new bull market. **Wave two will generally retrace 50%, 61.8% and 78.6% of the wave one advance.**

Wave structure in second waves is the best guide to the retracement level. A simple zig zag correction can take on the following appearance; phase (a) corrects between 25% and 38.2% of the wave one advance, phase (b) retraces 61.8% of wave (a), wave (c) for [2] terminates at the 61.8% or 100% projection level of wave (a). It will normally depend on the depth of the first (a) wave to determine if a correction of over 50% to wave one can be expected.

A careful study of corrective wave structures is recommended because identifying wave two bottoms is one of the best ways to become rich trading leveraged markets. **Call option premiums are virtually given away as a wave two terminates and registered traders are convinced that the bear market is still in progress.**

FIG 12.5 ILLUSTRATES WAVE (2) AS A 61.8% PRICE RETRACEMENT TO WAVE (1) IN 50% OF TIME.

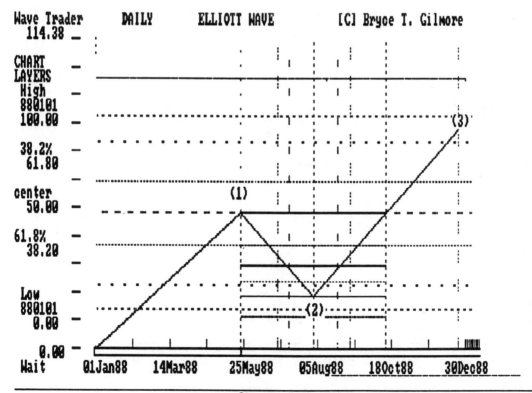

## WAVE THREE OF A BULL MARKET

Third waves are often long and broad. The trend is unmistakable. Fundamental news is entering the market and instilling confidence in the future. As they progress market sentiment will be so high one would think there will never be an end to the current trend. Third waves are the best waves to identify and trade for the long haul. Minor corrections are often very shallow affairs as the move really gets going.

Third waves, IF SIMPLE, usually advance to the 161.8% level of the wave one advance, either measured from the wave two low or the wave one high. 61.8% advance on the wave one expansion is a minimum target.

**WAVE THREE TARGETS BASED ON WAVE ONE PROJECTIONS SHOULD BE 61.8% THEN 100% THEN 161.8% THEN 200% THEN 223.6% THEN 261.8%**

**WAVE THREE CAN COMMONLY TERMINATE AT 100% 200% 300% SQUARES OF THE ORIGINAL LOW PRICE WHERE THE ADVANCE BEGAN.**

FIG 12.6 ILLUSTRATES WAVE (3) AS A 61.8% PROJECTION OF WAVE (1).

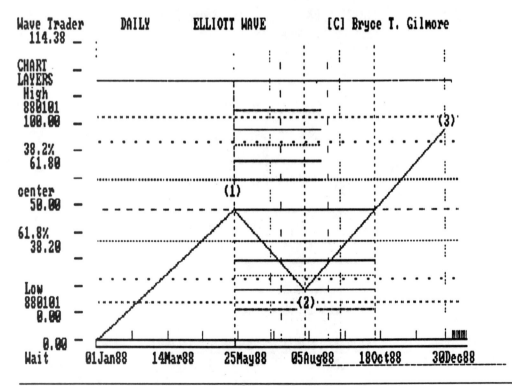

**FOURTH WAVES IN THE OLD BULL MARKET**

Fourth waves are predictable in as much as they see the sentiment turn from one of hope to one of despair. The bullish index will fall to the lowest readings seen for months. Soothsayers will be predicting the end of the bull market and further falls as the fourth wave terminates. Johnny come latelys to the market will be in a state of nervousness. The public have usually entered at the late stages of the third wave.

Fourth waves often take on a triangular appearance due to the fight backwards and forwards between the longer term trend and the frightened traders. When the local share market (Australian All Ordinaries Index) was distributing in (1987) before the final advance, a head and shoulders pattern emerged as the previous intermediate fourth wave low was tested. Many chartists were tricked into believing that the top had been attained, instead the next advance gained 33% in value from the wave four low. A word of warning regards the count in a fourth wave is this, sometimes wave (1) of wave five will double bottom with the wave four low giving the appearance that it is part of the fourth wave structure, this can often leave you a wave short on your fifth wave count. This can be disasterous when you believe a market has one more upswing to complete a valid Elliott wave count.

FIG 12.7 S&P 500 INDEX - FOURTH WAVES IN PRIMARY AND INTERMEDIATE DEGREE.

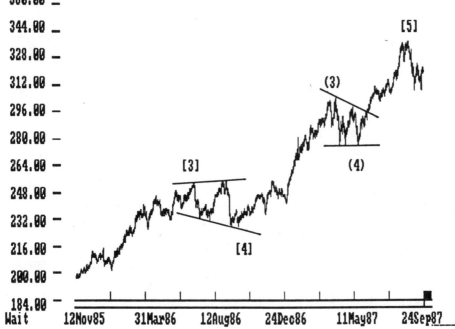

Fourth waves usually retrace only 14.6% or 23.6% of the range advanced during the third wave or sometimes of the total range from the bull market start. A 38.2% retracement in fourth waves of lesser degree is common when measured off the 3rd wave.

If a fourth wave retraces more than 38.2% of wave three or the total bull market range wave 5 will often result in a failure. A failure occurs when the next advance fails to trade above the previous high point prior to the correction.

Whenever you identify a triangular formation it is nearly always signaling a base for one more advance. This is the distribution phase catching all the latecomers. Once a fifth wave breaks above the third wave high even the traders who exited through the distribution phase are attracted back into the market.

In figure 12.7 on the previous page you will see two examples of fourth wave structures. The primary wave [4] unfolded as an expanding triangle and the intermediate wave (4) unfolded as a symetrical triangle.

**FIFTH WAVES THE END OF THE BULL MARKET**

Fifth waves can be either dynamic or mild. The market will be pessimistic to the future and the first wave of the fifth will be a laboured affair as the so called experts continue to sell into the advance, refusing to believe that the bull market is still intact.

Primary fifth waves can fail to reach the high point of the third primary wave, this will be signaled only if a clear five wave count can be identified. This event is more common if the third primary wave contains an extended fifth intermediate wave, ie., wave 5 is greater in price amplitude to wave 3.

Once a fifth wave breaks above the previous third wave top the fundamentals will be changing yet the market is not listening. Human nature will be buying the market as greed becomes more apparent. No one will be predicting the top, quite the contrary, the so called experts will be advocating that the market is headed for even more ridiculous highs. The public will be fully invested and the commercials will be distributing as much as they can. No one will listen to sensible advice when it comes to investments, brokerage houses will be recording huge profit results.

A dynamic fifth wave will expand 161.8% of the first three waves above the third wave high.

WAVE FIVE TARGETS BASED ON PROJECTIONS OF THE TOTAL ADVANCE TO WAVE THREE SHOULD BE 61.8% THEN 100% THEN 161.8% THEN 200% THEN 261.8%

THE BULLISH INDEX IS AT AN ALL TIME HIGH

There were two fundamentals that warned me prior to the Australian share market high in September 1987. One was the way the market kept advancing whilst the Dow Jones and S & P 500 were in the first stage of their decline. The other was the way the old established brokerage houses were selling off their businesses to the banking corporations. Distribution right at the top!

FIG 12.8 POSSIBLE LAYER STRUCTURE FOR A DYNAMIC BULL MARKET.

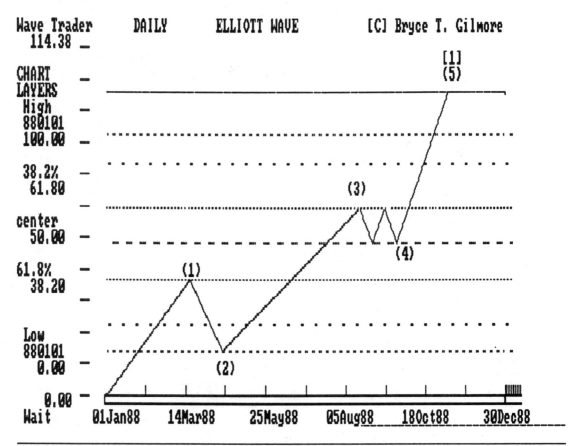

# BEAR MARKETS

## WAVE A OR ONE OF THE NEW BEAR MARKET

A waves are usually viewed as corrections to an overheated market they are generally short and swift, it depends upon the volume of trading that takes place that determines the amount of panic that they create. The A wave will generally take out the bull market fourth wave low, this is the confirmation of the new bear market. At the conclusion of the A wave the regulatory authorities and the media will make all the excuses about the place for the sudden fall. Before the bear market can continue a sizeable retracement to the crash wave must be completed. As the retracement progresses it will seem to the casual observer that all is well. [FAR FROM IT]

**DYNAMIC [A] WAVE TARGETS SHOULD BE A 50% DECLINE OF THE TOTAL ADVANCE OF THE BULL MARKET or A 50% DECLINE IN VALUE FROM THE HIGH.**

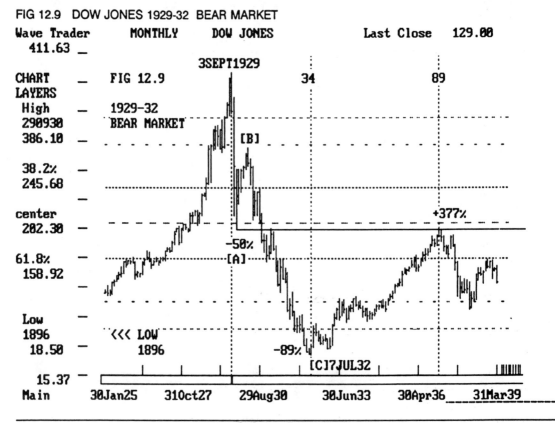

## WAVE B OR TWO OF THE NEW BEAR MARKET

This is a short covering rally and could also contain fresh buying by the traders who now consider prices are at their correct level. This is the last hurrah ! The attitude is that things have been overdone and the bargain hunters come out of the woodwork. Most major B waves often become triangular in appearance as the people caught by the fall slowly unload positions on the rallies. Sometimes as they are nearing completion the sentiment will become more bullish than it was at the top of the preceeding fifth wave.

[B] WAVE TARGETS SHOULD BE A 38.2%, 50%, 61.8%, 66.6%, 85.4% even 100% RETRACEMENT OF THE [A] WAVE DECLINE. ALSO TRY PERCENTAGE RATIOS OF THE [A] WAVE LOW VALUE.

FIG 12.10 DOW JONES INDUSTRIAL AVERAGE 1974- JUNE 1989

One must be careful not to presume that this market will duplicate the bear market of 1929-32. The economic conditions surrounding the two eras are totally unrelated.

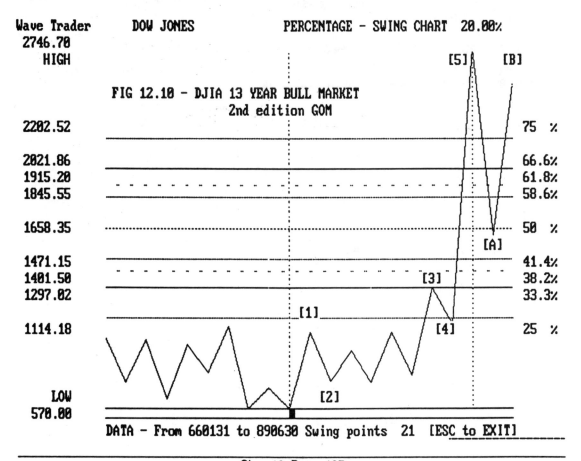

Chp. 12 Page 137

## WAVE C OR THREE OF THE NEW BEAR MARKET

**[C] WAVES CAN BE DYNAMIC OR AS WITH [5] WAVES, FAIL TO REACH THE EXTREMES OF PREVIOUS IMPULSE WAVES.** A failed [C] wave will form a triangle and indicate a new bull market of extreme strength.

**DYNAMIC** [C] waves start off slowly and build up as the fundamental news turns from bad to worse (similar in the reverse to third waves of a bull market). Media attention turns the sentiment around to one of despair, forced sellings accentuate the fall in prices.

Finally complete desperation takes over causing even the most stable investors to abandon positions close to the bottom. The bullish index is at an all time record low.

WAVE C CAN BE CALCULATED ONCE THE A WAVE AND THE B WAVE HAVE BEEN IDENTIFIED. THE TOTAL GROUND LOST FROM THE BEGINING TO THE B WAVE TOP WILL END UP BEING 25% 33.3% 38.2% 50% 61.8% OR 66.6% OF THE TOTAL GROUND LOST TO THE TERMINATION OF THE BEAR MARKET.

FIG 12.11 AUSTRALIAN DOLLAR valued in US cents per $ 1974-1988

Wave [B]-[C] = 66.6% of total bear market. From 1974 high to the 1986 low was a decline in value of 61.8%. Wave [B]-[C] was exactly 61.8 US cents.

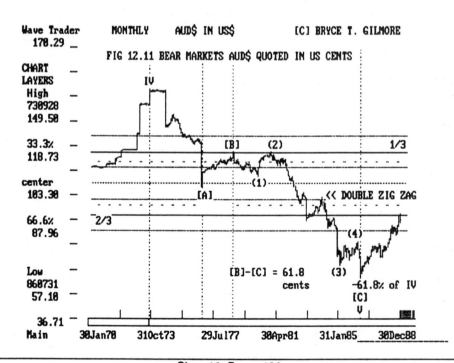

## WAVE ANALYSIS PROCEDURES

**If possible keep a yearly or quarterly price chart of each stock or commodity for as long back as it is possible to gather data.**

**Maintain a monthly price history as far back as you can.**

**Maintain a weekly price history from 1970 if possible.**

**Maintain geometric daily price histories from 1970 if possible.**

**Establish ELLIOTT WAVE counts on all charts and determine the state of each stock or commodity on a long term cycle basis, a primary wave term basis, an intermediate term basis and a minor wave basis.**

**Analyze the probabilities of future moves based on the past. Always consider an alternative wave count, your expectations could bias your opportunity to profit.**

**Follow the mathematical relationships of past markets for a guide to the future.**

FIG 12.12 SWING CHART SHOWING ELLIOTT WAVE FORMATIONS IN VARYING DEGREES.

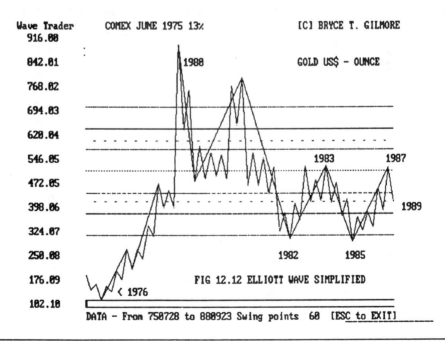

## ELLIOTT WAVE IN PRACTICE

Elliott wave analysis is an extraordinary tool when used in the manner promoted by Ralph Elliott in the early thirties. Just the same one has to treat theory and practice with respect. If you believe that each wave will fall into the same pattern as the theory you will become horribly disillusioned with the whole concept.

The Elliott wave theory was formulated around the Dow Jones Industrial Averages, primarily Elliott intended its use in determining price levels of support and resistance in the stock market. The stock market is an ever growing monster of capitalization and as such will continue to advance as long as the civilization behind that market is intact. This is not the case with commodities as they are expendable and prices rise and fall during periods of over and under supply. Substitutes become more viable at times of high prices and this in turn keeps the lid on further advances. Wave structures in commodities unfold obeying the basic tenets of time and price, but more often than not, many Elliott wave rules have to be broken if one is to apply a long term wave count over more than 10 years. Another characteristic common to commodities is that they move in the more complex wave structures outlined in the theory.

The best guide to a wave count on commodities is the mass psychology readings taken at extreme turning points in trend, if you label your waves accordingly you will have a better chance at forecasting the future direction of that market.

To quote a friend "Elliott wave analysis is similar to a love affair with a beautiful woman! Until something goes wrong."

My recommendation is to consider your **preferred** wave counts as having a 65% probability and your **alternate** wave counts a 35% probability. By keeping a balance you will be able to adjust quite quickly **IF** your alternate count becomes the most preferred count.

Follow markets that interact with each other for confirmation and non-confirmation of major trend changes. For instance the stock market and the gold complex historically move "contra cyclical", the DJIA and the BOND market have a relationship, foreign currency investment can drive a market if currency fluctuation is extreme.

As an example I have included two long term wave counts for gold and two for the DJIA.

## ELLIOTT SPEAKS ON GOLD as interpreted by Bryce Gilmore

"The Elliott Wave Principle is a law of probability and relative degree, not a law of inevitability". ELLIOTT WAVE PRINCIPLE. 1981 Frost and Prechter, page 124.

My **preferred** wave count as of now (9th June 1989) is for the current downtrend that began at the high of US$ 502.30 (marked (A) on the chart fig 12.13) on 14th December 1987 to either be completed or have one more minor wave down to a level of US$ 337.00 where upon a reversal of trend will take gold prices up in 5 minor waves to the US$ 576 or to the US$ 645 level.

FIG 12.13 - SPOT GOLD MONTHLY.

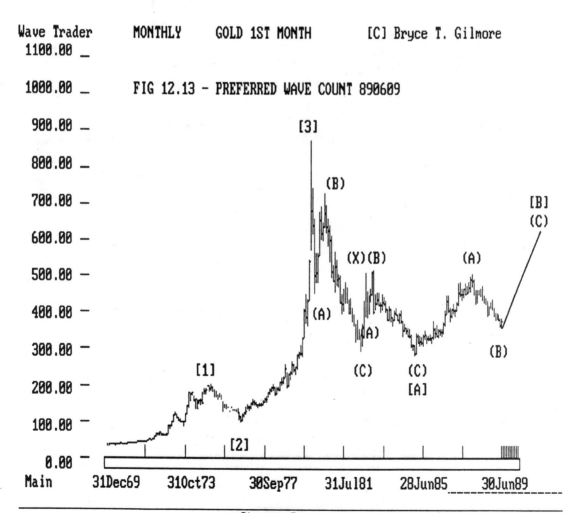

Chp. 12 Page 141

The main reason I have for calling the 1987 high an intermediate (A) wave is very clear to me. Gold prices rose from February 1985 to December 1987 on the back of a depreciating US dollar. This in effect was a corrective fundamental as at the same time gold continued to decline in Japanese Yen, Swiss Francs and Deutche Marks. Currently gold has made convincing lows when charted in most major foreign currencies, given that the US dollar has shown considerable strength since January 1988.

**THE ALTERNATE WAVE COUNT.**

If US$ 337.00 is broken on the downside I would expect price to fall into the high 200's before the current downtrend is over. Long term the bullish scenario for new highs is still in place once the wave [2] is completed.

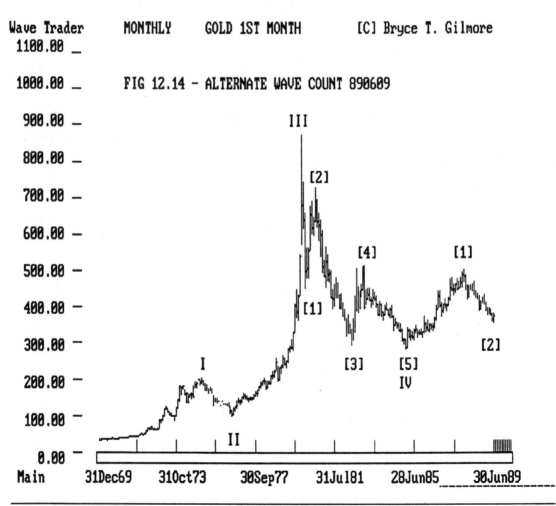

## DJIA Wave count probability

My preferred count for the DJIA index is calling for a wave IV of cycle dimension to complete a symetrical or ascending triangle that will terminate at around 1910 points. After which new highs will be made in the vicinity of the 3600 call made by Robert Prechter Jr. some years ago.

The relative fundamental factors for the amazing bull market of 1982 to 1987 were inflationary and currency related presures. These presures are still far from resolved and it would appear that they will re-emerge again, once the current recession that is in progress has ended.

FIG 12.15 - DJIA PREFERRED COUNT 890604

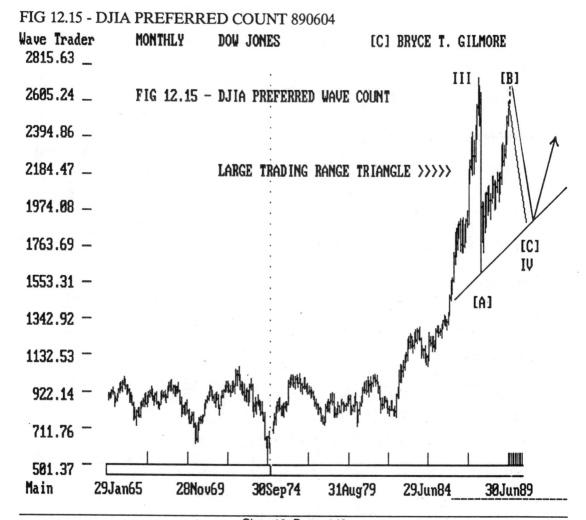

## DJIA ALTERNATE WAVE COUNT 890604

It is very important to have an alternate wave count just in case things don't unfold as planned. This alternate count could reap huge profits if the preferred wave count fails to hold good.

This scenario calls for a DEFLATIONARY DEPRESSION which is a remote possibility at this time. My feelings are that this fate is some way off just yet, maybe 1993.

I can't imagine the politicians committing suicide just yet, especially when they can still turn on the power (boost up the money supply) one more time.

FIG 12.16 - DJIA ALTERNATE WAVE COUNT 890604

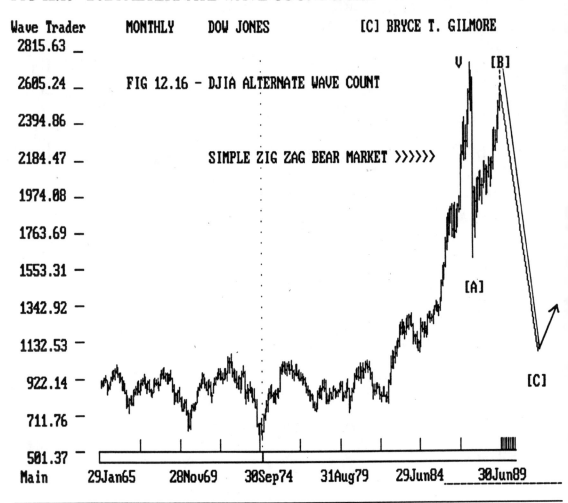

# 13. TIME PRICE & SPACE

## CORRECTLY RECORDING STOCK OR COMMODITY PRICE HISTORY

Time, price and space analysis charts are prepared from past records of stock and commodity price history. If we wish to maintain absolute accuracy it is imperative that our data base records are correct.

## COMMODITY PRICE HISTORIES

There are numerous ways to plot commodity prices correctly.

1. **CASH PRICES**

2. **1st MONTH FUTURES** continuous

3. **SEASONAL DELIVERY MONTH** continuous

W.D. Gann discovered that seasonal commodities maintain geometric relationships with the past when plotted on a continuous basis. For instance you will have seen examples earlier in this book for the NYCSE SUGAR MARCH delivery or the COMEX GOLD DECEMBER delivery, each of these charts were constructed using only prices from their respective contract months.

To maintain a seasonal history for a particular contract delivery month we must gather the price history for that contract on the active delivery month. This means that for 12 months out from delivery we are geometrically relating forward price. On long-term charts we are relating previous years of continuous price history for a particular delivery month.

To correctly maintain a COMEX GOLD DECEMBER chart requires data only from the December delivery, ie., we start the chart when the exchange first began trading the December contract, this was in early 1975. At the end of December 1975 when that contract expired we continue with prices from the December 1976 contract, when that expires we plot December 1977 and so on until our chart is up to date.

CHARTS CONSTRUCTED IN THIS STYLE ARE TERMED **GEOMETRIC CHARTS**, commonly referred to in the industry as **Gann style charts**.

**With commodities, forward prices can run at a premium or discount to the cash price, this will mean that a geometric chart could have its important highs or lows on different dates to the cash market. When working with a particular commodity it is important to keep at a minimum two geometric charts, for instance with Gold I keep both DECEMBER and JUNE continuous. The best idea is to keep two contract delivery months 180 degrees apart (six months), this way you will always have a reasonably active market to trade. When it comes to trading signals work only from your geometric chart. Other price series such as CASH or 1st MONTH FUTURES can be used to confirm ones opinion derived from the geometric data.**

**Do not mix data from two exchanges or different locations, if you wish to stick strictly to these rules.**

If a contract specification is ever changed then all previous prices will need to be adjusted to remain geometric. This seldom occurs these days but the case I had in mind was COCOA, originally prices were quoted in cents per pound, currently prices are quoted in dollars per tonne. I had to convert old data to reflect the current contract specification some years ago.

## STOCK PRICE HISTORIES

The geometric relationship for particular stock prices is their ratio of value to market capitalization. For instance on inception a company could issue 10 million shares at $1.00, for a capitalization of $10,000,000. Whilst these shares are trading above or below the original $1.00 they are registering the perception of that companies value in relationship to the $10,000,000 capitalization.

When an issue changes a companies capitalization, past share price data must be adjusted to maintain the true geometric relationship of past price to the new market capitalization.

Companies can change their market capitalization by issuing bonus shares to shareholders in several ways.

Shares can be issued at no charge, for example as a 1 for 4 bonus. This will mean that in future we will now have 5 shares for every 4 that existed in the past. All prices prior to the issue will have to be adjusted by 20%. If a share was trading at $1.00 prior to a 1 for 4 bonus issue that price when adjusted would equate to 80 cents.

To explain this further so there is no confusion, 4 shares at $1.00 equal $4.00, now 5 shares equal $4.00 since each shareholder has been given 1 extra share for every 4 previously held. $4.00 divided by 5 equals 80 cents.

One way a company can raise extra capital is to offer an issue at a reduced price. Generally they will strike the issue price well below the market value of the existing shares. A form of issue could be 1 for 4 at 50 cents, when a share is trading at $1.00. This means that 4 shares are worth $4.00 before the issue, after the issue 5 shares are worth $4.50. It requires a slightly more complicated equation to adjust the earlier data.

## CALCULATING A RIGHTS ISSUE ADJUSTMENT

Rights issue is 1 for 4 at 50 cents. Last close prior to issue date equals $1.00.

**The correct procedure is to calculate the BONUS content implied by the issue.**

Before issue 4 shares at $1.00 equals $4.00 or $1.00 per share.

After issue 5 shares now equal $4.50 or 90 cents per share.

Bonus content is $1.00 divided by 90 cents equals a 1 to 1.1111 stock split with the past.

Past prices must be adjusted accordingly, this means that for every old 10,000 shares we adjust their value as if there were 11,111. **A reduction of 10% per share.**

## PRICE IN TIME FROM PAST SHARE PRICE

I have found that if a stock has split regularly, as happens on the Australian share market, then it is not such a good idea to place any faith in converting static price values to time. All other methods of analysis are valid as the percentage relationships between past and future price maintain strict geometric relationships. Best results in any analysis are achieved through the use of range vibration techniques in any case.

## CORRECT DATA MEANS ACCURATE ANALYSIS

Before embarking on a career of speculation using the methods outlined in this text be sure that you have your facts straight. Double and triple check your data base for accuracy, correct price history and no days missing. **A workman is only as good as his tools.** I lost some money recently on a trade, simply because my data file contained an incorrect price. The time and price squaring off that incorrect price, was so strong, I jumped the gun and cut a long position well ahead of time. It was only when I mentioned the trade to another analyst that I became aware of the incorrect price. My ex-assistant had entered this incorrect price in my data file while I was away on holiday.

## TIME PRICE & SPACE

The bottom line objective of wave analysis is to correctly predict when a market will make or has made a significant high or low, which results in a significant change of trend.

Most of the techniques put forward in this text to date are guidelines and approaches that will lead us to the ultimate answer we are seeking.

At every cycle, primary, intermediate and minor degree trend change a geometric relationship with the past must exist to confirm that TIME, PRICE and SPACE have been satisfactorally balanced out.

Geometry of markets is the term I use to describe the relationship of past waves of price movement in time to future price movements in time. Price can be squared two ways, ie., first by counting units of price and secondly by counting percentage changes to price. Time is simple as it only has one axis, ie., units of hours, days, weeks, months or years.

Time, Price and Space can be represented as a triangular formation that contains a 90 degree angle. Time is the first known side of the equation. Price is the second known side of the equation. Space however could be represented as the area, hypotenuse, height or base of the triangular equation.

When comparing one market campaign (bull to bear, impulse to correction, et cetera.) with another, we need to look at all the contingent possibilities.

1. How do the time factors for each campaign relate?
2. How do the price units moved in each campaign relate?
3. How do the price percentage changes in each campaign relate?
4. How does space when expressed as the hypotenuse of each campaign relate?
5. How does space relate when time is expressed as the hypotenuse?
6. How does space relate when price is expressed as the hypotenuse?
7. How does space relate when the area of each triangular formation is compared?

Units of price are equated with units of time, primarally we can consider time as the base axis and price as the height axis, space is the area or hypotenuse formed from the triangular formation created when height and base are 90 degrees opposed.

## TIME PRICE & SPACE RATIO ANALYSIS

*The primary guide to prudent investment decisions.*

Market movement is merely a reflection of the ongoing battle between buyers and sellers. The underlying forces motivating buyers and sellers can be divided into three categories; primary fundamentals, intermediate fundamentals and minor fundamentals. Primary fundamentals are the prevailing economic conditions, together with the longer term supply and demand forces underlying all markets. Intermediate fundamentals are the psychological forces at work which effect the trading decisions of market participants, in any medium term market trend. The minor fundamentals result from the action and reaction of buyers and sellers to news items, constantly bombarded on the public.

The minor fundamentals have added a new dimension to markets since we are now living in an age of instant worldwide communication. For this reason our judgement can be somewhat clouded when it comes to applying the strict mental discipline necessary for success.

Human nature nevertheless has not changed and never will. Everything in nature works to a rule, these rules have been with us from the beginning of time and will hold good until the end of time, whenever that is.

The basis of market wave analysis is simply the application of mathematical laws passed down since time began. Mathematical ratios are manifested in sound waves, plant growth, ancient architecture, art, the human body, marine life, stock and commodity price activity and planetary cycles. Strict ratios found in the geometric forms, square, cube, circle, golden rectangle and the logarithmic spiral are the strongest binding relationships found in all forms of nature.

In the following examples I will use the June Comex Gold continuous futures price action to demonstate how each intermediate wave in the price series, starting at the 1982 low (US$ 295) and terminating at the 1983 high (US$ 528), signaled time, price and space squarings at each high or low prior to a change of trend.

Market swing highs and lows are points in time, price and space where the psychological imbalance between buyers and sellers reaches its zenith. Reversals of trend are an imminent result.

**Figure 13.01  COMEX JUNE GOLD CONTINUOUS.**

Standard Bar chart of price movement March 1982 to May 1983. Each intermediate degree price swing point is labeled with the date in yymmdd format. Scale is drawn to $1.00 per trading day.

The horizontal lines are fibonacci range layers of the chart high to low price, ie., in order from the high they are graduated in ratios .146, .236, .382, .5, .618, .764, .854.

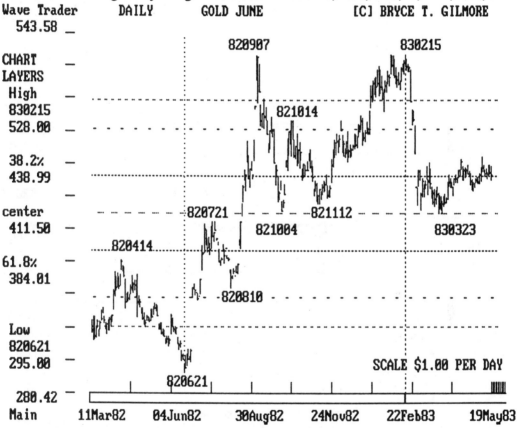

Range layers give a visual perspective to the wave ratios in a completed campaign. This particular campaign was a bear market rally. I can remember at the time of the high thinking to myself that this market has no reason being here, yet everyone around seemed to be saying that gold would never fall below the psychological $ 500 level. I started trading a breakout system with a partner in early August of 1982 and have contract notes testifying to profits of over US$ 20,000 per contract from August 1982 through to March 1983. In fact we took US$ 120,000 from the market on the crash wave in February 1983.

**Figure 13.02  10% SWING CHART.**

WAVE TRADER 10% price swing analysis of the wave structure March 1982 to May 1983.

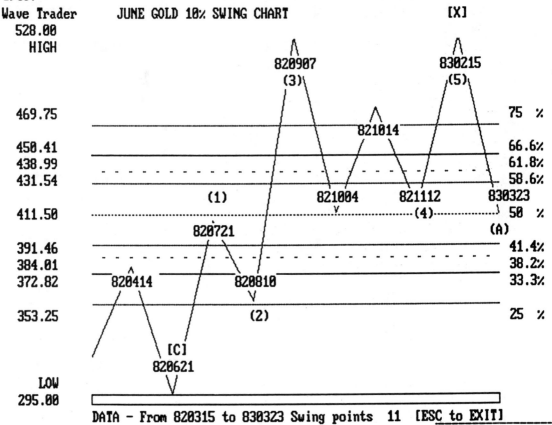

This routine measures when a minimum price change has occured from a previous high or low price dependent on the current trend. Values can be selected between 3 and 50% to break wave formations down in degrees that reflect cycle, primary, intermediate, minor, minute and minuette ELLIOTT WAVES. I often find that 10% plus or minus 2% will give an instant appraisal of the intermediate market swing points. 25% to 33.3% normally outlines the primary degree swings over longer periods of time.

**Table 13.1**

Information relative to each swing point illustrated in Fig. 13.02.

| DATE | WAVE # ELLIOTT | SWING POINT | PRICE RANGE | DAYS DURATION | % SWING | SPACE | AREA |
|------|----------------|-------------|-------------|---------------|---------|-------|------|
| 820414 |              | $377.50     | $ 58.50     | 30            | 18.34%  | na.   | na.  |
| 820621 | Start         | $295.00     | $ 82.50     | 68            | 21.85%  | 106.9 | 2805 |
| 820721 | (1)           | $407.50     | $112.50     | 30            | 38.20%  | 116.4 | 1688 |
| 820810 | (2)           | $356.00     | $ 51.50     | 20            | 12.50%  | 55.2  | 515  |
| 820907 | (3)           | $527.00     | $171.00     | 28            | 48.00%  | 173.2 | 2394 |
| 821004 | A of (4)      | $413.00     | $114.00     | 27            | 21.60%  | 117.2 | 1539 |
| 821014 | B of (4)      | $481.00     | $ 68.00     | 10            | 16.50%  | 68.7  | 340  |
| 821112 | C of (4)      | $415.50     | $ 65.50     | 29            | 13.60%  | 71.6  | 950  |
| 830225 | (5)           | $528.00     | $112.50     | 95            | 27.10%  | 147.3 | 5344 |

* % SWING is the percentage price increase from the last low or the percentage decrease from the last high. For instance wave (5) range up equals $112.50 divided by wave (4) low $415.50 = 0.271
* SPACE is the length of the hypotenuse of a right angled triangle formed when height is units of price and time in calendar days is units of base. Space = square root of [(range * range) + (days * days)].
* AREA is the area in the triangle formed in the space equation. Area = Half of days * range.

By definition whenever strict relationships are formed between one SPACE or AREA and another SPACE or AREA then both TIME and PRICE have squared important esoteric relationships.

**Price movement patterns formed on your bar charts.**

Before reviewing the ratios present at each intermediate trend change it bears mentioning that one of the cleverest tools introduced to market analysis this century was the simple bar chart itself. By plotting price movement against time, telltail patterns develop before your eyes. These patterns give a solid foundation to expectations in the near to medium term. If you review the bar chart in Fig. 13.01 you will clearly identify a simple Elliott zig zag for wave (2) (three minor waves), followed by an accelerating dynamic wave (3) containing 5 minor waves. Next you will see a large trianglular adjustment phase for wave (4) [alternation with wave (2)], followed by a fifth wave that ends in a diagonal triangle formation. Wave (5) just manages to rise above wave (3) after forming 5 waves. Wave 5 of (5) fails to continue the advance. Wave (5) is a weak structure and consequently the market crashes back to the 50% level of the overall advance from the low. Another clear observation was the depth of wave (4) which not only overlapped the 4th wave of (3) but retraced 50% of the whole advance to the wave (3) high. Formations such as these are more common in bear market rallies than in bull market trends.

**Obvious Elliott wave calculations at the termination of the 5th intermediate wave were :-**

Wave (1) $ 112.50 and Wave (5) $ 112.50 are equal in price length.

The entire bull market phase of 5 waves advanced **$ 233** from June 21st, 1982 to February 15th, 1983 in exactly **34 weeks** (239 calendar days to be precise). 233 is a Fibonacci number and so is 34. This could not have been more precise if it tried.

Wave (5) endured 95 days from the wave C of (4) low 821112. (96 is .666 of the square of 144). 144 is of course 12 squared the base of the ancient imperial measurement system. 144 also a Fibonacci number is the strongest number in the solar system. The harmonic of the speed of light is 144,000 feet per second$^2$.

Time from wave (2) 820810 to wave (4) 821112 equals 94 days. Squares 100% of time with wave (5).

Wave (5) $112.5 as a percentage of wave (3) $171.00 was just short of 66.6% relationship.

The wave (5) advance increased in value from (4) by 27.1%. The value at (4) $415.50 multiplied by root Phi (1.618), ie., 1.272 * $415.5 gives the top of $528.00. The Great Pyramid of Giza has a height to half its base in this ratio 1.272.

Time from Wave (3) high to the wave (5) high equals 161 days. Time from the wave (3) high to wave C of (4) equals 66 days, A harmonic relationship between the wave (4) and wave (5) exists on the square of root 2 (1.414). It takes two parts to make a whole, if one part was 1 and the other part was 1.414 times the first part we would have two parts totaling 2.414 (1 + 1.414). The ratio of each part to the other when compared as a whole is 1 = 0.414 + 0.586. For instance 0.414 and 0.586 equals 161 days therefore 0.414 equals 66.6 days and 0.586 equals 94.34 days.

**AREA CALCULATIONS IN THE IMPULSE WAVES.**

Wave (5) = 5344, Wave (1) = 1688 ; 5344 divided by 1688 = 3.16 (root 2 [1.414] multiplied by root 5 [2.236] equals 3.161).

Wave (5) = 5344, Wave (3) = 2394 ; 5344 divided by 2394 = 2.232 (root 5 = 2.236).

Wave (3) = 2394, Wave (1) = 1688 ; 2394 divided by 1688 = 1.418 (root 2 = 1.414).

These facts should have been enough to alert a dedicated wave technician to an inevitable change of trend especially when the bigger picture was taken into account. The June continuous contract registered an all time high in January 1980 of $ 916.00. The range from this high to the June 1982 low of $ 295.00 was $ 621 in 882 days. $621*0.382 = $ 237, $621*0.375 = $ 233 and 882 * 0.272 = 239.9 (34 weeks). See figure 13.03.

**Figure 13.03.** Weekly June Gold continuous bar chart showing the major price retracement levels of the 1980 to 1982 range.

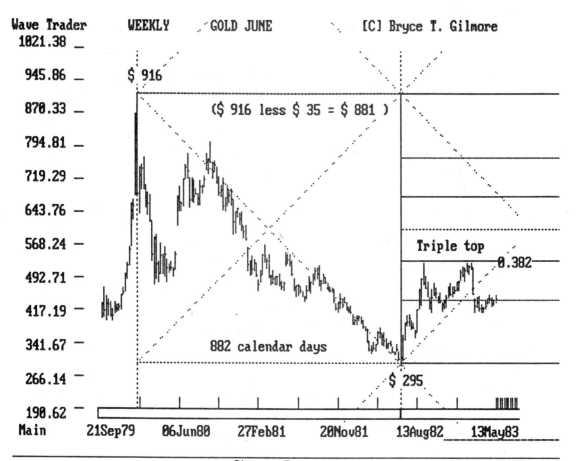

The wave structures that began from the 21st June 1982 (summer solstice) low of $295 and terminated on the 25th February 1983 at $528 were:-

**Wave (1)** terminated 820721, $407.50, range $112.50, time 30 days.

The low of $295 to the high of $407.50 represented a gain of 38.2% in value.

Time alternated with the previous advancing wave at 30 days (100% time vibration in the alternate wave).

**Wave (2)** terminated 820810, $356.00, range $51.50, time 20 days.

Time for (2) equals 66.6% of (1).

Percentage decline in value from (1) was 12.5%.

Wave (2) range of $51.50 divided by the previous alternate wave range of $82.50 equals 0.624, a strict Gann ratio of 3/8ths. Also close to 0.618 the strongest Elliott wave ratio.

**Wave (3)** terminated 820907, $527.00, range $171.00, time 28 days.

28 days squared root 2 (1.414) with wave (2) 20 days. ie., 20*1.414 = 28.2

Time from wave (1) to wave (3) was (20+28) 48 days. Wave (1) 30 days * PHI (1.618) = 48.5

Time of the previous 3 waves squared 0.236 at wave (3), ie., 68+30+20 = 118 ; 118* 0.236 = 28

Wave (3) had a range of $171.00 (this was approximately 1.5 times the wave (1) range).

The percentage increase in value at the wave (3) top measured up from the low of $295.00 was 78.6%, the total time from low to high was 78 days. 0.786 is an interesting ratio and appears quite often in Elliott wave structures. 0.786 is the reciprocal of root PHI (1.618) ; 1 divided by 1.272 = 0.786

All expansion waves squared in Golden logrithmic spiral relationships ; wave (1) 38.2%, wave (3) 78.6%, wave (5) 27.2%

**Wave A of (4)** terminated 821004, $413.00, range $114.00, time 27 days.

Wave A's are generally swift and devestating when they follow a dynamic impulse wave. This one was no exception to the rule.

In 27 days 50% of the gains made from $295 to the wave (3) high of $527.00 were retraced.

Time balanced 100% (27/28 days) with the wave (3) impulse.

Price balanced 66.6% of the wave (3) advance, ie., $171 * .666 = $114.00

**Wave B of (4)** terminated 821014, $481.00, range $68.00, time 10 days.

B waves always created an analysis problem for me until I found a means to rotate space measurements . The market is invariably in a state of confusion, as buyers and sellers evaluate their current positions. This B wave advanced 16.5% (1/6 th) in value from the A wave low of $413.00. The retracement of the A wave range ($114.00) was 59.6%, just short of a perfect 61.8%.

The time, 10 days also fell just short of an ideal 38.2% of the A wave. Actual time ratio was 37% (10 divided by 27).

Sometimes you can home in on squarings of time and price by working several ranges together. For instance if you add the price ranges of Wave (3) [$ 171.00] and wave A [$ 114.00] you get a total of $ 285.

Wave B of $ 68.00 as a percentage of $ 285.00 equals 23.6%.

**Wave C of (4)** terminated 821112, $ 415.50, range $ 65.50, time 29 days.

Wave C completed a triangle, terminating slightly higher than the A wave low. In classic Elliott wave fashion this wave related to Wave (2) as a 1.272, ie., $51.50 * 1.272 = $ 65.50. Also this wave was exactly 38.2% the length of wave (3), ie., $ 171.00 * 0.382 = $ 65.30
The time of wave C came within a day of wave (1) and (3).


By now you may be thinking that time and price analysis is a time consuming and tedious effort. Your right! But if you do the work you will be richly rewarded. I have divised many time saving routines within WAVE TRADER to alert me to the FACTS. Tables 13.2 and 13.3 are just an example of how simple you can make Elliott Wave Analysis, given the right tools.

**Table 13. 2** Elliott wave ratios of PRICE in a completed INTERMEDIATE degree wave.

### WAVE RELATIONSHIPS WORKING BACK FROM INDICATOR DAY

| SWING | PIVOT | TIME | RANGE | %CHANGE | VIBRATION | PRICE | TIME |
|---|---|---|---|---|---|---|---|
| 820621 | 295.00 | 68 | 82.50 | 21.85 | 1.2132 | 1.4103 | 2.2667 |
| 820721 | 407.50 | 30 | 112.50 | 38.14 | 3.7500 | 1.3636 | 0.4412 |
| 820810 | 356.00 | 20 | 51.50 | 12.64 | 2.5750 | 0.4578 | 0.6667 |
| 820907 | 527.00 | 28 | 171.00 | 48.03 | 6.1071 | 3.3204 | 1.4000 |
| 821004 | 413.00 | 27 | 114.00 | 21.63 | 4.2222 | 0.6667 | 0.9643 |
| 821014 | 481.00 | 10 | 68.00 | 16.46 | 6.8000 | 0.5965 | 0.3704 |
| 821112 | 415.50 | 29 | 65.50 | 13.62 | 2.2586 | 0.9632 | 2.9000 |
| 830215 | 528.00 | 95 | 112.50 | 27.08 | 1.1842 | 1.7176 | 3.2759 |

### PRICE RELATIONSHIPS IN PAST SEVEN WAVES

| waves 7-1 | 112.50 | 51.50 | 171.00 | 114.00 | 68.00 | 65.50 | 112.50 |
|---|---|---|---|---|---|---|---|
| WAVE 7 | 1.000 | 0.458 | 1.520 | 1.013 | 0.604 | 0.582 | 1.000 |
| WAVE 6 | 2.184 | 1.000 | 3.320 | 2.214 | 1.320 | 1.272 | 2.184 |
| WAVE 5 | 0.658 | 0.301 | 1.000 | 0.667 | 0.398 | 0.383 | 0.658 |
| WAVE 4 | 0.987 | 0.452 | 1.500 | 1.000 | 0.596 | 0.575 | 0.987 |
| WAVE 3 | 1.654 | 0.757 | 2.515 | 1.676 | 1.000 | 0.963 | 1.654 |
| WAVE 2 | 1.718 | 0.786 | 2.611 | 1.740 | 1.038 | 1.000 | 1.718 |
| WAVE 1 | 1.000 | 0.458 | 1.520 | 1.013 | 0.604 | 0.582 | 1.000 |

Press any key to return to CHART ...

**Table 13.03** Elliott wave ratios of TIME in a completed INTERMEDIATE degree wave.

```
WAVE RELATIONSHIPS WORKING BACK FROM INDICATOR DAY

SWING    PIVOT    TIME   RANGE   %CHANGE  VIBRATION  PRICE   TIME
820621   295.00    68    82.50    21.85    1.2132   1.4103  2.2667
820721   407.50    30   112.50    38.14    3.7500   1.3636  0.4412
820810   356.00    20    51.50    12.64    2.5750   0.4578  0.6667
820907   527.00    28   171.00    48.03    6.1071   3.3204  1.4000
821004   413.00    27   114.00    21.63    4.2222   0.6667  0.9643
821014   481.00    10    68.00    16.46    6.8000   0.5965  0.3704
821112   415.50    29    65.50    13.62    2.2586   0.9632  2.9000
830215   528.00    95   112.50    27.08    1.1842   1.7176  3.2759

TIME RELATIONSHIPS IN PAST SEVEN WAVES
waves 7-1      30       20        28         27       10        29       95

WAVE 7       1.000    0.667     0.933      0.900    0.333     0.967    3.167
WAVE 6       1.500    1.000     1.400      1.350    0.500     1.450    4.750
WAVE 5       1.071    0.714     1.000      0.964    0.357     1.036    3.393
WAVE 4       1.111    0.741     1.037      1.000    0.370     1.074    3.519
WAVE 3       3.000    2.000     2.800      2.700    1.000     2.900    9.500
WAVE 2       1.034    0.690     0.966      0.931    0.345     1.000    3.276
WAVE 1       0.316    0.211     0.295      0.284    0.105     0.305    1.000
```

Press any key to return to CHART ...

Table 13.2 - Price relationships between ranges of a completed bull market. The top half of the page lists the relevant details of each swing high or low greater than 10%. Vibration is calculated by dividing range by time. The price column contains the direct relationship to the previous range. The time column contains the direct relationship of this wave time to the previous wave time.

The ratio matrix in the lower half of the report lists the past seven waves in order. In each row you will see a ratio 1.000, this represents the primary range and all other ranges are compared to this range. A quick scan of the matrix will enlighten even the most bigoted sceptic of this science.

## Ratios of extreme importance

If you refer to chapter 2 you will see illustrations of the important geometric forms and their interrelating ratios.

There are three groups of common relationships that occur in nature, music and space. These are known as the trinity of trinities.

The relationships known as the trinity of trinities are the divisions of 1 in ARITHMETIC, HARMONIC and GEOMETRIC MEANS.

The ARITHMETIC MEANS of 1.000 are 0.333 and 0.666 (1 to 2).

The HARMONIC MEANS of 1.000 are 0.414 and 0.586 (1 to 1.414).

The GEOMETRIC MEANS of 1.000 are 0.382 and 0.618 (1 to 1.618).

In addition to these important ratios we have the Great pyramid of GIZA which contains the ratios of the geometric progression. (see page 15, figure 2.7).

The pyramid has a height 1.272 times half its base. The hypotenuse of the pyramid is 1.618 times half its base. ie., height = 1.272, side = 1.618 and base = 2.000

The right angled triangle formed from half a pyramid reduces the ratios to base = 1.000, height = 1.272 and side = 1.618. Each side relates in a similar ratio of progression, ie., 1.272 divided by 1.000 = 1.272, 1.618 divided by 1.272 = 1.272. By the same token 1.272 divided by 1.618 = 0.786 and 1.000 divided by 1.272 = 0.786.

You could refer back to page 156 and review the expansions that occured in the gold market example just presented.

The price value at the wave (1) high $407.50 was 38.2% greater than the beginning price of $295.00

The price value at the wave (3) high of $527.00 was 78.6% greater than the beginning value of $295.00

Just as a quick example of how I use these ratios we can do some forward thinking. The February 1985 low for spot gold was $281.20, 78.6% increase in value calculates to $502.30 the exact high made on 14th December 1987. There is an illustration of the bear market that has been in progress since this high on page 141, fig 12.13. Assumming the current downtrend in the gold price arrests itself without breaking below the 1985 low we would have sufficient reason to think that the future uptrend will expand above the 1987 high. Infact if it does we would like to have an approximate idea where it may rise to. Considering that the last increase from the 1985 low expanded 78.6% maybe the next long term rise will square 127.2% with the same low. A quick calculation of $281.2 increased in value 127.2% gives a target of $638.80. My records show the 1980 all time high for spot gold as $871.00, the lowest low since then has been the February 1985 low at $281.20, this gave the total decline high to low a range of $589.80 ($871 less $281.60). A 61.8% retracement of this range gives an upside target in a new bull market of $645.70 which is very close indeed to the 127.2% expansion of the $281.20 low price. If price were to rise $144.00 above the 1987 high of $502.30 it would go up to $646.30.

You can see how easy it is to combine several methods to arrive at a similar conclusion.

As the circle or wheel of time continues forward, reactions to the past occur as both time elapsed and price moved either attract or repulse themselves from one gravity vortex to another.

Unfolding cycles of price movement in time will balance minor, intermediate and primary degree. A cycle could be viewed for our purposes as the swing points in a wave series, ie., Chart high-low-high-low or low-high-low-high.

Each cycle contains impulses and reactions to impulses. Impulses will relate to impulses, reactions will relate to reactions, reactions will relate to impulses and impulses will relate to reactions.

Relationships between price, time and space can alternate as the wheel continuously rolls along. To predict future probabilities ahead of time I simply calculate all of the possibilities and investigate the strongest clusters. If the market arrives at these points in the future in an overbought or oversold condition I can take the signal as valid.

Gann was reputed to have said, "When time, price and space are square a change in trend is imminent".

## WAVE RELATIONSHIPS IN MINOR DEGREE AT THE 1985 LOW

Figure 13.04 June Gold continuous prices.

```
WAVE RELATIONSHIPS WORKING BACK FROM INDICATOR DAY
```

| SWING  | PIVOT  | TIME | RANGE  | %CHANGE | VIBRATION | PRICE  | TIME    |
|--------|--------|------|--------|---------|-----------|--------|---------|
| 830711 | 473.50 | 41   | 63.50  | 15.49   | 1.5488    | 1.4941 | 1.9524  |
| 831117 | 392.00 | 129  | 81.50  | 17.21   | 0.6318    | 1.2835 | 3.1463  |
| 831130 | 428.50 | 13   | 36.50  | 9.31    | 2.8077    | 0.4479 | 0.1008  |
| 840126 | 374.00 | 57   | 54.50  | 12.72   | 0.9561    | 1.4932 | 4.3846  |
| 840305 | 418.50 | 39   | 44.50  | 11.90   | 1.1410    | 0.8165 | 0.6842  |
| 840615 | 368.00 | 102  | 50.50  | 12.07   | 0.4951    | 1.1348 | 2.6154  |
| 840629 | 419.50 | 14   | 51.50  | 13.99   | 3.6786    | 1.0198 | 0.1373  |
| 850225 | 287.00 | 241  | 132.50 | 31.59   | 0.5498    | 2.5728 | 17.2143 |

PRICE RELATIONSHIPS IN PAST SEVEN WAVES

| waves 7-1 | 81.50 | 36.50 | 54.50 | 44.50 | 50.50 | 51.50 | 132.50 |
|-----------|-------|-------|-------|-------|-------|-------|--------|
| WAVE 7    | 1.000 | 0.448 | 0.669 | 0.546 | 0.620 | 0.632 | 1.626  |
| WAVE 6    | 2.233 | 1.000 | 1.493 | 1.219 | 1.384 | 1.411 | 3.630  |
| WAVE 5    | 1.495 | 0.670 | 1.000 | 0.817 | 0.927 | 0.945 | 2.431  |
| WAVE 4    | 1.831 | 0.820 | 1.225 | 1.000 | 1.135 | 1.157 | 2.978  |
| WAVE 3    | 1.614 | 0.723 | 1.079 | 0.881 | 1.000 | 1.020 | 2.624  |
| WAVE 2    | 1.583 | 0.709 | 1.058 | 0.864 | 0.981 | 1.000 | 2.573  |
| WAVE 1    | 0.615 | 0.275 | 0.411 | 0.336 | 0.381 | 0.389 | 1.000  |

Press any key to return to CHART ...

On 25th February 1985 the gold complex bottomed, from here a protracted bullish trend took prices to the 14th December 1987 high of $521.00 basis the June contract.

The last minor wave down in this bear market when compared to the seven previous waves had an equality with each.

On the bottom line of the matrix the final wave of $132.50 is represented as 1.000. The previous wave squared 0.389 in price, the wave prior to that squared 0.381 in price, the wave prior to that squared 0.333, need I say more. The low of $287.00 was twice 144 in value. Look across further there is a 0.272 and a 0.618 relationship in the earlier waves.

# TIME PRICE & SPACE RELATIONSHIPS TO LOOK FOR

## ARITHMETIC RELATIONSHIPS

| | | | |
|---|---|---|---|
| 1/8th = 0.125 | 1/6th = 0.166 | 1/4th = 0.250 | 1/3rd = 0.333 |
| 1/2th = 0.500 | 5/8th = 0.625 | 2/3rd = 0.666 | 7/8th = 0.875 |
| Unity = 1.000 | 1.50 = 1.500 | 1.66 = 1.666 | 2.000 = 2.000 |

## HARMONIC RELATIONSHIPS

**Sacred roots**   1.414 (Root 2)   1.732 (root 3)   2.236 (root 5)

0.707  (1/2 of 1.414 and the reciprocal of 1.414)
0.577 (reciprocal of root 3 (1.732))
0.447 (reciprocal of root 5 (2.236))
1.118 (half of root 5)
2.449 (root 2 by root 3)          3.1618 (root 2 by root 5)

## GEOMETRIC SPIRAL RELATIONSHIPS

| | | | | | | | |
|---|---|---|---|---|---|---|---|
| 0.146 | 0.185 | 0.236 | 0.300 | 0.382 | 0.486 | 0.618 | 0.786 |
| 1.000 | unity | | | | | | |
| 1.272 | 1.618 | 2.058 | 2.618 | 3.33 | 4.236 | 5.39 | 6.85 |
| 11.1 | 14.1 | 17.9 | 22.8 | 29 | 36.9 | 47 | 60 |
| 76 | 97 | 123 | 157 | 199 | 254 | 322 | 411 |
| 522 | 665 | 846 | 1076 | 1368 | 1740 | 2214 | 2817 |

## OTHER IMPORTANT RATIOS..

| | | | |
|---|---|---|---|
| 0.276 | (0.618 divided by 2.236 (root 5)) | 1.382 | (2.236 by 0.618) |
| 0.309 | (0.618 divided by 2 (root 4)) | 1.236 | (2 by 0.618) |
| 0.357 | (0.618 divided by 1.732 (root 3)) | 1.07 | (1.732 by 0.618) |
| 0.437 | (0.618 divided by 1.414 (root 2)) | 0.874 | (1.414 by 0.618) |

0.726 (hypotenuse of a 90 right angle triangle - height 0.618, base 0.382)
0.874 (hypotenuse of a 90 right angle triangle - height 0.618, base 0.618  ALSO 0.618 * 1.4142)
1.176 (hypotenuse of a 90 right angle triangle - height 0.618, base 1.000)
1.902 (hypotenuse of a 90 right angle triangle - height 1.618, base 1.000)
3.141593 (PI )          1.571 (half PI)

# 14. STEPS REQUIRED FOR COMPREHENSIVE TIME & PRICE ANALYSIS

This chapter uses Australia's number one company, BHP LTD, to demonstrate the steps I would take to create a base for future analysis.

Before we can undertake any analysis we need to procure a long-term monthly price history for at least 20 years, longer if the information is available. In this case we will be making a study of a stock that has had many share splits and bonus issues throughout its history so it is imperative that the data be free of any errors. If you do not have accurate data then it is impossible to implement time and price analysis with reliability. Do not take someone else's word that new data is correct until you have checked its accuracy yourself, this may involve some research but I have learnt through bitter experience that this must be done.

## STEP 1. RECORD ALL IMPORTANT HIGHS AND LOWS

The first thing we need to do is record all cycle and primary waves high and low turning points, actual traded price, current adjusted price and the date of each swing point. As we approach current times we can record intermediate and minor wave swing highs and lows of importance.

**A major swing high or low market day is the day that the psychological imbalance between buyers and sellers reached its zenith.** The price recorded is a measure of buyer support or resistance that is extremely important for the future, examples throughout this text attest to this fact. The time period between each swing of cycle and primary degree is even more important for our future calculations.

Creating a history **fact file** can be done quickly if you have the tools; run a percentage change swing chart on your daily data. You could use monthly data, but this will require extra work in locating the exact date the market made its high or low. Primary waves and cycle waves should be generated on swings greater than 15%.

## ANALYSIS PROCEDURES

## BHP LTD - RECENT HISTORY FACT FILE

| DATE | TRADED PRICE | ADJUSTED TODAY | DILUTION FACTOR |
|---|---|---|---|
| 1968-JUN-28 | $25.75 | $ 3.12 | 0.1213 |
| 1974-SEP-30 | $ 4.10 | $ 0.72 | 0.1756 |
| 1980-NOV-18 | $17.60 | $ 4.17 | 0.2369 |
| 1982-DEC-10 | $ 5.90 | $ 1.44 | 0.2450 |
| 1984-APR-09 | $12.37 | $ 3.73 | 0.3014 |
| 1984-JUN-27 | $ 9.20 | $ 2.77 | 0.3014 |
| 1985-NOV-11 | $ 9.26 | $ 6.27 | 0.6779 |
| 1986-MAR-26 | $ 6.12 | $ 4.97 | 0.8134 |
| 1986-MAY-29 | $ 9.00 | $ 7.32 | 0.8134 |
| 1986-SEP-01 | $ 7.30 | $ 5.93 | 0.8134 |
| 1987-SEP-16 | $11.10 | $11.10 | 1.0000 |
| 1987-DEC-11 | $ 5.98 | $ 5.98 | 1.0000 |
| 1988-JUN-01 | $ 8.90 | $ 8.90 | 1.0000 |

An initial observation I have just made is this. The highest physical price BHP LTD has ever traded was $25.75 in June 1968, the second highest level was $17.60 in November 1980. Both of these levels will retain a psychological barrier for the future, irrespective of the current price dilution caused by share issues and splits.

## CALCULATE TIME VIBRATIONS BETWEEN FACT FILE DATES

| DATE | PRICE | DAYS | WEEKS | MONTHS | APPROX TRADING |
|---|---|---|---|---|---|
| 1968-JUN-28 | $ 3.12 | 0 | | | |
| 1974-SEP-30 | $ 0.72 | 2285 | 326.4 | 75.1 | 1577 |
| 1980-NOV-18 | $ 4.17 | 4526 | 646.6 | 148.7 | 3125 |
| 1982-DEC-10 | $ 1.44 | 5278 | 754.0 | 173.4 | 3650 |
| 1987-SEP-16 | $11.10 | 7019 | 1002.7 | 230.6 | 4850 |

| DATE | PRICE | DAYS | WEEKS | MONTHS | APPROX TRADING |
|---|---|---|---|---|---|
| 1974-SEP-30 | $ 0.72 | 0 | | | |
| 1980-NOV-18 | $ 4.17 | 2241 | 320.1 | 73.6 | 1548 |
| 1982-DEC-10 | $ 1.44 | 2993 | 427.6 | 98.3 | 2069 |
| 1987-SEP-16 | $11.10 | 4734 | 676.3 | 155.5 | 3273 |

| DATE | PRICE | DAYS | WEEKS | MONTHS | APPROX TRADING |
|---|---|---|---|---|---|
| 1980-NOV-18 | $ 4.17 | 0 | | | |
| 1982-DEC-10 | $ 1.44 | 752 | 107.4 | 24.7 | 521 |
| 1987-SEP-16 | $11.10 | 2493 | 356.1 | 81.9 | 1725 |

## ANALYSIS PROCEDURES

| DATE | PRICE | DAYS | WEEKS | MONTHS | TRADING DAYS |
|---|---|---|---|---|---|
| 1982-DEC-10 | $ 1.44 | 0 | | | |
| 1984-APR-09 | $ 3.73 | 486 | 69.4 | 16.0 | 334 |
| 1984-JUN-27 | $ 2.77 | 565 | 80.7 | 18.6 | 387 |
| 1985-NOV-11 | $ 6.27 | 1067 | 152.4 | 35.1 | 737 |
| 1986-MAR-26 | $ 4.97 | 1202 | 171.7 | 39.5 | 830 |
| 1986-MAY-29 | $ 7.32 | 1266 | 180.9 | 41.6 | 873 |
| 1986-SEP-01 | $ 5.93 | 1361 | 194.4 | 44.7 | 939 |
| 1987-SEP-16 | $11.10 | 1741 | 248.7 | 57.2 | 1204 |

## WORK TIME BACKWARDS FROM HISTORY HIGH

| DATE | PRICE | DAYS | WEEKS | MONTHS | TRADING DAYS |
|---|---|---|---|---|---|
| 1987-SEP-16 | $11.10 | 0 | | | |
| 1986-SEP-01 | $ 5.93 | 380 | 54.3 | 12.5 | 265 |
| 1986-MAY-29 | $ 7.32 | 475 | 67.9 | 15.6 | 331 |
| 1986-MAR-26 | $ 4.97 | 539 | 77.0 | 17.7 | 374 |
| 1985-NOV-11 | $ 6.27 | 674 | 96.3 | 22.1 | 467 |
| 1984-JUN-27 | $ 2.77 | 1176 | 168.0 | 38.6 | 817 |
| 1984-APR-09 | $ 3.73 | 1255 | 179.3 | 41.2 | 870 |
| 1982-DEC-10 | $ 1.44 | 1741 | 248.7 | 57.2 | 1204 |
| 1980-NOV-18 | $ 4.17 | 2493 | 356.1 | 81.9 | 1725 |
| 1974-SEP-30 | $ 0.72 | 4734 | 676.3 | 155.5 | 3273 |
| 1968-JUN-28 | $ 3.12 | 7019 | 1002.7 | 230.6 | 4850 |

ANALYSIS PROCEDURES

## STEP 2. ELLIOTT WAVE COUNT

The next analysis procedure is establishing possible Elliott wave counts on the price history.

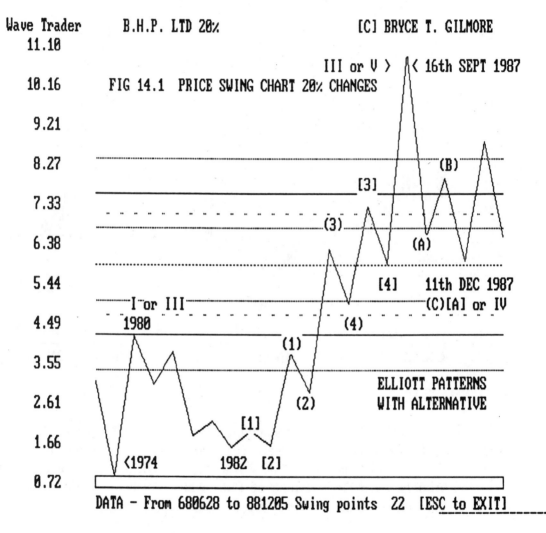

**FIG 14.1  20% MINIMUM PRICE SWINGS FROM 1980 HIGH**

Elliott wave formations are pronounced using the percentage swing procedure.

## ANALYSIS PROCEDURES

**FIG 14.2  1968-1982 MONTHLY CHART**

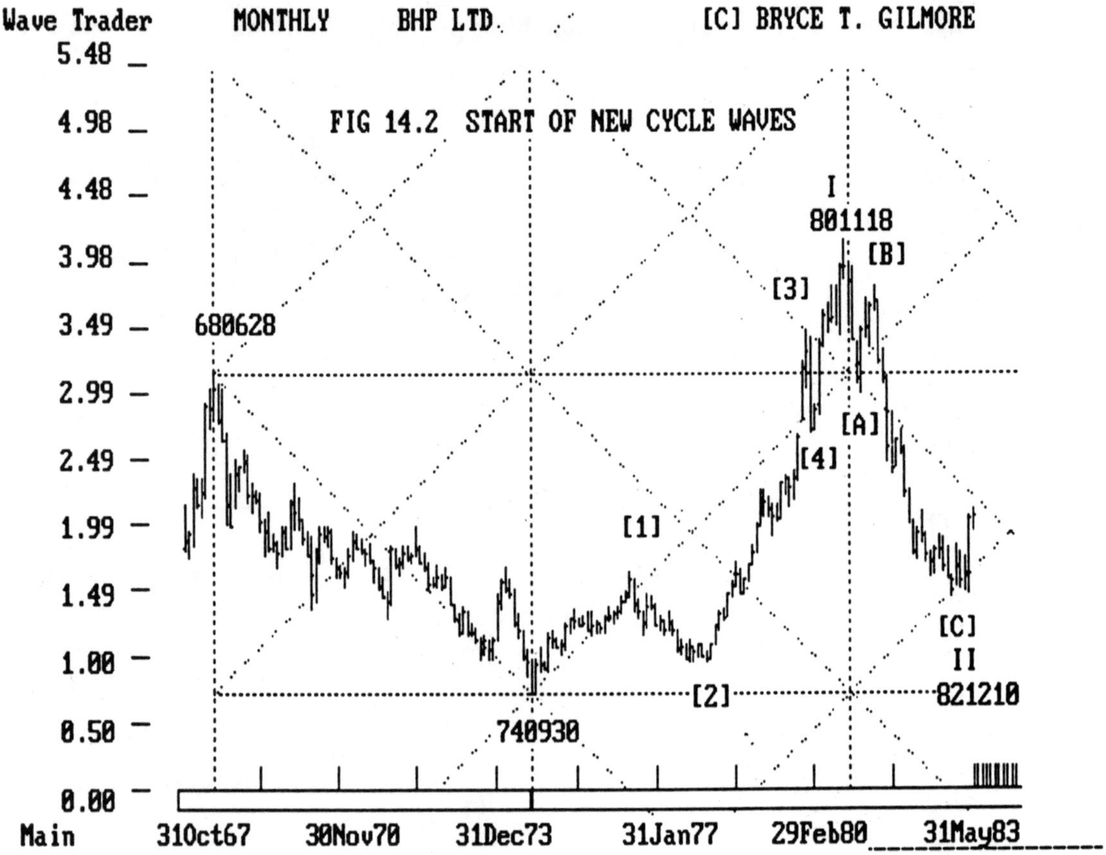

```
Wave Trader     MONTHLY    BHP LTD.              [C] BRYCE T. GILMORE
```

FIG 14.2  START OF NEW CYCLE WAVES

### CYCLE PHASE I-II

The major bear market from 1968 concluded on 30th September 1974, here a new cycle began so I have started a fresh wave count. In my opinion the bull market cycle that started in 1974 and finished in 1980 was a cycle I. The 1982 low at $ 1.44 overlapped the primary wave [1] of I high of $1.64 which normally (under Elliott strict rules) discounts this low being a cycle IV wave.

The loss in value from the 1980 high to the 1982 low was 65.5% an ideal ratio between 61.8% and 66.6% for a second wave. The time period for the fall was 752 calendar days against a bull market period from 1974 to 1980 of 2241 calendar days, in percentage terms 33.5%.

## FIG 14.3   PRICE SWING CHART 1968 TO 1982

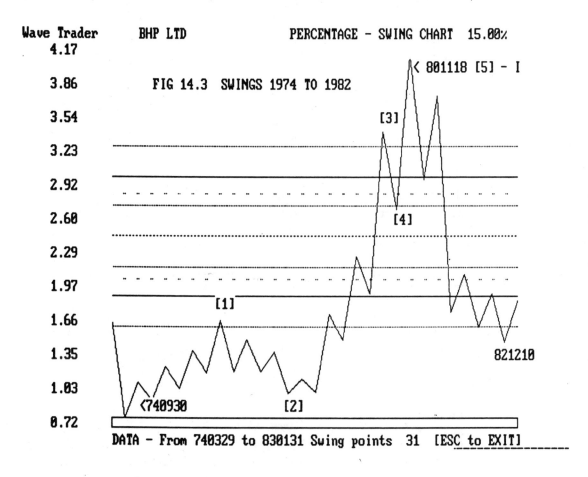

## CYCLE PHASE III  1982-1987

The next cycle phase from 1982 to 1987 unfolded in five major waves. Cycle high III or V of $11.10 fell exactly on the second price square projection of cycle I or III ($0.72 to $4.17 = $3.45), ($4.17 plus 2 times $3.45 = $11.07). An arithmetic progression of 0.333 to 0.666 [See FIG 14.1 page 167 for wave I or III on the 1/3 layer division line]

The crash wave of 1987 followed a bull market from 1974 that ran 13 years, a 50% retracement of the overall advance from $0.72 to $11.10 calculated to a price target of

# ANALYSIS PROCEDURES

$5.91, the low at [A] was $5.98 and the low at [4] was $5.93, these waves were nearly 100% square in price and both equal to 50% of the 1974 to 1987 range.

My conclusion to date is that this particular option is either in a new bull market or just starting a (C) of a [B] wave of cycle IV. Considering that the cycle II wave from 1980 to 1982 was a simple zig zag formation, then under the Elliott wave interpretation of alternation between corrective waves in a sequence, we should be expecting a triangular formation to unfold. So long as the low at $5.98 holds then a cycle degree V wave could take this option to new highs sometime in the distant future or fail as a primary [B] at a higher high than $ 8.90.

The test will be to see how long prices continue to trade above the $5.91 mid point of the 1974-1987 range. If we project the time of the 1982-1987 range forward 38.2% we get July 1989, if this stock continues to trade above the [A] wave low up until this time it will be fairly certain that this count is the correct one.

You will notice that I have not labeled the last high of $8.90 of June 1988 as yet, it is possible that $8.90 is a (1) of a V, we will discuss this as we move on.

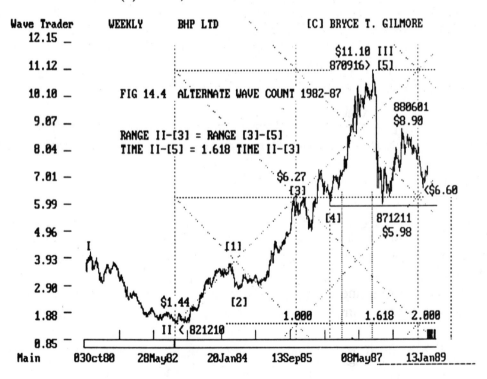

FIG 14.4 ALTERNATIVE WAVE COUNT FOR CYCLE III

The weekly chart (FIG 14.4) shows even more interesting time and price relationships unfolding between the primary and cycle waves. The range of the 1982 low (II) $1.44 (which incidentally was 100% square in price with the 1974 low of $0.72) to the wave [3] high of $6.27 was $4.83. $4.83 added to $6.27 gave a price range square target of $11.10 (which was the exact high made on the 16th September 1987).

Wave [A] or IV ($5.98 871211) of my cycle IV has held above wave [4] of III (fig 14.1) indicating that the long-term trend is still intact.

Also this may just be a coincidence but the range of the 1974 low $0.72 to the [3] of III at $6.27 in 1985 (fig 14.4) was $5.55, this range doubled ie $5.55 times 2 equals $11.10 (the III wave high price).

## WHERE TO FROM HERE

**Firstly** we must verify all of the support zones post Cycle wave III. This will surely tell us what the possibility is of another crash wave emerging in this wave series.

We need to identify the last intermediate swing high and low. From there we can apply a short term Elliott wave count and evaluate where we are likely to go from here.

**Secondly** we can calculate all of the cycle and primary wave SQUARES of PRICE and RANGE for future support and resistance estimates.

**Thirdly** we calculate all time vibration measurements forward so we have an idea where to expect trend changes.

**Fourthly** we will conduct research on Minor and Intermediate waves to evaluate which vibration ratios this option tends to vibrate around in lesser degree waves.

**Fifthly** we can examine the fundamental position of this company as a guide to its future standing among investors.

Some chartists will probably not bother with the last exercise as they believe this information will be reflected in the price. Please don't follow their guide, if you intend to trade your own advice and expect to make a profit.

ANALYSIS PROCEDURES

FUNDAMENTALS WILL BE REFLECTED IN THE PRICE LONG BEFORE THE NEWS HITS THE STREET, SO THINK AHEAD. STUDY THE LONGER TERM FUNDAMENTALS, NOT THE DAY TO DAY NOISE.

Treat each commodity or stock that you trade, AS A BUSINESS.

**MARKETS CAN ONLY DO THREE THINGS, MOVE UP IN PRICE, DOWN IN PRICE OR SIDEWAYS IN PRICE.**

WHEN THE TIME COMES FOR A CHANGE IN TREND WE WILL KNOW FROM OUR TIME VIBRATIONS - IT WILL ALSO BE OF ASSISTANCE IF WE CAN CONFIRM A PRICE SQUARING AT THE SAME TIME.

## WAVE STRUCTURE POST 1987 HIGH $11.10

Once we have formed a long-term opinion on the state of an option we can proceed to analyze the closer in price action to see if it is telling the same story.

By running a percentage swing chart in ratios that reflect the Minor degree waves we can see the shorter term market vibrations unfolding in a very clear manner.

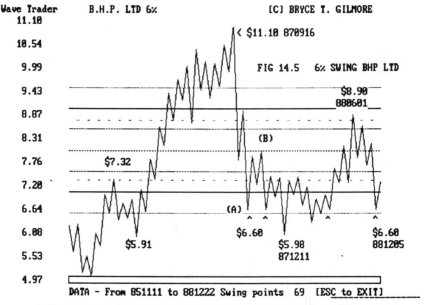

FIG 14.5   6% MININIMUM PRICE SWING CHART 1985 TO 1988

This chart Fig 14.5 certainly has a message that is important to the longer term cause. The low of $5.98 (December 11th, 1987 formed a double bottom with the primary wave [4] of III low) which lies on the 50% level of the 1974-1987 range, this chart is indicating strong support at this level. It is always possible that this market could trade below this level, yet since the rally to $8.90 we have had 4 lows registered at $6.60, this level is now indicating major support. Another thing is that the rally from February 1988 expanded in five waves. (See Fig 14.6)

### FIG 14.6  6% SWING CHART WAVE III to JANUARY 13th, 1989

Five waves formed in an impulse move that adhered to strict Elliott wave rules. Wave

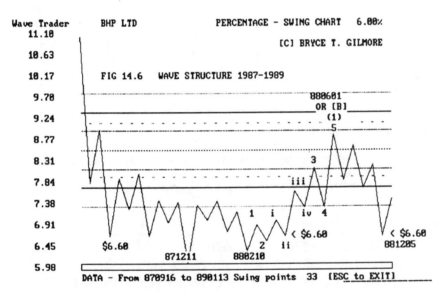

4 found support at the iv wave low of lesser degree before the 5 wave blasted up to $8.90 (50% square with $5.91 [50% of the 1974 to 1987 range]).

Is the high of $8.90 a [B] (primary bear market rally in a sustained bear market or a (1) wave of a new expansion). Looks more like a (1) to me, even though the wave 1 has been overlapped at the last low of $6.60 indicating a large diagonal triangle. The importance of this will, of course, be found out in the near future. An important point worth mentioning is the discipline that we can now apply to these findings. If $6.60 breaks then we will need to reassess the present scenario I have put forward and accept the alternative. If $8.90 is broken on the upside then we can project new highs forming at a rapid rate, as fund managers and traders who have been sidelined, rush to build up their portfolios once again, wondering why they bailed out at the bottom of a crash wave.

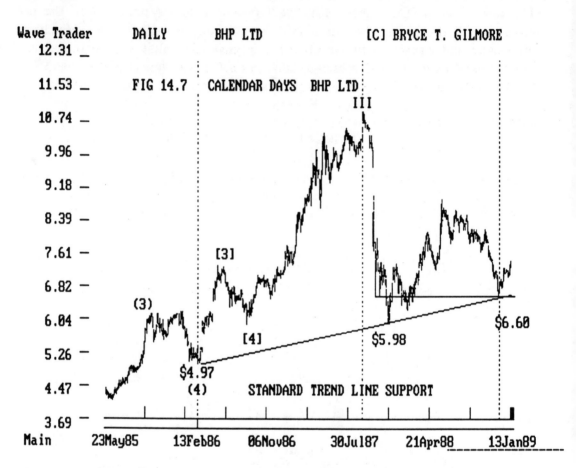

FIG 14.7  HOW STRONG WAS THE LOW AT $6.60 ON DECEMBER 5TH 1988

If you were to use the supports previously mentioned, $6.60 for a wave (2) seems to be an impenetrable barrier at this time. By combining standard charting practice and drawing a trend line, you find that this aspect also added to the geometric support. What was even more important was the time duration from $5.98 to $6.60, low to low, at twelve months (360 days exactly [degrees in a circle]) and 985 calendar days from $4.97 (close on the Fibonacci number [give a day or two] 987). Time was present at this low, this adds an almighty weight to my analysis at any time.

The alternative of course, should the market break below $6.60, is for support at $5.90 (50% of the 1974-87 range) or $5.55 (50% square of the 1987 high $11.10).

ANALYSIS PROCEDURES

## LAST INTERMEDIATE AND MINOR ELLIOTT WAVE SWING POINT

To remain on the conservative side, at least until we receive more conformation, I will assume that $8.90 (880601) is still a [B] of primary degree. To disprove this analysis $6.60 (881205) would need to be confirmed as a (2) [intermediate wave two] or a (B) of a [B] of IV (under this scenario $8.90 is a (A) of [B]).

**question..** What would need to happen to confirm $6.60 (881205) as a (2) or a (B) of [B].

**answer..** A retracement greater than 38.2% of the range $8.90 to $6.60.

**reason..** If we are currently in a [C] (primary bear market impulse wave) then $6.60 (881205) has to be counted as a (3) [intermediate wave three of five]. It then follows that we are now in a (4) [intermediate wave four]. Wave four (normally) in an impulse wave sequence should not retrace more than 38.2% of its advance.

**FIG 14.8 $6.60 LOW DECEMBER 5TH, 1988 as a wave (3) of [C].**

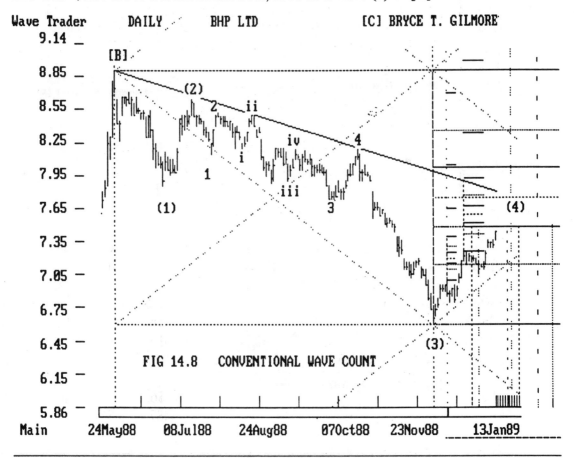

# ANALYSIS PROCEDURES

The moment of truth is close at hand, it is now January 13th, 1989 and the market has traded within 2 cents of the 38.2% retracement level.

More importantly this market appears to be impulsing. Study the wave formations unfolding in the minor wave from the low. It may of course come to pass that a correction will occur here just to keep us in suspense for a little longer.

The final outcome will be known for sure just as soon as the downtrend angle is broken (see fig 14.9). We are either, in a bull market on a convincing break of $7.48 or in a confirmed bear market on a break of $6.60.

**FIG 14.9  $6.60 LOW DECEMBER 5TH, 1988** as a wave (2) of [1]

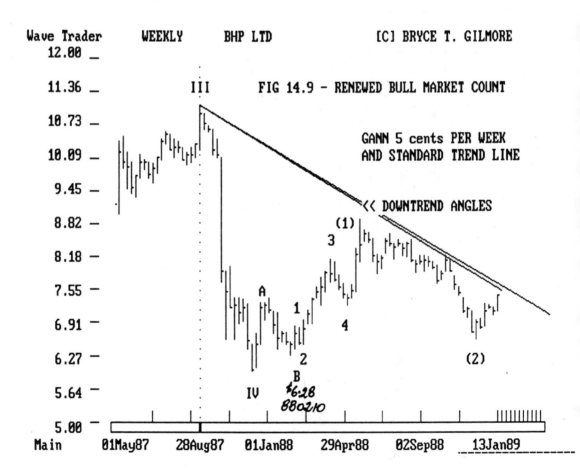

## ANALYSIS PROCEDURES

Careful observation of this wave count will illustrate an anomaly mentioned in R.N. Elliott's thesis. A-B formations can form between the end of a bear market and the begining of the new bull market. Mention is made of this wave form in "THE ELLIOTT WAVE PRINCIPLE", Frost and Prechter 1981 (page 48).

To accept this wave count and of course to have arrived at it in the first place, one needed to experience the pschological factors present at the time both the bottom labeled IV and B were registered.

This market was in proverbial tatters on the days both bottoms were recorded. Bullish concensus was reading ZERO. Every indicator was hard down. This still did not stop me from buying a parcel of 50 call options in another stock at the February low (wave B) on this chart (fig 14.9). My profit was $5150 for an investment of $2972 in 6 weeks.

## STEP 3. RECORDING SQUARES OF PRICE SUPPORT AND RESISTANCE

### SQUARES OF PRICE

1. HIGHEST RECORDED PRICE IN CURRENT CYCLE WAVE SERIES - $11.10

2. LOWEST RECORDED PRICE IN CURRENT CYCLE WAVE SERIES - $0.72

3. HIGHEST OR LOWEST PRICE APPLICABLE IN LAST 7 YEARS - $1.44

4. MOST RECENT CYCLE OR PRIMARY WAVE HIGH OR LOW - $5.98
The high at $11.10 is covered by selection 1.

### SQUARES OF RANGE

1. HIGHEST AND LOWEST CYCLE TOPS AND BOTTOMS - 1974 to 1987

2. LAST MAJOR BULL OR BEAR PHASE - 1987 high $11.10 TO 1987 low $5.98

3. PROJECTIONS OF RANGE  (0)-(I)

4. PROJECTIONS OF RANGE  (0)-(III)

# ANALYSIS PROCEDURES

These prices and ranges would be the most important to monitor for the future. Of course recent ranges, minor highs and lows can be calculated as the market moves along.

## SQUARES OF PRICE

The simplest way to continually monitor these important levels is on long term monthly charts. I have several cork boards strategically placed around my office walls, on these I keep updated long term charts for the stocks and commodities I wish to trade. After a while support and resistance levels in markets are committed to memory. This way it is highly unlikely the markets can arrive at these levels and be overlooked. The first rule when it comes to trading is, **KNOW YOUR BUSINESS**.

**FIG 14.10   BHP LTD SQUARES OF 1974 (0), 1982 (II) AND 1987 (IV) LOWS**

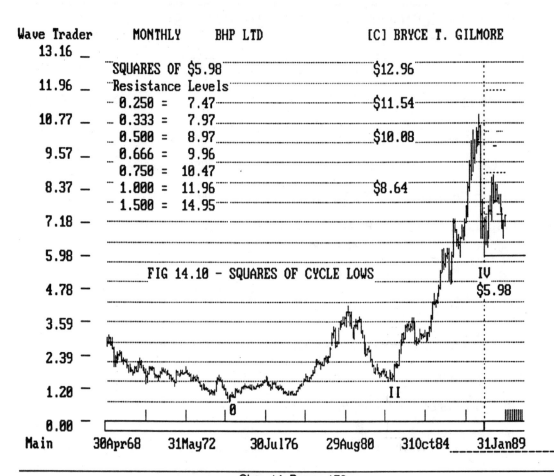

## ANALYSIS PROCEDURES

**FIG 14.11   BHP LTD SQUARE OF HIGH (III) $11.10 16th SEPTEMBER 1987**

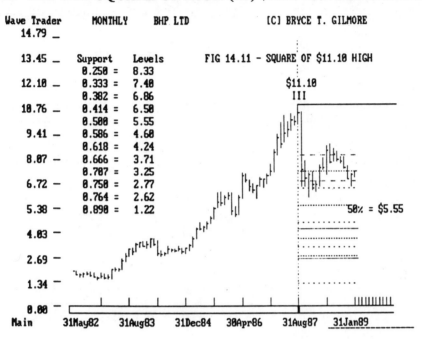

**FIG 14.12   BHP LTD SQUARE OF 1974 (0) TO 1987 (III) TRADING RANGE**

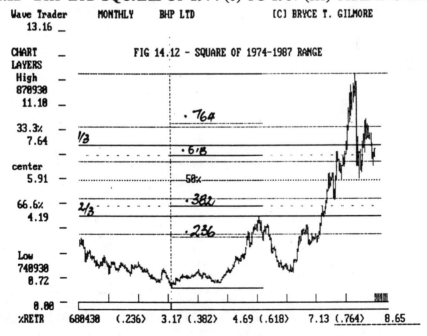

## ANALYSIS PROCEDURES

### FIG 14.13 BHP LTD SQUARE OF CRASH WAVE (III)-(IV)

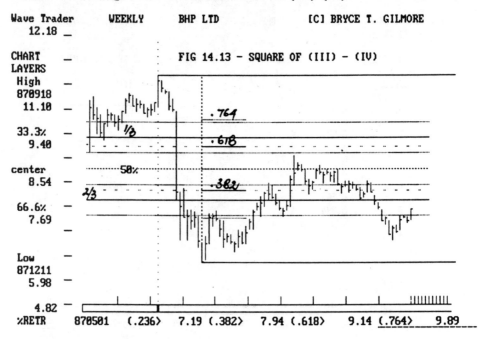

### FIG 14.14 BHP LTD PROJECTIONS OF 1974-1980 BULL MARKET (0)-(I)

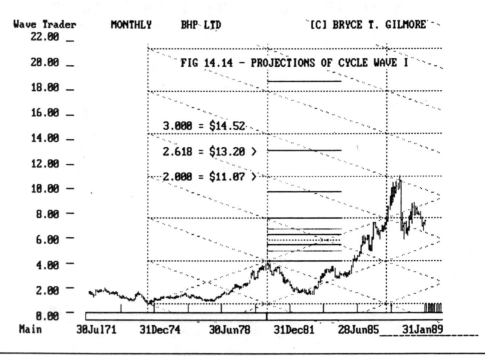

## ANALYSIS PROCEDURES

**FIG 14.15   BHP LTD PROJECTIONS OF 1974-1987 RANGE (0)-(III)**

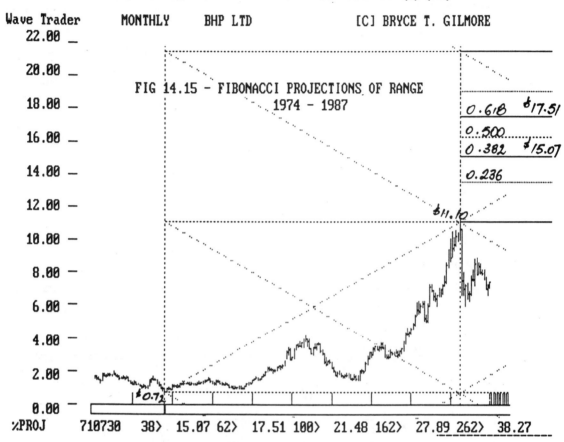

Now that we have recorded all of the major price levels we can move on to major time vibrations that may square in the near future.

## STEP 4. RECORDING MAJOR TIME VIBRATIONS FOR THE FUTURE

Fundamental input and investor psychology determine the strength in price rises or falls, yet, time is the ruler of markets. Time has only one axis, always moving forward. Experiences from the past vibrate forward under cover of the mass subconscious actions of investors. Once time is overbalanced a reaction to trend will be almost certain. The universe vibrates about three major sets of ratios; Arithmetic, Geometric and Harmonic. In terms of cycles (total time of an action and the reaction) we can use these ratios to determine a logical end to a current trend. Of course within all markets the vibration of minor, intermediate, primary and cycle degree waves are going on at all times. The strongest areas for a reaction to a current trend are when clusters of vibrations fall around a future date. For instance, the most important event that is imprinted in the investors memory is the crash of 1987, this will take time to erase. Each time a market begins a correction to any upward move nervousness will abound. This will continue until all of those jittery stock holders have quit the market. It then follows that vibrations of the crash wave are the most important to monitor.

**VIBRATIONS OF RANGE TIME THAT I WOULD TRACK WITHOUT DEVIATION:-**

1. Range vibrations of 1987 high (III)[$11.10 on 870916] to crash wave low $ 5.98 on 871211. (for analytical purposes we will tag the crash low as IV).

2. Squares of total vibration from 1974 [740930] to 1987. Low $0.72 (0) to high $11.10 (III).

**FIG 14.16** Wave Trader TIME ANALYZER menu

```
V1.51  W A V E  T R A D E R tm - T I M E  &  P R I C E  M O D U L E
       (C) Copyright  Bryce T. Gilmore 1987,1988  - All rights reserved


       TIME  and  PRICE calculations applicable to market trends

        1 -  WAVE TRADER IMPORTANT DATES - fact file required.
             Fact files can contain  100 past market swing dates
             between 1910-1999.   (see % SWING CHART MODULE)
        2 -  GANN VIBRATION DATES OF PRICE IN TIME -  fact files
             are required with details of important price and
             price range between swing highs and lows.
        3 -  Future dates squaring any VALUE from a starting date
             Used for RANGE time, LOW \ HIGH value, a set period
        4 -  DATE CALCULATOR
             Calculate time in days, weeks and months between two
             dates or project time forward or backwards.
        5 -  VIEW details of a FACT FILE to SCREEN or PRINTER
        6 -  PLANETARY POSITIONS - Heliocentric aspects 1910-99
        7 -  PRICE SQUARING  PROJECTIONS AND RETRACEMENTS MODULE

        Select by number [1-2-3-4-5-6-7] or [ESC] to exit....?
        [F10 Advance printer to a new page]  [F1 Abort any routine]
```

## ANALYSIS PROCEDURES

3. Squares of cycle wave I vibration. $0.72 to $4.17  (740930 to 801118).

4. Squares of cycle wave III vibration $1.44 to $ 11.10 (821210 to 870916).

5. All current waves of minor, intermediate and primary degree.

I shall list a few of these that have been prepared by the WAVE TRADER TIME MODULE.

**FIG 14.17  VIBRATIONS OF CYCLE WAVE IV (870916 to 871211 = 86 days)**

Wave Trader report using selection 3. Notice that the first vibration of 5 (Fibonacci) falls on February 13th, 1989. This is also 430 days (3x144=432) and 61.8 weeks. This forward date 890213 is within days of the 1 year anniversary from the wave labeled B (begining of my new bull market count - see Fig 14.9 page 176 - low was $6.28 on 880210).

```
              TIME AND PRICE  FORECASTING ANALYSIS
            Project squarings of a PRICE or RANGE forward.


       Enter  begining DATE to start SQUARING  ( yymmdd ) .. ? 871211
       Is this Squaring to be in (D)ays  (W)eeks  or (M)onths ? D
       Enter VALUE that is to be squared forward  (999.99) .. ? 86
       Do you wish to print a report    ENTER    (Y) or (N).. ? N
       Place a limit year on report     START    (1901) etc . ? 1989
       Place a limit year on report     FINISH   (1999) etc . ? 1989
The VALUE   86.00 squared in time period from 871211    in D    periods.
   5.000   time vibration    430 days    61 weeks   forward is 1989 Feb 13   *
   6.000   time vibration    516 days    74 weeks   forward is 1989 May 10
   6.180   time vibration    531 days    76 weeks   forward is 1989 May 25
   6.850   time vibration    589 days    84 weeks   forward is 1989 Jul 22
   7.000   time vibration    602 days    86 weeks   forward is 1989 Aug  4
   8.000   time vibration    688 days    98 weeks   forward is 1989 Oct 29

Press any key
```

## ANALYSIS PROCEDURES

**FIG 14.18 VIBRATIONS OF CYCLE WAVES 1974 (740930) TO 1987 (870916)**- see calculations of time as per schedule prepared on page 166.

```
              TIME AND PRICE  FORECASTING ANALYSIS
              Project squarings of a PRICE or RANGE forward.


        Enter  begining DATE to start SQUARING  ( yymmdd ) .. ? 870916
        Is this Squaring to be in (D)ays  (W)eeks  or (M)onths ? D
        Enter VALUE that is to be squared forward  (999.99) .. ? 4734
        Do you wish to print a report    ENTER    (Y) or (N).. ? N
        Place a limit year on report    START    (1901) etc . ? 1989
        Place a limit year on report    FINISH   (1999) etc . ? 1992
The VALUE 4734.00 squared in time period from 870916    in D   periods.
   0.146   time vibration    691 days     99 weeks   forward is 1989 Aug  7
   0.168   time vibration    795 days    114 weeks   forward is 1989 Nov 19
   0.204   time vibration    966 days    138 weeks   forward is 1990 May  8
   0.272   time vibration   1288 days    184 weeks   forward is 1991 Mar 26
   0.333   time vibration   1576 days    225 weeks   forward is 1992 Jan  9
   0.382   time vibration   1808 days    258 weeks   forward is 1992 Aug 28

Press any key
```

-------------------

The first vibration of this report falls on 7th August 1989, when we review the report for the crash wave vibrations (previous page Fig 14.17) we find that also on 4th August 1989 we will run the 7th vibration of that range.

This means that a cluster of timing vibrations is being formed in the first week of August 1989. It is not so important right at this moment, but when we get closer to this time we can investigate lesser degree vibrations from the Minor wave formations that will unfold between now and then.

ANALYSIS PROCEDURES

**FIG 14.19** VIBRATIONS OF CYCLE WAVE I (740930 to 801118 = 2241 see schedule page 165).

```
               TIME AND PRICE  FORECASTING ANALYSIS
              Project squarings of a PRICE or RANGE forward.


     Enter begining DATE to start SQUARING  ( yymmdd ) .. ? 801118
     Is this Squaring to be in (D)ays  (W)eeks  or (M)onths ? D
     Enter VALUE that is to be squared forward  (999.99) .. ? 2241
     Do you wish to print a report    ENTER      (Y) or (N).. ? N
     Place a limit year on report     START      (1901) etc . ? 1989
     Place a limit year on report     FINISH     (1999) etc . ? 1992
 The VALUE 2241.00 squared in time period from 801118    in D   periods.
    1.382  time vibration  3097 days     442 weeks  forward is 1989 May 12
    1.414  time vibration  3169 days     453 weeks  forward is 1989 Jul 22
    1.500  time vibration  3362 days     480 weeks  forward is 1990 Jan 31
    1.618  time vibration  3626 days     518 weeks  forward is 1990 Oct 22
    1.666  time vibration  3734 days     533 weeks  forward is 1991 Feb  7
    1.902  time vibration  4262 days     609 weeks  forward is 1992 Jul 20
 Press any key
```

---

**BINGO** two clusters with the crash wave vibrations are evident (Fig 14.17 page 183). These are 12th May 1989 and 22nd July 1989.

1.382 is a Geometric relationship and 1.414 (root 2) is a Harmonic vibration.

On July 22nd 1989 to the exact day the crash wave (Fig 14.17) runs a 6.85 Geometric vibration as this wave runs a Harmonic. I would consider July 22nd an extremely important vibration point even at this time.

**FIG 14.20 VIBRATIONS OF CYCLE WAVE III (821210 to 870916 = 1741 see schedule page 166).**

```
               TIME AND PRICE  FORECASTING ANALYSIS
             Project squarings of a PRICE or RANGE forward.


     Enter  begining DATE to start SQUARING  ( yymmdd ) .. ? 870916
     Is this Squaring to be in (D)ays  (W)eeks  or (M)onths ? D
     Enter VALUE that is to be squared forward  (999.99) .. ? 1741
     Do you wish to print a report    ENTER    (Y) or (N).. ? N
     Place a limit year on report     START    (1901) etc . ? 1989
     Place a limit year on report     FINISH   (1999) etc . ? 1990
The VALUE 1741.00 squared in time period from 870916   in D   periods.
  0.272   time vibration     474 days       68 weeks  forward is 1989 Jan  1
  0.333   time vibration     580 days       83 weeks  forward is 1989 Apr 17
  0.382   time vibration     665 days       95 weeks  forward is 1989 Jul 12
  0.437   time vibration     761 days      109 weeks  forward is 1989 Oct 15
  0.500   time vibration     871 days      124 weeks  forward is 1990 Feb  2
  0.618   time vibration    1076 days      154 weeks  forward is 1990 Aug 26
  0.666   time vibration    1160 days      166 weeks  forward is 1990 Nov 18
```

Press any key

-------------------

Nothing on this report exactly fits the previous reports (Figures 14.17 to 14.19) although the 0.382 vibration falling on July 12th, 1989 is an important benchmark for the future. Should the price of BHP LTD stay trading above $ 5.98, I am positive that my expectation for a new expansion will be correct. 666 is the number of man and this date is 665 days from the HIGH $11.10, the period July 12th to July 22nd seems to be an extremely important time period to monitor.

One interesting aspect I have noticed is the reoccurence of November 18th, anniversaries of the 1980 bull market high, form, vibrations on this report at the .666 vibration and a 1/6th vibration on the report Fig 14.18 page 184.

ANALYSIS PROCEDURES

One of the most important Gann teachings on TIME is to watch for changes in trend around anniversaries of previous major market tops or bottoms.

## MONITORING STATIC TIME AND VIBRATIONS ON A DAY TO DAY BASIS

By preparing a fact file using the details from my price swing charts I can keep track of long term market vibrations as well as short term vibrations easily.

I have already prepared a long term fact file using the details from the swing chart FIG 14.1 page 167.

For the shorter term I am now preparing a 10% price swing file back to the pre-crash high $11.10 (870916). This is illustrated in Fig 14.21, Elliott wave analysis made easy.

### FIG 14.21  ELLIOTT WAVE ANALYSIS MADE EASY

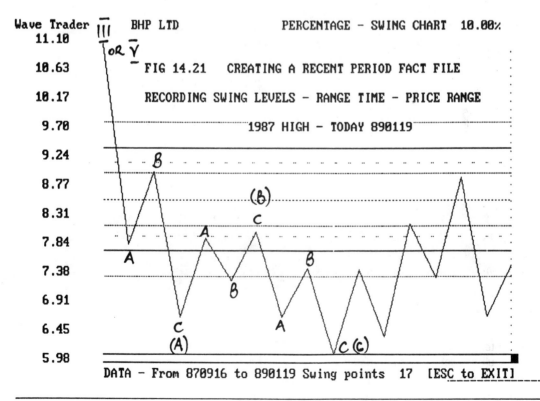

Chp. 14 Page. 187

Here is a print out of the relevant swing levels shown in fig. 14.21. FIG 14.22 shows the date of swing high or low, the price extreme recorded that day, the time in calendar days from the last swing or an edited record that reflects a completed series of waves, the price range of the swing in cents (this will be used for translating units of price range to time) and notes.

**FIG 14.22  FACT FILE OF MARKET SWINGS at 10% FROM 870916 HIGH**

```
Print your fact file details to printer (Y or N) ...
Fact file details for  BHP 10% 87 HIGH ON
DATE,    SWING,     HI/LO,    CYCLE,     RANGE,     IMPORTANT NOTES
870916    11.10     HIGH        380      517.00     HISTORY HIGH
871020     7.80     LOW          34      330.00     SWING = 29.73 %
871022     9.00     HIGH          2      120.00     SWING = 15.38 %
871027 *   6.60 *   LOW           5      240.00     SWING = 26.67 %
871028     7.90     HIGH          1      130.00     SWING = 19.7 %
871029     7.20     LOW           1       70.00     SWING = 8.86 %
871102     8.00     HIGH          4       80.00     SWING = 11.11 %
871111 *   6.60 *   LOW           9      140.00     SWING = 17.5 %
871113     7.40     HIGH          2       80.00     SWING = 12.12 %
871211     5.98     LOW          86      512.00     CYCLE WAVE BOTTOM IV
880106     7.38     HIGH         26      140.00     SWING = 23.41 %
880210     6.28     LOW          35      110.00     SWING = 14.91 %
880414     8.14     HIGH         64      186.00     SWING = 29.62 %
880512     7.24     LOW          28       90.00     SWING = 11.06 %
880601     8.90     HIGH        112      262.00     41.7% INCREASE $6.28
881205 *   6.60 *   LOW         187      230.00     SWING = 25.84 %
890119     7.46     HIGH         45       86.00     SWING = 13.03 %

Press any key to exit
```

The next step is to run static time counts from each high or low and vibrations of each swing phase. From this information we will be alerted to forthcoming dates to watch. The strongest dates are when we have many clusters falling together.

## FIG 14.23   WAVE TRADER TIME REPORT FOR SUNDAY, JANUARY 22th, 1989

This report makes the necessary calculations for static time periods and vibration ratios of previous swing points and time ranges that we should monitor. It needs to be viewed in two parts. Firstly, time is measured forward from the swing points to the date of this report. Secondly, squares (Gann methodology) are calculated on the actual time elapsed. Thirdly, approximate trading days elapsed are calculated, a quick perusal by a trained eye would alert an experienced analyst to any Fibonacci or Lucas relationships falling close at hand.

```
Time Analysis of BHP 10% 87 HIGH ON      on 890122
DATE    PRICE           TIME   SQR DAYS   SQR WKS   T/DAYS       NEXT  NEXT DATE
870916  11.10 HIGH       494    22.23       8.40     341          505  1989 Feb  2
871020   7.80 LOW        460    21.45       8.11     317          465  1989 Jan 27
871022   9.00 HIGH       458    21.40       8.09     316          465  1989 Jan 29
871027   6.60 LOW        453    21.28       8.04     313          455  1989 Jan 24
871028   7.90 HIGH       452    21.26       8.04     312          455  1989 Jan 25
871029   7.20 LOW        451    21.24       8.03     311          455  1989 Jan 26
871102   8.00 HIGH       447    21.14       7.99     308          448  1989 Jan 23
871111   6.60 LOW        438    20.93       7.91     302          441  1989 Jan 25
871113   7.40 HIGH       436    20.88       7.89     301          441  1989 Jan 27
871211   5.98 LOW        408    20.20       7.63     281          408  1989 Jan 22
880106   7.38 HIGH       382    19.54       7.39     264    *     385  1989 Jan 25
880210   6.28 LOW        347    18.63       7.04     239          350  1989 Jan 25
880414   8.14 HIGH       283    16.82       6.36     195    *     288  1989 Jan 27
880512   7.24 LOW        255    15.97       6.04     176          261  1989 Jan 28
880601   8.90 HIGH       235    15.33       5.79     162    *     238  1989 Jan 25
881205   6.60 LOW         48     6.93       2.62      33           48  1989 Jan 22
890119   7.46 HIGH         3     1.73       0.65       2           11  1989 Jan 30
Press any key to exit OR [S] for next 7 days dates...
```

Lastly, the next possible important number is selected from the number bank and the date calculated for its due day.

## FIG 14.24 WAVE TRADER DATE SORT OF STATIC TIME AND VIBRATION TIME, PREPARED ON REPORT FIG 14.23

```
SELECTION 1, Sort of closest dates in next 7 days for BHP 10% 87 HIGH ON

1989 Jan 22   WT time           408 days   58 weeks from 871211    5.98 LOW
1989 Jan 22   WT time            48 days    7 weeks from 881205    6.60 LOW
1989 Jan 23   WT time           448 days   64 weeks from 871102    8.00 HIGH
1989 Jan 24   WT time           455 days   65 weeks from 871027    6.60 LOW
1989 Jan 24   vibration* 0.272 time         7 weeks from 881205    6.60 LOW
1989 Jan 25   WT time           455 days   65 weeks from 871028    7.90 HIGH
1989 Jan 25   WT time           441 days   63 weeks from 871111    6.60 LOW
1989 Jan 25   WT time    *      385 days   55 weeks from 880106    7.38 HIGH
1989 Jan 25   WT time           350 days   50 weeks from 880210    6.28 LOW
1989 Jan 25   vibration 10.000 time        50 weeks from 880210    6.28 LOW
1989 Jan 25   WT time    *      238 days   34 weeks from 880601    8.90 HIGH
1989 Jan 25   vibration  0.146 time         1 weeks from 890119    7.46 HIGH
1989 Jan 26   WT time           455 days   65 weeks from 871029    7.20 LOW
1989 Jan 27   WT time           465 days   66 weeks from 871020    7.80 LOW
1989 Jan 27   WT time           441 days   63 weeks from 871113    7.40 HIGH
1989 Jan 27   WT time    *      288 days   41 weeks from 880414    8.14 HIGH
1989 Jan 28   WT time           261 days   37 weeks from 880512    7.24 LOW
1989 Jan 29   WT time           465 days   66 weeks from 871022    9.00 HIGH
Press any key to exit ...
```

PART TWO

Time is clustering on the 25th January 1989, from a fact file of effectively 16 entries time is vibrating 6 times on this date (I am not taking any notice of the 0.146 vibration from 890119). Two of the entries are pinpointing 55 and 34 week periods. 55 weeks from the post crash short covering rally high of $7.38 (880106) and 34 weeks from the $8.90 high of 880601 (Intermediate wave (1) on my preferred count, fig 14.9). This date requires investigation on the daily price chart. See Fig 14.25

## ANALYSIS PROCEDURES

**FIG 14.25 PRICE SERIES FROM $8.90 (880601) TO CURRENT (890119)**

```
Wave Trader    DAILY       BHP LTD              [C] BRYCE T. GILMORE
   9.00 _
                                                              890125
   8.77 _              FROM HIGH $11.10                       238 CAL
                                                              166 TRD
   8.55 _                   << RESISTANCE ANGLES              (3*55)
                                                              34 WEEKS
   8.32 _

   8.09 _

   7.86 _
                                                              .500
   7.64 _
           FIG 14.25 TECHNICAL RESISTANCE LEVELS              .382
   7.41 _

   7.18 _
                  187*1.272 = 238 = 34 WEEKS
   6.95 _         1.272 = ROOT PHI(1.618)

   6.73 _         132 T DAYS AND 187 CAL DAYS       34/51 DAYS

   6.50 _
  Main      30May88    14Jul88   30Aug88  13Oct88  29Nov88  19Jan89
```

Interesting position, this market has now formed more than three waves (normally in a correction phase only 3 waves should form) from the $6.60 low. This certainly does not appear to be a (4) as my conventional count FIG 14.8 page 175 would have us believe. However my bullish scenario still has several technical obstacles to overcome before my preferred count can be substantiated. January 25th will most likely signal a swing high that will usher in a correction that will terminate on or about February 13th, the major time frame illustrated in FIG 14.17 - vibration 5 of the crash wave. If the picture unfolds this way then we could expect the next expansion to last until the major date of May 10-12 as per Fig 14.17 and Fig 14.19.

Technical time resistance present next week :-

890125 = 55 weeks and 34 weeks time vibration discussed in FIG 14.24

890125 = 34 trading days from low $6.60, 5th December 1988.

890125 = 1.272 vibration of time $8.90 to $6.60, total time 34 weeks. (appears as 0.272 in fig 14.24).

## FUNDAMENTAL OUTLOOK FOR THIS STOCK

Most pure chartist's would shudder when I mention fundamental analysis! They consider it is not at all necessary, don't make their mistake. Markets are vibrating from shock to shock on the pschological action of traders, underlying all of these price actions a basis of value exists. What are the general economic conditions? Has this stock a solid balance sheet? Is it earning profits on a consistent basis? What are the future prospects for continued growth and profits? Is the management secure and in tune with investor needs? What is the long term history of this stocks performance? Poor? Mediocre? Good? Excellent?

**THE ANSWER TO THESE QUESTIONS ARE SIMPLE!**

BHP LTD has managed to fragment the share holding and increase capitalization at every share offering it has ever made, investors have long term confidence in this enterprise. Continually it increases it's earnings and divests it's holdings.

During the past several years it has been a target for takeover offers, its management has fought, dealt with and resisted all such attempts.

BHP LTD is now well positioned since the crash of 1987, two record profit performances of over one billion dollars per year.

Australia's number one company, large holdings in producing oil fields, mining iron ore for export, producing steel and other building materials, together with diversified investments in many other areas, the most prominent of these being a 50% plus holding in the new Gold producer BHP GOLD LTD which has 3.7 million ounces of Gold in proven reserves (December 1988) and presently geared to produce 250,000 plus ounces per annum.

Another plus BHP pays a dividend that includes imputation tax.

At current price levels I would assume that downside risk is at a minimum, this conclusion certainly helps sway me in the direction of my preferred wave count.

There is no point investing in anything unless it has a pedigree, forget about get rich schemes that presumably will work overnight. The secret to the business (investing for

## ANALYSIS PROCEDURES

profit) is investing and trading for the longterm. Search out ships to trade that always remain afloat, even after capsizing in a storm.

One lesson in investments I have learnt over the years, having participated in the 1970-74 bear market, the 1981-82 bear market, thankfully through knowledge and good judgement not the 1987-88 bear market, is that when the proverbial *shit hits the fan* or the wave breaks over the ship no amount of hope will ever recover your money. You will have to rely on the ship uprighting itself and adjusting to the new environment.

If you lose all of your capital you will be bankrupt and out of business. Don't let this happen to you. Plan, study, analyse, prepare and attack. If it becomes necessary, retreat and attack another day.

If you wish to trade in speculative areas, make sure that you continually monitor these investments, trade only for the short term when every fundamental, be it real or imaginative, is in your favor.

No matter what you see, read or hear, **unless it is an atomic bomb**, markets will continue to expand and contract on the expectations of traders.

These fundamentals have been with us for several millennium or longer, they will not desert us now just because it is 1989. The technical approaches I have outlined in this book and chapter will hold good *ad infinitum. They have already stood the test of time.*

Always remember this, whenever things are confused, or not going according to plan, you have not been doing enough analysis work! Start again from scratch and replan your attack.

Throughout this chapter I have been discussing BHP Ltd, before concluding I would like to make it clear that any commodity or stock should be approached in the same manner.

Earlier chapters outline many examples of my methods for the gold market. I will probably make this the sole subject of my next book. However at present I am writing a bi-weekly Wave Trader Digest on the day to day technical events that come to pass, together with future price and time projections. Wave Trader Digest is purely devoted to the gold complex. (call me or your local distributor if you are interested in subscribing).

## GEOMETRY OF MARKETS - 2nd Edition JUNE 1989

All of the material presented earlier in this chapter first went to print in late January 1989. I now have the opportunity to review the events that have unfolded since then. This should prove to you the value of time, price and space analysis.

The chart displayed in Fig. 14.26 shows how precise the market followed my earlier preferred probabilities. The rally in progress on January 19th, 1989 expired at $7.58 (now shown as $6.89 due to an adjustment in price for a 1 for 10 bonus issued on 20th April 1989. All prior data was reduced in value by a factor of 11 to 10, ie., 10 shares = 10 times $7.58 or $75.80, after bonus 11 shares = $75.80 or $6.89 each).

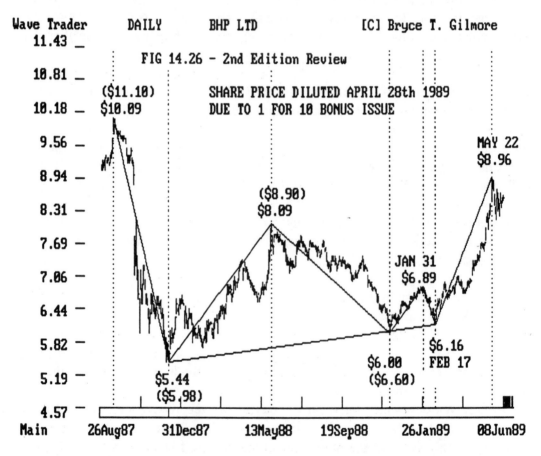

**FIG 14.26 - BHP Ltd 1987 HIGH TO June 8th, 1989** using adjusted price data after the 1 for 10 bonus issue went ex-bonus on 21st April 1989.

## ANALYSIS PROCEDURES

In the first edition of "GEOMETRY OF MARKETS", January 1989, I felt strongly towards a renewed bull market wave unfolding in BHP Ltd. However not enough time has elapsed to confirm a fully fledged bull market. What happened since January has nevertheless enabled me and other wave traders to reap substantial profits by following the previous analysis.

I traded the market long for a substantial part of the rise between $6.16 and $8.96. I went short this market the day after the $8.96 high and made some fast profits, 100%+ in less than 2 weeks.

After the high of $8.96 which occured on 22nd May 1989. I shorted this market first thing the next day for the following reasons.

The RSI 10 day indicator was reading 90+ with the following time and price squarings.

1) Price rise from $6.00 to $8.96 = $2.96 ($2.96 as a ratio of the previous intermediate decline $8.09 to $6.00 = $2.09 [2.96 as a ratio of 2.09 = 1.414]. The day after the high prices began to decline without looking like making a higher high. I could count a five to seven wave advance using Elliott wave rules.

2) Price increase from the crash low now shown as $5.44 to the high $8.09 was $2.65 in adjusted dollars. [2.96 divided by 2.65 = 1.117] 1.118 equals half of root 5 (2.236). A definite price squaring occured at the $8.96 high of immeasurable strength. The triangle formed by dividing a square into two has an hypotenuse equal to 1.414 times the side. If you divide this triangle into two parts then the hypotenuse will be equal to 1.118 times the side of the square. See fig 14.27 which contains a diagram.

3) Price expansion from the $6.00 low to $8.96 equals approximately 50%?

4) Fundamental changes to the economy were currently taking place. Interest rates have risen from 15% p.a. in January to 21% p.a. today, this alone should make even the shrewdest investor look in other directions to the stock market for the time being.

Nevertheless the current correction is triangular in pattern, this under Elliott wave technique suggests another wave up in the present wave series. The next major price squaring, were this market to keep expanding upwards, would suggest a high at or just short of the 1987 high. This area should it be reached would represent an excellent opportunity to short this market or buy it on a break above the 1987 high.

## ANALYSIS PROCEDURES

### FIG 14.27 - BHP LTD. WAVE RELATIONSHIPS POST 1987 CRASH LOW $5.44

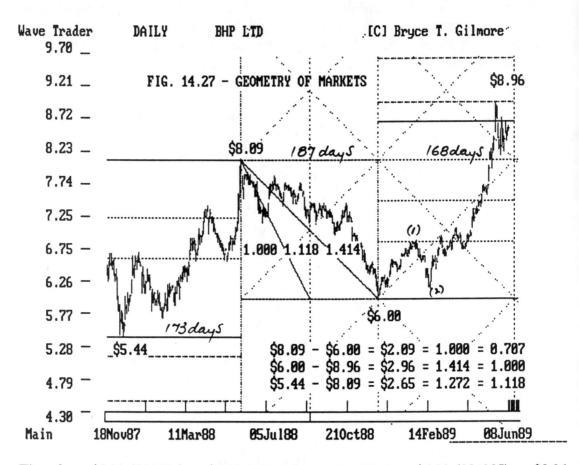

Time from $8.09 (880601) to $6.00 (881205) equals 187 days, $6.00 (881205) to $8.96 (890522) equals 168 days. 187 divided by 168 equals 1.118 (1/2 root 5). This market appears to be travelling in some type of contracting mode. I would not be to sure given the wave structures, but we could have been tracing out a complex type of [B] wave starting at the $5.44 low. After all we now have an (A) (B) (C) formation with each wave bound together geometrically with time and price relationships.

Study this chart and observe how bull and bear trends in markets can relate. Form an opinion as to the most probable direction prices will take, yet remain flexible should an alternative probability become real. Stay on top of the stocks or commodities that you follow. They will signal you their intentions when it is time to trade.

## 15. TRADING WITH TIME AND PRICE ANALYSIS

As one cannot be sure of the market volatility prior to important time and price signals, it pays to monitor the market sentiment as a barometer of what to expect. I see trading markets as a chess game. We have many valuable tools to use in our plan of attack, yet in the final analysis if we are foolish traders we will never make any money from our knowledge. No two traders are the same. Each must have a plan that makes them comfortable. Develop particular strategies for specific market conditions; sometimes an option play can be extremely rewarding with low risk in a fast moving market. At other times a move will ultimately go in your favor, yet the time taken will be too long, options can expire before your analysis is proven correct. I have found several approaches are needed if one is to continually profit from the markets. Another word of advice, only follow a limited number of markets. Keep up with the fundamental news for each market, when important news reaches the public and the chart price patterns have reflected this news, a counter trend reaction often occurs.

The procedures I follow for trade selection are:-

My primary indication for a trade is a balancing of time and price using Gann & Elliott Wave Ratio Analysis. At least three important squarings must be present.

Secondly, I watch the natural cycle periods of the year, equinox, solstice and mid points.

Thirdly, I look for time and price occurrences in Fibonacci or Lucas degree.

Next, I monitor the market bullish consensus poll, I will not trade any market unless it is overbalanced and subject to volatile action. The greater the volatility the greater the opportunity.

As a balance I monitor relative strength indices and momentum indicators for mathematical indications of overbought and oversold market conditions. Indicators can also give a sound guide to the position of system traders. You would be amazed how many people blindly follow oscilator indicators. Trading directly from oscillators, without a filter, is equivalent to driving a car with only one gear; reverse. You see where you have been, instead of where your going.

It may only take a limited time period to learn the methods outlined in this book, but to trade successfully is an art, requiring a professional approach.

Prepare a check list, employ a risk reward money management system, take frequent breaks to recharge your batteries, rid yourself of any personal problems that could influence bad decisions, have confidence and resolve before entering a trade. Most importantly of all <u>set your goals</u> and <u>stick</u> to them. Trading markets for profit requires discipline, as does any other occupation if you intend to be successful. Nothing is easy until you become an expert, this can only be accomplished by hard work, study and dedication. If you are not mentally prepared to commit yourself fully then do not proceed. I can guarantee that you will become a casualty of the market, if you apply a half baked approach to trading.

Markets have a way of deceiving the majority of players, most of the time. This is because the professionals are at the other end of each trade made. It is their business to make a profit out of you. It is my business to make a profit out of them. By understanding markets you can sit aside and pick and choose your trades. Trades will be signalled when the appropriate times comes. There is no need to force the issue, approximately 70% of the time markets will be in a state of equilibrium, either distributing or accumulating. The other 30% of the time markets will be offering highly leveraged opportunity to profit. I would rather be in the market 30% or less of the time, than 100% any day. This way I have time to plan and research future opportunities.

Use your brain before making a trading decision, set your stops upon entry and stick to them, don't hope! If in doubt stay out.

## BULLISH CONSENSUS

A bullish consensus poll is a good barometer of the mass psychological forces underlying a particular commodity or stock. Expert advisors are polled for their opinion on future market direction, overall opinion is rated between 0% and 100%. 100% readings would mean that everybody thought the market was going up, 0% readings would indicate everybody thought the market was going down. However these extremes are rarely reached and 80% to 20% is the general range. The higher or lower the bullish consensus reading when a change in trend is indicated, the more volatile the ensuing move will be. Remember vibration up equals vibration down.

Many books have been published on bullish consensus and the power of contrary thinking. My advice is to purchase one for your library and refer to it **regularly**.

My logic, when it comes to the bullish consensus, is that if everyone is bullish then they have all bought. Who else is left to buy? Only the uneducated public, whose funds will soon be depleted at high prices. When the bullish consensus is very bearish everyone has sold out and selling pressure is reducing. Sooner or later prices will appear to be at bargain levels and new buyers will emerge to reverse the downward path. A study of past volume and open interest charts will confirm this observation.

## RELATIVE STRENGTH INDICES

There are many different indicators that can be used under this heading, they are all mathematical calculations based on the past market ranges over specific time frames. From my experience it is only necessary to have one or two trend indicators. They all tell you the same thing, some faster or slower than others.

To reduce the conflict of opinion I use the popular indicator made famous by J. WELLES WILDER Jr. A 7 day, 10 day and 14 day RELATIVE STRENGTH INDEX can tell you all you need to know regarding the strength of the current trend.

The detailed interpretation for this index can be found in the book "NEW CONCEPTS IN TECHNICAL TRADING SYSTEMS" by J. Welles Wilder Jr. One of the better features of this index is the way it diverges at major swing highs and lows in the market. A divergence is seen when the price rises to a new high yet the oscillator fails to make a higher reading than it did at the last peak in price.

## FILTER DAILY NEWS

It is most important that intermediate, primary and cycle time and price squarings are accompanied by overbought or oversold sentiment readings. Besides using mathematical equations to monitor these conditions it is also important to actually identify them in the true sense (ie., watch the fundamental news). Never act without first thinking.

Sometimes oscillators can remain overbought or oversold for weeks on end as a move virtually doubles previous gains, the only filter will be your perception of the prevailing market strength. This area alone could decide whether you win or lose when it comes to placing money on the line.

Let the market tell you where it is going, don't you tell the market where it has to go.

THE MARKET WILL EVENTUALLY BALANCE IMPORTANT RATIOS OF TIME AND PRICE WITH THE PAST, WHEN IT DOES AND YOU ARE CONFIDENT IT HAS! THEN TRADE- NOT BEFORE.

I HAVE NEVER SEEN A MARKET TURNING POINT OF ANY IMPORTANCE THAT I COULD NOT JUSTIFY TECHNICALLY, USING THE METHODS OF TIME AND PRICE RATIO ANALYSIS COVERED IN THIS BOOK.

## TIME PRICE & PATTERN

Market activity has three dimensions, TIME, PRICE AND SPACE. These "VIBRATIONS" are graphically represented by the sides of a triangle that adhere to a sacred geometric form.

As the circle or wheel of time continues forward, reactions to the past occur as both time elapsed and price moved either attract or repulse themselves from one gravity vortex to another.

The cycles of the solar system are programmed into nature, the cycles of 1 year, 1 month (lunar cycle), 1 day or 1 week should be considered as wheels within wheels. Equinox, Solstice, solar eclipse, lunar eclipse, planetary cycles of time, new moons, full moons are also wheels within wheels that effect the human psyche and have a bearing on market behaviour.

Market swing highs and lows are points in time, price and space, where the PSYCHOLOGICAL imbalance of supply and demand, dictated by traders, reaches its zenith.

**TIME** calculations that can balance vibrations of previous trends are measured by extending ratios of previous ranges or cycles, as well as high and low prices forward to the future. Strong future dates are identified by multiple clusters vibrating from a series of previous waves of varying degree. Time measured off in Fibonacci, Lucas, multiples of important numbers, combinations of Fibonacci and Lucas numbers in days, weeks and months are very important. Sacred ratios of 1 year, ie., 225 days (0.618), 287 days (0.786), 465 days (1.272), 516 days (1.414), 590 days (1.618) et cetera.

**PRICE** calculations in terms of range retracements and projections, percentage increases in value from lows and highs of importance, percentage decreases in value from past highs of importance are all necessary to follow.

### PRICE CALCULATIONS FOR RESISTANCE IN A BULL MARKET IMPULSE

1. Percentage increases in price from an important low or series of lows in the bull market campaign.

2. Projections of price range of previous impulse waves upwards, eg., wave 1, wave 3 et cetera.

3. Old highs and retracement levels of previous bull market campaigns.

### PRICE CALCULATIONS FOR SUPPORT IN A BULL MARKET CORRECTION

1. Percentage calculations of the last major high price.

2. Retracements levels of the last impulse wave.

3. Retracement levels of the complete bull market advance to the last major high.

### PRICE CALCULATIONS FOR SUPPORT IN A BEAR MARKET IMPULSE

1. Price retracements of the completed bull market.

2. Percentage declines from the bull market high.

3. Projections down from the bull market high and bear market correction highs.

## PRICE CALCULATIONS FOR RESISTANCE IN A BEAR MARKET CORRECTION

1. Retracements of the last impulse wave down.

2. Retracements of the total bear market impulse high to low completed to date.

3. Retracement to the previous bear market support zone that produced a correction.

## PRICE CALCULATIONS FOR SUPPORT AND RESISTANCE IN A SIDEWAYS MARKET

1. Wave equality with the alternate wave in the series, could be lesser or greater but more often than not both a price and time ratio will balance out at the turn.

**SPACE** calculations are a third dimension, and may not necessarily be easily recognized.

The first important area to watch is specific times of the year which are historically important, static seasonal anniversaries such as Equinoxes, Solstices, Perigees and Apogees, Solar eclipses and interplanetary aspects such as conjunctions and oppositions.(see chapter 16 for further detailed explanation) Not surprisingly, these times can be confirmed usually by squarings of time of previous trend vibrations, as they are repetitive and cyclical in nature.

The second method of identifying space squarings are at the crossings of time and price vibration angles of previous trends. Some may be quite obscure but as each individual method will confirm clusters at strong points in the future, we should work all methods in unison. It is not necessary that vibration angles actually pinpoint a price intersection to be valid, although if they do they are more convincing.

The third method of confirming a space squaring is when price or time of a previous trend squares in reflection. Ie., A price range in units squares to the future in time. For instance a previous trend may have advanced 144 points, when 144 days has elapsed from the change in trend that price range will square 100%. Conversely a previous trend may have lasted 144 days so that when the new trend has advanced or declined 144 points from its beginning it will square price 100%. These methods of monitoring space are extremely important and should not be discounted under any circumstances.

**TIME AND PRICE VIBRATIONS** of a move MUST SQUARE out in definite proportions to past waves of SIMILAR DEGREE if they are to signal the completion of that market phase and the beginning of a new trend.

**IMPULSE WAVES** generally expand and contract in direct relationship to the Golden Mean (PHI 1.618) or 100% levels in time and price, ie 38.2%, 61.8%, 100%, 161.8%, 200%, 261.8% et cetera.

**CORRECTIVE WAVES** generally do not conform to any particular set of ratios. Although once they have run their race they will be easily identified by multiple time and price squarings with previous waves of larger degree. Each wave in the corrective series should relate and conform to the underlying theory of markets.

**OVERLAPPING CORRECTIVE WAVES** in a move signal weakness of trend, these are usually a forewarning of exhaustion and an imminent reversal. These formations are commonly known as diagonal triangles.

**CYCLES IN TIME OF TRENDS** are not static, cycles expand and contract in direct relationship to the subconscious action of traders. In a bull market phase corrections will be much swifter and shallower as the expansion progresses. The same principle applies in reverse to a fully fledged bear market. Bear markets start off fast then make labouring protracted corrections before entering their final phase.

## TIME & PRICE RELATIONSHIPS OF EXPANSIONS AND CORRECTIONS MUST RELATE TO PAST WAVES OF SIMILAR DEGREE.

The major ratios of time are strictly determined using ancient geometry. The Circle, Square, Pyramid of Giza and Golden Rectangle are the only means of explaining the apparent irrational connection in this regard.

Unity of a cycle is 1, 100% time periods forward from high to high or low to low that mark a new high or low are convincing areas for a reversal of trend.

Because CYCLES ARE NOT ALWAYS STATIC, divisions and expansions of 1 in strict natural ratios must always be monitored.

Most Important ratios are :-

| PYRAMID | GEOMETRIC | ARITHMETIC | HARMONIC |
|---|---|---|---|
| 0.185 | 0.146 | 0.250 | 0.3535 |
| 0.3 | 0.236 | 0.333 | 0.414 |
| 0.486 | 0.382 | 0.500 | 0.447 |
|  | 0.618 | 0.666 | 0.586 |
| 0.786 | 0.764 | 0.875 | 0.707 |
|  | 0.854 | 1.00 | 1.118 |
| 1.272 | 1.618 | 1.50 | 1.414 |
|  | 1.902 | 2.00 | 1.732 |
| 2.058 | 2.618 | 3.00 | 2.236 |
| 3.333 | 4.236 | 4.00 | 2.449 |
| 5.39 | 6.854 | 5.00 | 3.1618 |

At every major turn in market trend a natural triangular relationship between time and price will exist in strict ratios. These relationships may at first seem difficult to recognize. Only study and a clear appreciation for the aesthetic side of the market will be the answer to this problem. The right brain (which has the intellectual capacity to identify patterns in space) will recognize these situations once we have the knowledge. All we need to do is convince the left brain (the emotive and analytic side of our intelligence) that action is required.

There is a book "SACRED GEOMETRY"*, by Robert Lawlor, which goes into great depth explaining natural ratios and their history, this should be considered a must for any student of time and price market analysis.

* Thames and Hudson Ltd. London, 1982, reprinted 1987.

# MONITOR UNFOLDING RATIOS OF WAVES WITHIN CYCLES

Each completed two phase cycle, ie., High-low-high-low or Low-high-low-high, should contain relationships in waves of similar degree.

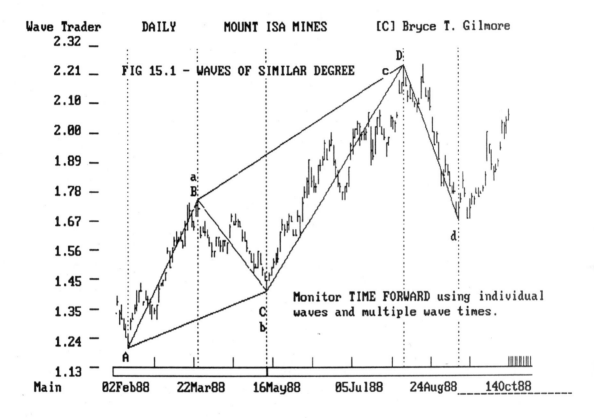

For instance if we were to label wave turning points as A = start of first impulse, B = first exhaustion point, C = reaction exhaustion point, D = end of next impulse.

Price relationships between waves could exist in the following way :-
PRICE ADVANCE B to D as a percentage of A-B range, eg., 0.382, 0.618, 1.00, 1.618, 2.00, 2.618.
PRICE ADVANCE C to D as a percentage of A-B range, eg., 1.00, 1.414, 1.618, 2.236.
PRICE ADVANCE C to D as a percentage of B-C range, eg., 1.414, 1.618, 1.732, 2.00, 2.236, 2.618.
PRICE ADVANCE C to D as a percentage of A-C range, eg., 2.00, 3.00, 5.00 et cetera.

Time relationships between waves could exist in the following ways:-

TIME PERIOD A to B projected forward to locate C and D, eg., 0.382, .5, 0.618, 1.00, 1.272, 1.414, 1.618, 2.00, 2.618.
TIME PERIOD A to C projected forward to locate D, eg., .5, 0.618, 1.00, 1.618, 2.00 et cetera.
Time and price of (c to d) could relate to C-D or A-D.
In a corrective pattern (c-d) could relate to (a-b) the alternate wave in the series.

Always investigate each option as waves may be impulsing or alternating depending upon the market forces at work. Practical experience and the study of past markets will guide you to appreciate what is important.

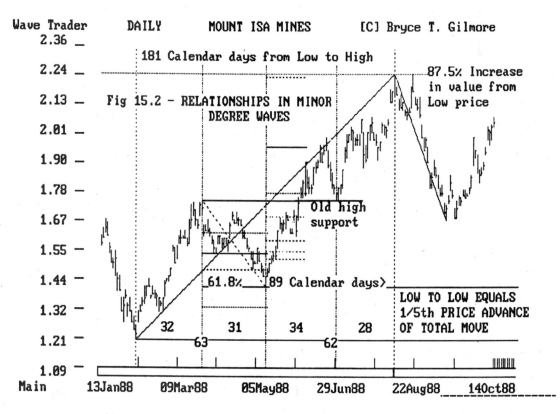

From the low this market made a three wave advance, this action was followed by a three wave correction. The correction retraced 0.618 of the price advance in 100% of the time. The first wave of the correction terminated at the 0.382 retracement level of the first minor wave advance from the chart low.

By following a momentum indicator as you approach time and price intersections of importance, you will be guided towards the true position of the market.

Time and price analysis, to be used successfully, requires personal judgement. Personal judgement is an acquired art.

By the completion of the first wave advance (see fig. 15.3), momentum had slowed to a crawl, this was indicated by the flag pattern of the RSI.

At the exact squaring of 61.8% price retracement in 100% of time, the RSI made a classic divergence pattern as the low came in.

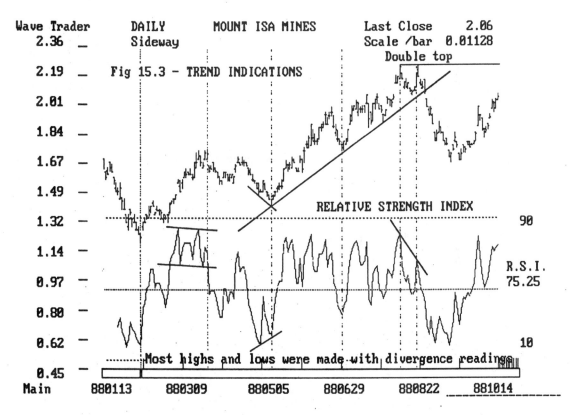

This market had approached similar levels of overbalance (oversold readings of the RSI), as it had done at the chart low. More often than not, a divergence will be signalled between price movement and momentum at any important change of trend. Seldom do markets unfold in only one advance. Mostly they will trace out between two and four major advances in any primary degree campaign. Blow off tops or bottoms will be signalled by extremely high readings of the RSI. I will only look for blow off tops when I see the RSI go above 90 or spike bottoms when the RSI goes below 10.

Unless you expect a spike top or bottom to occur it is generally a good idea to let the market confirm the time and price squaring before entering a trade. There will be plenty of time to plan out a strategy and make profitable trades in any intermediate degree wave that is about to unfold.

As a move progresses and adds further confirmation to your analysis, you will gain the opportunity to pyramid extra positions, as the market makes minor corrections.

This market gave a classic re-entry to the buy side when it retraced back to the level of the first wave advance (see figure 15.2 page 206 - Old high = new support).

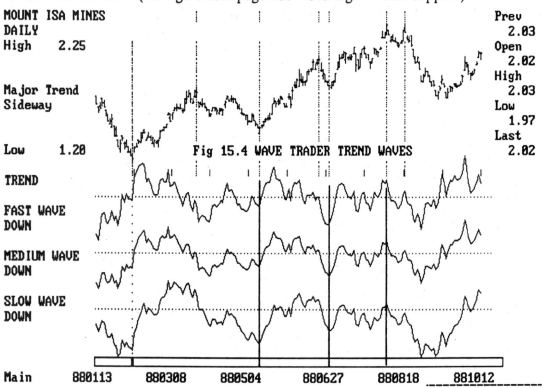

As an added market tool to track momentum, velocity and acceleration. I have an indicator that I call the WAVE TRADER TREND WAVES. This indicator confirms a new trend, if all waves turn in the same direction. I really only monitor this indicator at time and price intersections. If all three waves turn in the direction of the expected trend within a couple of days, of a time and price squaring, I have a good reason to expect that all is well with my analysis. If not, I know to get out and think again.

In figure 15.5 the correction that unfolded after the high labeled (A) traced out a protracted diagonal triangle with quite large trading ranges. The bottom labeled (B) turned in a repeat performance of the price ratio observed in the minor correction labeled A-B. Before discussing the correction (B) I would like to remind you of the high at (A). This was the high of $2.25 that occurred on the 9th August, 1988. See chapter 11, page 115, figure 11.7 and page 123, figure 11.15 for an illustration of the major time and price intersections that signalled this top.

The correction (B) terminated 244 days (0.666) of a year from (A). This time coincided with the 1.666 vibration of the bull market square shown in figure 15.6.

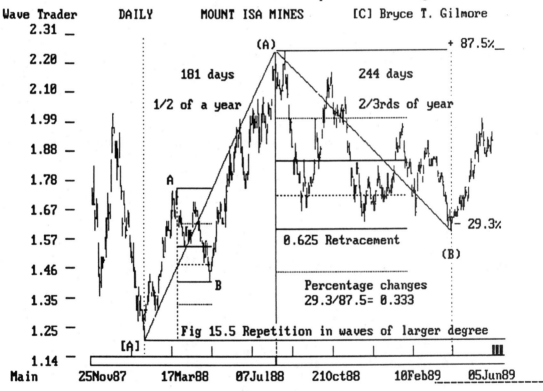

The price rise from [A] ($1.20) to (A) ($2.25) was an 87.5% increase in value, the decline from (A) ($2.25) to (B) ($1.59) was a discount of 29.3%. The ratio of the decline to the advance in percentage terms was 0.333 (29.3% divided by 87.5%).

This example demonstates the integration of ratios between waves of similar degree.

FIG 15.6 - Long term time vibrations still working in Mount Isa Mines

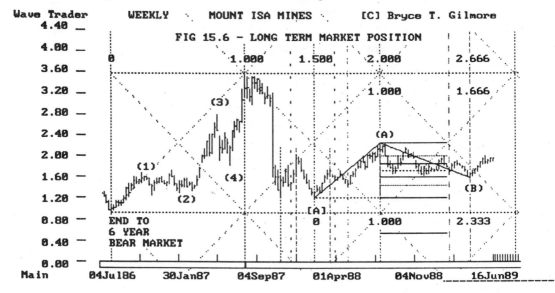

The low marked (B) Fig. 15.6 above, $1.59 occurred on the 10th April, 1989. Below a Wave Trader vibration schedule for the waves of lesser degree, shows the many clusters surrounding this date. It's no surprise the trend changed at this point.

```
SELECTION 1. Sort of closest dates in next 7 days for MIM 15%

1989 Apr  9   WT time    243 days   35 wks    0.665 yrs   HIGH   880809   2.25
1989 Apr  9   WT time     68 days   10 wks    0.186 yrs   HIGH   890131   1.98
1989 Apr  9   3/4 vib     68 days   10 wks    0.486 vib   HIGH   890131   1.98
1989 Apr  9   2/4 vib     53 days    8 wks    0.726 vib   LOW    890216   1.65
1989 Apr  9   3/4 vib     53 days    8 wks    0.447 vib   LOW    890216   1.65
1989 Apr  9   WT time     34 days    5 wks    0.093 yrs   HIGH   890306   1.92
1989 Apr  9   1/4 vib     34 days    5 wks    1.902 vib   HIGH   890306   1.92
1989 Apr  9   3/4 vib     35 days    5 wks    0.382 vib   HIGH   890306   1.92
1989 Apr 10   WT time    987 days  141 wks    2.702 yrs   LOW    860728   0.93
1989 Apr 10   WT time    516 days   74 wks    1.413 yrs   LOW    871111   1.24
1989 Apr 10   3/4 vib    473 days   68 wks   11.000 vib   HIGH   871224   2.02
1989 Apr 10   WT time    333 days   48 wks    0.912 yrs   LOW    880512   1.41
1989 Apr 10   WT time     53 days    8 wks    0.145 yrs   LOW    890216   1.65
1989 Apr 10   1/4 vib     53 days    8 wks    3.330 vib   LOW    890216   1.65
1989 Apr 11   3/4 vib    819 days  117 wks    7.000 vib   HIGH   870113   1.72
1989 Apr 11   3/4 vib    539 days   77 wks    7.000 vib   LOW    871020   1.69
1989 Apr 11   1/4 vib    210 days   30 wks    6.000 vib   LOW    880913   1.67
1989 Apr 11   4/4 vib    128 days   18 wks    0.618 vib   LOW    881205   1.63
1989 Apr 11   1/4 vib     70 days   10 wks    1.236 vib   HIGH   890131   1.98
1989 Apr 11   4/4 vib     37 days    5 wks    0.272 vib   HIGH   890306   1.92
Press any key to continue
```

By keeping up your time and price calculations you will be ready to act when the market dictates. Develop a daily work schedule and stick to it.

As a further example of the integration of price ratios, between waves of similar degree, that can occur at the expiry of a trend. I would like to detail some of the minor and intermediate wave relationships that occurred at the high of BHP Ltd of $8.96, 22nd May 1989 as mentioned in chapter 14, page 196, figure 14.27.

### WAVE RELATIONSHIPS WORKING BACK FROM INDICATOR DAY

| SWING | PIVOT | TIME | RANGE | %CHANGE | VIBRATION | PRICE | TIME |
|---|---|---|---|---|---|---|---|
| 860901 | 5.39 | 95 | 1.26 | 18.95 | 0.0133 | 0.5915 | 1.4844 |
| 870916 | 10.09 | 380 | 4.70 | 87.20 | 0.0124 | 3.7302 | 4.0000 * |
| 871027 | 6.00 | 41 | 4.09 | 40.54 | 0.0998 | 0.8702 | 0.1079 |
| 871102 | 7.27 | 6 | 1.27 | 21.17 | 0.2117 | 0.3105 | 0.1463 * |
| 871211 | 5.44 | 39 | 1.83 | 25.17 | 0.0469 | 1.4409 | 6.5000 |
| 880601 | 8.09 | 173 | 2.65 | 48.71 | 0.0153 | 1.4481 | 4.4359 |
| 881205 | 6.00 | 187 | 2.09 | 25.83 | 0.0112 | 0.7887 | 1.0809 |
| 890522 | 8.96 | 168 | 2.96 | 49.33 * | 0.0176 | 1.4163 * | 0.8984 |

### PRICE RELATIONSHIPS IN PAST SEVEN WAVES

| waves 7-1 | 4.70 | 4.09 | 1.27 | 1.83 | 2.65 | 2.09 | 2.96 |
|---|---|---|---|---|---|---|---|
| WAVE 7 | 1.000 | 0.870 | 0.270 * | 0.389 * | 0.564 | 0.445 * | 0.630 * |
| WAVE 6 | 1.149 | 1.000 | 0.311 | 0.447 * | 0.648 | 0.511 | 0.724 * |
| WAVE 5 | 3.701 | 3.220 * | 1.000 * | 1.441 * | 2.087 | 1.646 | 2.331 * |
| WAVE 4 | 2.568 | 2.235 | 0.694 | 1.000 | 1.448 | 1.142 | 1.617 * |
| WAVE 3 | 1.774 | 1.543 | 0.479 | 0.691 | 1.000 * | 0.789 * | 1.117 * |
| WAVE 2 | 2.249 | 1.957 | 0.608 | 0.876 * | 1.268 * | 1.000 * | 1.416 * |
| WAVE 1 | 1.588 | 1.382 * | 0.429 | 0.618 * | 0.895 * | 0.706 * | 1.000 * |

Press any key to return to CHART ...

FIG 15.11 - INTERMEDIATE PRICE SWINGS IN BHP LTD. up to 890522 $8.96.

Swings are registered from the 1987 high point, prior to the crash, up until the high at $8.96. I have highlighted the ratios of importance, take a close look.

I went short on the opening, the day after the high of $8.96. I recognized the importance of the inter-relationships that had unfolded in the wave structure.

BHP not only squared time and price at $8.96 it was reading 96 on the RSI signalling an extremely overbought condition that would result in a quick blowoff.

```
WAVE RELATIONSHIPS WORKING BACK FROM INDICATOR DAY

SWING     PIVOT   TIME   RANGE   %CHANGE   VIBRATION   PRICE     TIME
880512    6.58    28     0.82    11.08     0.0293      0.5503    0.5833
880601    8.09    20     1.51    22.95     0.0755      1.8415    0.7143
880630    7.15    29     0.94    11.62     0.0324      0.6225*   1.4500
880718    7.85    18     0.70     9.79     0.0389      0.7447    0.6207*
881205    6.00   140     1.85    23.57*    0.0132      2.6429    7.7778
890131    6.89    57     0.89    14.83*    0.0156      0.4811    0.4071
890217    6.16    17     0.73    10.60     0.0429      0.8202    0.2982
890522    8.96    94     2.80    45.45     0.0298      3.8356    5.5294

PRICE RELATIONSHIPS IN PAST SEVEN WAVES
waves 7-1    1.51    0.94    0.70    1.85    0.89    0.73    2.80

WAVE 7   1.000*   0.623*   0.464    1.225   0.589   0.483*  1.854
WAVE 6   1.606    1.000    0.745    1.968   0.947   0.777   2.979
WAVE 5   2.157    1.343    1.000*   2.643   1.271*  1.043   4.000*
WAVE 4   0.816    0.508*   0.378*   1.000*  0.481*  0.395   1.514
WAVE 3   1.697    1.056    0.787*   2.079   1.000*  0.820   3.146*
WAVE 2   2.068    1.288    0.959    2.534   1.219   1.000   3.836
WAVE 1   0.539    0.336*   0.250*   0.661*  0.318   0.261   1.000*
```

Press any key to return to CHART ...

FIG 15.12 - MINOR DEGREE PRICE SWINGS IN BHP LTD AT $8.96

Time and price analysis affords several luxuries. Firstly, we have a decision point to work off. Secondly, we can place close stoplosses on our positions. Thirdly, if we are proven wrong we can reverse position and flow with the continuing trend as it has proven its strength.

When you master the methods of time and price analysis, you will be totally selfsufficient. You will not need other peoples advice. In fact, you will be in the perfect position to offer critizism where others are concerned. You will become master of your own destiny. You will be sort after for advice, simply because you will have the knowledge that inspires confidence in your ability to beat the market.

# 16. HELIOCENTRIC PLANETARY CYCLES

This book would not be a complete work unless I were to publish my findings in this area. In modern times there has been a popular trend towards market analysis using the age old art of astrology. Astro-economics as it is known remains in my view a subjective subject. Although the basis of astrology, (the movement of the planets in their respective cycles), holds an intriguing connection to the numbers and ratios put forward earlier in this text.

I am not convinced from a market analysis viewpoint that one needs to know more than the basics in this area as the methods and procedures already discussed will pinpoint areas for change in markets more precisely. In the interests of a better understanding of time cycles and human nature it is better to include this section rather than leave it out.

Firstly, it would appear that the planetary positions are important in as much as the psychological factor they generate. This alone warrants watching their progressions. Astrology in its various forms is probably the most written about subject in this world. Passed down through the ages, records of events have been connected with the aspects of certain planets in the universe. Some aspects are interpreted as having favorable meanings whilst others portray adverse meanings. The belief, by so many indivuals, that planetary aspects have a bearing on the the day to day events causes one to at least investigate this phenomena.

ASTRO ECONOMICS is the study of regular economic cycles as they relate to planetary positions. Some schools of thought have devised ways of weighting planetary aspects as either positive or negative, by using a cumulative total an oscillator can be plotted and compared with the past. Future predictions are based on past observations.

MUNDANE astrology is the study of planetary aspects for a particular place or institution, ie., a town, country, stock exchange et cetera. Astrologers prepare a birth chart to interpret the future effects of planetary aspects in general relationship to the masses of a town or country in a similar way to NATAL astrology.

## ELECTRO MAGNETIC FORCES

Scientific evidence exists to say that ELECTRO MAGNETIC forces surrounding the EARTH's surface go through regular periods of change associated with the movement of the MAJOR planets. The SUN SPOT cycle is also another area of interest to students of ASTRO ECONOMICS. The SUN SPOT cycle goes through two phases in each 22 3/4 year period, the popular belief that a cycle only lasts 11.11 years has been disproved by Dr G. E. HALE who discovered the MASTER sun spot cycle. 2.5 cycles is very close to 55 years and the KONDRATIEFF 54 year cycle, also 5 half cycles make up an important harmonic vibration.

## HELIOCENTRIC ASTRONOMY

From a scientific viewpoint and the study of cycles the approach I have made is in the area of HELIOCENTRIC PLANETARY POSITIONS. Heliocentric means the relationship of the planets to the SUN. These cycles of planetary movement are not distorted by retrogression of planets as occurs in GEOCENTRIC ASTRONOMY. Geocentric astronomy tracks the position of the planets relative to the planet Earth. One of course needs to keep an open mind as these periods of retrogression could have some psychological effect on the masses, in fact some work to light compares the stock market corrective cycles each year with the phases of retrogression experienced by JUPITER and SATURN.

>The planets of our universe, which is SUN centered, are positioned in the following order:-
>
>SUN - MERCURY - VENUS - EARTH - MARS - JUPITER - SATURN - URANUS - NEPTUNE - PLUTO

The relative distances of the planets from the SUN are measured in Astronomical Units (A.U.), with one A.U. equal to the mean distance of the Earth to the Sun. The exact distance of a planet from the Sun is called the Radius Vector by astronomers. As each planet moves through its orbit around the Sun it travels in an ellipse, this causes variations in its radius vector. The shortest radius vector is referred to as the Perihelion of the planet whilst the Aphelion is the point of greatest distance from the Sun. The shortest and longest distances are known as PERIGEE and APOGEE. As a planet moves through each orbit its velocity varies in proportion to the area of the el-

## HELIOCENTRIC PLANETARY CYCLES

lipse that it transits (KEPLERS LAW) and these velocities can be calculated with amazing mathematical accuracy. The exact time of each orbit around the Sun is constant yet the time of each transit through a star sign (12 signs of the Zodiac) will vary depending upon the radius vector at that time. Planets travel at their slowest as they approach their Aphelion and at their fastest as they approach their Perihelion. There is some thought that planetary aspects that occur at times when velocity is at its greatest have a stronger effect.

My current research is based on the planets VENUS, EARTH, MARS, JUPITER and SATURN. To give you an idea of the variations in these planets velocity one needs to understand the star signs that the progressions move through.

Looking from the Sun a planet will travel through 360 degrees for each full planetary year, one orbit. If we assign 0 degrees to the entry point into ARIES (as viewed from the Sun) then each 30 degree progression will have the planet progressing into another star sign.

In order from 0 degrees ARIES we have TAURUS, GEMINI, CANCER, LEO, VIRGO, LIBRA, SCORPIO, SAGITTARIUS, CAPRICORN, AQUARIUS and PISCES. The orbit is complete as the phase has then returned to 0 degrees ARIES and starts again. An EPHEMERIS plots the planets positions as viewed from 0 to 30 degrees of each star sign.

I have found that the average speed of a planet through each star sign will give its position within +1 or -1 degree thus allowing simpler calculations to be made to find the relative aspects of each planet to the Sun. I make my studies by viewing the planetary aspects below a bar chart to determine if any regular price trends are associated with the important aspects.

**ORBITAL TIME** -The actual time of the following planets orbits around the SUN are again as follows:-

| | |
|---|---|
| VENUS | 224.695 days (0.618 years) |
| EARTH | 365.2403 days (1.000658 years) |
| MARS | 686.936 days (close to 34x20) |
| JUPITER | 4331.242 days or 11.86 years |
| SATURN | 10736 days or 29.394 years |

## HELIOCENTRIC PLANETARY CYCLES

## TIME IN DAYS FOR EACH STAR SIGN TRANSIT

| POSITION | VENUS | EARTH | MARS | JUPITER | SATURN |
|---|---|---|---|---|---|
| ARIES | 18.815 | 30.36 | 49.37 | 327.61 | 870 |
| TAURUS | 18.719 | 29.87 | 53.26 | 332.37 | 828 |
| GEMINI | 18.612 | 29.54 | 58.54 | 344.39 | 806 |
| CANCER | 18.514 | 29.44 | 63.98 | 361.22 | 805 |
| LEO | 18.460 | 29.60 | 67.76 | 378.77 | 825 |
| VIRGO | 18.449 | 29.82 | 68.29 | 391.93 | 864 |
| LIBRA | 18.638 | 30.49 | 65.34 | 396.34 | 913 |
| SCORPIO | 18.758 | 30.99 | 60.16 | 390.41 | 958 |
| SAGITTARIUS | 18.899 | 31.35 | 54.66 | 376.27 | 990 |
| CAPRICORN | 18.969 | 31.45 | 50.28 | 358.52 | 992 |
| AQUARIUS | 18.962 | 31.28 | 47.80 | 342.21 | 966 |
| PISCES | 18.900 | 30.88 | 47.49 | 331.21 | 919 |

A quick observation will reveal that the Aphelion of EARTH occurs in the transit of Capricorn (as viewed from the Earth the Sun would be in Cancer, this is between June 21 and July 22). The Perihelion of EARTH occurs in the transit of Cancer (as viewed from the Earth the Sun would be in Capricorn, this is between December 22nd and January 20).

### SIMPLE PICTURE

If you could stand on the SUN and observe the rotations of the EARTH (heliocentric astronomy) in relation to the INNER and OUTER planets you would at regular intervals observe what is known as planetary CONJUNCTIONS and OPPOSITIONS. Conjunctions are the times when the planets line up outwardly from the SUN, oppositions occur at times when the Sun is between two planets. There are other configurations known as SEXTILE, SQUARE and TRINE used by astronomers. A planet is SEXTILE with another in heliocentric terms when the angle between the radius vectors from the Sun are at 60 degrees. SQUARE is 90 degrees and TRINE is 120 degrees. I feel from my research that other aspects such as 51.5 degrees SEPTILE (one seventh), 72 degrees PENTILE (one fifth) are areas that should be given consideration when studying cycles.

Relationships of the planets in any of these values are said to form hard and soft aspects. OPPOSITIONS and SQUARE are said to be hard aspects, CONJUNCTIONS can be either hard or soft, SEXTILE and TRINE are soft aspects. Donald Bradley in his book STOCK MARKET PREDICTION offers a table on the relative meaning of planetary conjunctions.

The planetary conjunctions of the SUN and planets with which EARTH participates are very regular in length and in fact Jupiter, Saturn, Uranus, Neptune and Pluto's conjunction cycles and opposition are between 13 months and 1 year.

Considering the number of OUTER planets that conjunct in roughly 1 year to 13 months or 55 weeks to 60 weeks or 367 to 400 days we have a solid foundation for the annual cycle of market performance. Gann theory explicitly tells us to watch anniversaries of previous major turning points for a change of trend. Both astronomically and psychologically these times have a sound basis.

Before we run off and program these time periods we must remember that these are average times only. Because of the ellipse type orbits of the planets we have them traveling faster and slower through their respective orbits as they are approaching their perigee and apogee (closest and most distant from the Sun).

This of course means that cycle times for future conjunctions and oppositions will be irregular. The correct manner of observation for these phenomena should be followed by a table from a HELIOCENTRIC EPHEMERIS. THE AMERICAN HELIOCENTRIC EPHEMERIS 1901-2000 prepared by Neil F. Michelsen is recommended.

## OBSERVATIONS THAT SUPPORT FURTHER STUDY IN THIS AREA

### FIG 16.1 - DOW JONES HIGH 1987

As an aside it is worth mentioning that the DOW JONES INDUSTRIAL AVERAGE high that occurred on August 25th 1987 at 2746.7 points intraday fulfilled a price projection target in Fibonacci degree of 1.618 times the rise from 1932 to 1973. Many other time factors were present such as 55 years from the 1932 low, 13 years from the 1974 low, 5 years from the 1982 low, what was absolutely amazing was that the number of days from the BULL MARKET HIGH of September 3rd 1929 to the high August 25th 1987 was exactly 21175 days or the square of 55 in weeks.  55x55 = 3025  3025x7 = 21175  55 as we know is a Fibonacci number and for two such important highs to fall to an exact time period of a natural square is perplexing to say the least.  Just the same what is even more thought provoking is the fact that also on the 23rd, 24th and 25th of August 1987 we had an EARTH SUN VENUS opposition, an EARTH SUN MARS opposition, a SUN VENUS MARS conjunction and a NEW MOON.

For a graphic picture of the planets positions at the time of the Dow high we can look at the following charts.

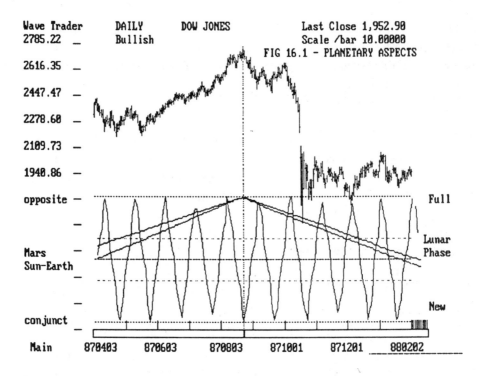

FIG 16.1 This bar chart of the DOW JONES INDUSTRIAL AVERAGES with the planetary cycle phases for Mars, Venus and the Moon relative to the Sun and Earth visually depicts an important cycle in time on the exact day of the top.

# HELIOCENTRIC PLANETARY CYCLES

FIG 16.2 - HELIOCENTRIC PLANETARY POSITIONS - 24th AUGUST 1987

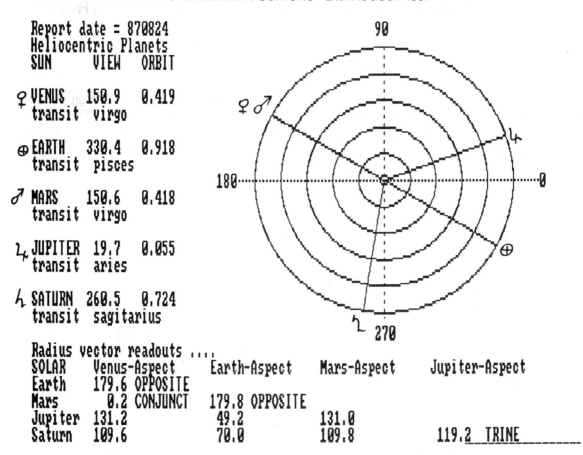

```
Report date = 870824
Heliocentric Planets
   SUN      VIEW    ORBIT

♀ VENUS    150.9   0.419
  transit  virgo

⊕ EARTH    330.4   0.918
  transit  pisces

♂ MARS     150.6   0.418
  transit  virgo

♃ JUPITER   19.7   0.055
  transit  aries

♄ SATURN   260.5   0.724
  transit  sagitarius

Radius vector readouts ....
SOLAR    Venus-Aspect    Earth-Aspect    Mars-Aspect    Jupiter-Aspect
Earth    179.6 OPPOSITE
Mars       0.2 CONJUNCT  179.8 OPPOSITE
Jupiter  131.2            49.2           131.0
Saturn   109.6            70.0           109.8          119.2 TRINE
```

If you imagine the planetary system lies on an horizontal plane this overlay depicts the positions of each planet in its orbit around the Sun. In addition to the so called hard aspects of Mars and Venus we also had a TRINE (120 degrees angle) between the radius vectors of Jupiter and Saturn.

## GOLD MARKET DECLINE - 14th DECEMBER 1987 TO 26th SEPTEMBER 1988

Whilst I have been working on the manuscript for this book I have been actively trading the Gold market. Its been very interesting following this decline and looking to pick the bottom. The low occurred on Monday 26th, September 1988 at $391.50 basis Comex 1st month futures, $395.50 basis Comex December futures and made a double bottom on the Comex June futures at $412.00 (a low of $412.00 was made two days earlier on the Equinox). The 1st month futures completed a 50% retracement within $1.00 of the total rise from 1985 to 1987, December futures made a 61.8% retracement of the same rise. Two standard price and time angles on the December chart at 50 cents a week emanating from the February 1985 low and the 8th October 1986 intermediate high crossed in that week at $395.00. A week prior to the low day I addressed a small band of analysts at a WAVE TRADER demonstration and alerted them to the time and price supports that were just around the corner. It took most of them several weeks before they acknowledged the accuracy of this form of analysis but I am used to that, in any case I positioned myself right at the bottom of the market and that what counts.

If one is patient all the signals for an imminent trend change will be telegraphed at the right time.

Using standard time and price procedures was ample in identifying this bottom. The total decline lasted 287 calendar days (2x144), trading time was 198 (lucas series), the price decline of the last wave down on the December contract was $89.50 (Fibonacci) and the three wave corrective formation adhered to a .382 and .618 relationship of GEOMETRIC mean which probably means that the next rise will unfold in an ARITHMETIC or HARMONIC relationship (see Sacred Geometry by Robert Lawlor page 84).

Insofar as the planetary observations were concerned the bottom was marked by a Mars-Earth-Sun conjunction which would have been common knowledge to any student of astronomy.

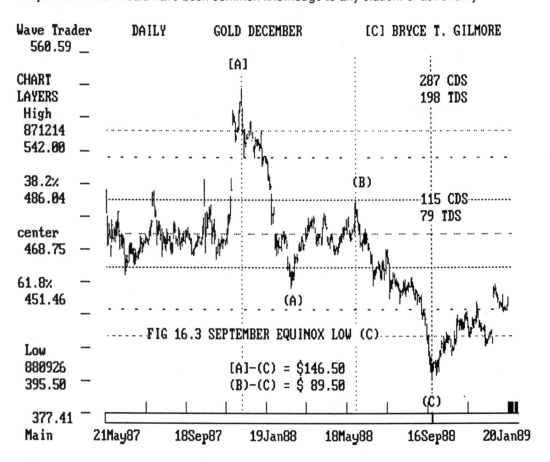

FIG 16.3 - GEOMETRIC AND FIBONACCI RELATIONSHIPS IN THE DECEMBER GOLD CONTRACT

FIG 16.4 - HELIOCENTRIC CYCLE PHASES OF MARS - SUN - EARTH

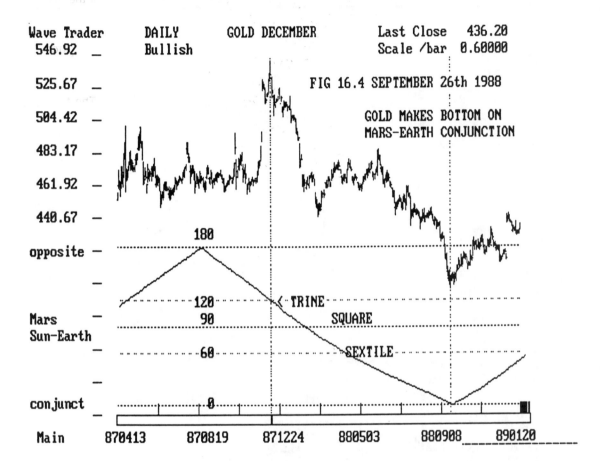

What I found extremely interesting about the whole corrective phase was the relationship in time of the Jupiter-Earth cycle.

If you look at the heliocentric overlay for the top on December 14th, 1987, (See FIG 16.5) you will see that Earth was SEPTILE Jupiter at a vector of 51.8 degrees (this is the angle of inclination of the Great Pyramid of GIZA). Also Saturn was in orb of opposition to Earth, we must not overlook that aspect.

# HELIOCENTRIC OVERLAY FOR 14TH DECEMBER 1987

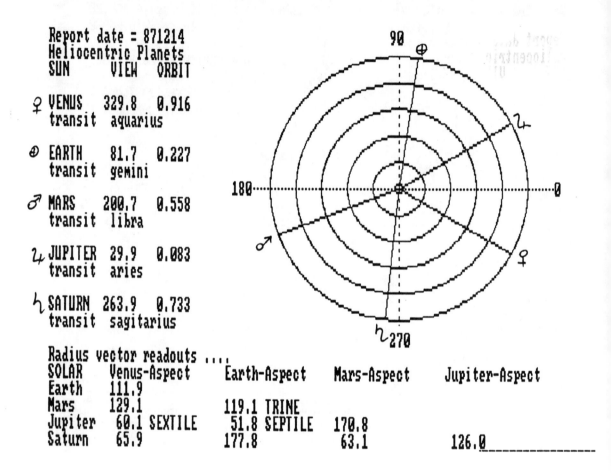

```
Report date = 871214
Heliocentric Planets
 SUN      VIEW    ORBIT

♀ VENUS    329.8   0.916
  transit  aquarius

⊕ EARTH    81.7    0.227
  transit  gemini

♂ MARS     200.7   0.558
  transit  libra

♃ JUPITER  29.9    0.083
  transit  aries

♄ SATURN   263.9   0.733
  transit  sagitarius

Radius vector readouts ....
SOLAR    Venus-Aspect    Earth-Aspect    Mars-Aspect    Jupiter-Aspect
Earth    111.9
Mars     129.1           119.1 TRINE
Jupiter  60.1 SEXTILE    51.8 SEPTILE   170.8
Saturn   65.9            177.8          63.1           126.0
```

FIG 16.5 - HELIOCENTRIC PLANETARY OVERLAY - AT TIME OF HIGH MADE IN THE GOLD MARKET PRIOR TO 287 DAY DECLINE.

# HELIOCENTRIC OVERLAY FOR 26TH SEPTEMBER 1988

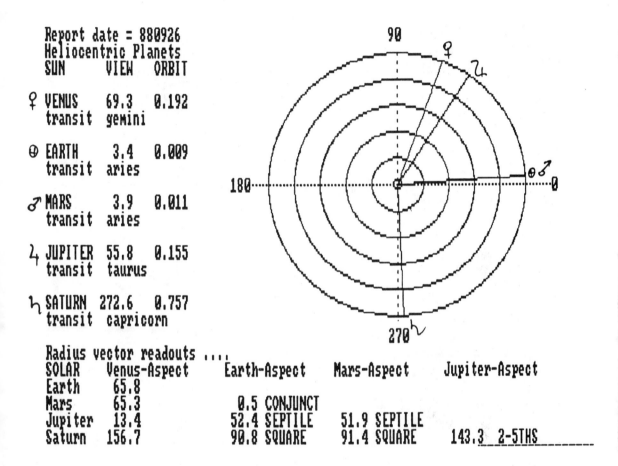

```
Report date = 880926
Heliocentric Planets
SUN      VIEW    ORBIT

♀ VENUS    69.3   0.192
  transit  gemini

⊕ EARTH    3.4    0.009
  transit  aries

♂ MARS     3.9    0.011
  transit  aries

♃ JUPITER  55.8   0.155
  transit  taurus

♄ SATURN   272.6  0.757
  transit  capricorn

Radius vector readouts ....
SOLAR    Venus-Aspect    Earth-Aspect    Mars-Aspect     Jupiter-Aspect
Earth    65.8
Mars     65.3            0.5 CONJUNCT
Jupiter  13.4            52.4 SEPTILE   51.9 SEPTILE
Saturn   156.7           90.8 SQUARE    91.4 SQUARE     143.3  2-5THS
```

FIG 16.6 - PLANETARY ASPECTS WHEN GOLD MAKES LOW AFTER 287 DAY DECLINE

Now look at the heliocentric overlay for the low day September 26th, 1988. Both Earth and Mars are SEPTILE Jupiter whilst conjunct each other. Earth had closed in on Mars from 120 degrees TRINE, one third of its cycle (Arithmetic mean). Earth had transited 5/7 ths of its cycle (.714 very close to half of root 2) with Jupiter at the same time.

## HELIOCENTRIC OVERLAY FOR 13TH JANUARY 1989

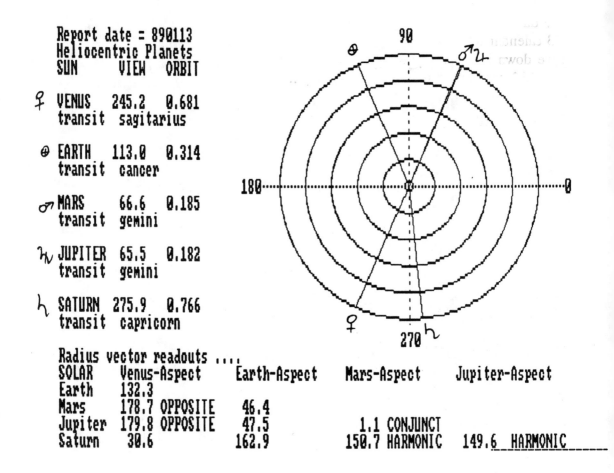

```
Report date = 890113
Heliocentric Planets
SUN        VIEW    ORBIT

♀ VENUS    245.2   0.681
  transit  sagitarius

⊕ EARTH    113.0   0.314
  transit  cancer

♂ MARS     66.6    0.185
  transit  gemini

♃ JUPITER  65.5    0.182
  transit  gemini

♄ SATURN   275.9   0.766
  transit  capricorn

Radius vector readouts ....
SOLAR    Venus-Aspect   Earth-Aspect   Mars-Aspect      Jupiter-Aspect
Earth    132.3
Mars     178.7 OPPOSITE  46.4
Jupiter  179.8 OPPOSITE  47.5          1.1 CONJUNCT
Saturn    30.6          162.9        150.7 HARMONIC    149.6 HARMONIC
```

FIG 16.7 - HELIOCENTRIC ASPECTS FOR FRIDAY 13TH JAUARY 1989

Whilst working my way forward to investigate when Earth and Jupiter reach SEPTILE again (I have a notion that the planetary cycles once in motion give a clear insight into the workings of Fibonacci numbers and cycle ratios amongst other things), I came across this planetary aspect on the 13th January 1989. Mars-Jupiter conjunction with Venus in opposition. I was alerted to several important time squarings falling in the Gold complex over the next week. This prompted an early issue of WAVE TRADERS DIGEST on the 12th January, 1989, which stated, QUOTE "Decline that began December 2nd, 1988 to end Monday 16th January 1989", "Maximum downside target US$ 392 (basis spot) - double bottom with 26th September 1988".

The date of the next SEPTILE Earth-Jupiter was 17th January, 1989 and a period of 113 calendar days from September 26th, 1988. This time has balanced 100% of the last wave down in the December 1987-September 1988 bear market. Wave (B)-(C) refer FIG 16.3 page 204. On cue a series of lows came in throughout the early part of this week at the US$ 400 level (basis spot), by Friday the 20th close, two days ago the market had made a respectable rally to US$ 408.50. All momentum indicators have now turned up.

My long term forecast for gold as you probably have read (Chapter 14, page 188) is for Gold prices to enter an inflationary spiral, the next major squaring of time, in cycle degree, will not be balanced until early April 1990. During the period from now until then I expect to see fireworks in the Gold market and the financial system generally.

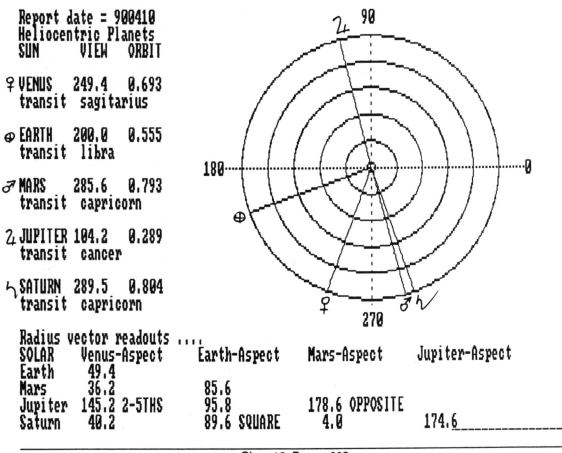

## COMBINING PLANETARY CYCLES WITH CONVENTIONAL TIMING AND ANALYSIS TOOLS

I have developed a practice of tracking heliocentric planetary cycles as a secondary timing tool. I would never try using the planets as a stand alone tool to forecast market highs and lows as some do; mostly with limited success. I have seen the same strong planetary aspects coincide with major turning points in two entirely different markets, the dilemma was that each market was trending in a different direction, one bearish the other bullish. The end result was that they both reversed and both went on to make extreme highs and lows. Who's to say whether a particular planetary aspect is hard or soft under those circumstances.

If you develop an opinion based on mere expectation of what an aspect may mean (this is pure astrology) you leave yourself open to miss a profitable move.

**WAVE FORM, MARKET SENTIMENT** and **GEOMETRY OF TIME AND PRICE** should be your primary guide to market direction. If the planets help identify a major **SUPPORT** or **RESISTANCE** zone in **TIME** then all the better.

## STUDY THE PLANETARY CYCLES AS A SCIENCE

Even if you never understand how to interpret planetary aspects you have lost nothing. The knowledge of **ORDER IN THE UNIVERSE** will be lesson enough to enrich your life.

**KNOWLEDGE IS POWER,** without it we are mere sheep. Sheep follow each other unwittingly, they allow themselves to be manipulated, they feel comfort in numbers and so long as they are all being treated the same, they are happy with their lot.

A Lion on the other hand is the master of his own destiny, he is a king, he can provide for himself and has no equal. The king of the jungle controls his own realm.

We live in a financial jungle.

WHICH IS IT GOING TO BE ?.... SHEEP OR LION.

## GEOMETRY OF MARKETS - EPILOGUE

Understanding this text may at first seem difficult and complex to new students. I can assure you, you will become a LION in regards to the financial markets, if you can grasp the principles outlined in GEOMETRY OF MARKETS. The techniques of analysis put forward here are within the grasp of any human being, given that they apply themselves and work for the knowledge. I wish I could have had an introduction such as this, it certainly would have saved me many years of hard work.

Trading commodity and stock markets for profit is akin to competing in a formula one motor racing championship. If you have the best car, any mishaps can only be due to your own lack of control and incompetence.

A champion driver smooths out the course by anticipating, when to accelerate, when to slow down. A novice or fool bounces from kerb to kerb until he either learns the circuit or the wheels fall off.

Spectators who have little knowledge of the skills involved, watch on, never realizing the work and effort a champion must go to in fulfilling his ambitions. I have realized this and so should you, hard work, study, common sense and dedication is the only answer.

The competition is ever changing, we must adapt to each new environment if we are to succeed. Every course is a little different, constant pressure is upon us to calculate the odds and act accordingly.

**To be a winner we must be trained and knowledgable, we must also be flexible and evaluate future events using known experiences from the past.**

*There are only three ingredients required for success, these are :-*

KNOWLEDGE - ABILITY - APPLICATION.

Good luck and successful trading,

BRYCE T. GILMORE.

# TRADERS PRESS, INC.®

**Publishes books exclusively
for traders and investors.**

• Publishes largest catalog collection of financial
classics in the U.S.
• Catalogs and publishes over 650 titles
for the successful trader.

*TRADERS PRESS INC.*® —order our 100-page catalog—hundreds of
books, tapes, courses and gifts of interest to all market traders
(Regular price $10)

Get a **FREE** copy by contacting
**TRADERS PRESS**

800-927-8222
864-298-0222
FAX 864-298-0221
*Tradersprs@aol.com*
*http://www.traderspress.com*

*25th Anniversary*
*1975~2000*
**Traders Press Inc.®**
**PO Box 6206**
**Greenville, SC 29606**